BREATH ON THE MIRROR

Breath
ON THE
Mirror

*Mythic Voices
& Visions of
the Living
Maya*

D E N N I S   T E D L O C K

*University of New Mexico Press
Albuquerque*

Portions of this book appeared originally in the following publications: "Writing and Reflection Among the Maya" in the 1992 *Lecture Series Working Papers 4,* College Park: University of Maryland Department of Spanish and Portuguese, 1989; "From Voice and Ear to Hand and Eye" in *Conjunctions* 13, 1989, and Journal of American Folklore 101, 1990; "Three Maidens at the Bath" in *Conjunctions* 18, 1993; "The Story of Evenadam" in *On the Translation of Native American Literatures,* ed. Brian Swann, Washington: Smithsonian Institution Press, 1992. All works reprinted by permission.

The drawings on pages 99 and 100 appeared previously in *The Quiché Mayas of Utatlán: The Evolution of a Highland Guatemala Kingdom* by Robert M. Carmack. Copyright © 1981 by the University of Oklahoma Press.

The drawing on page 19 appeared previously in *The Sculpture of Palenque: The Temple of the Inscriptions,* vol. 1, by Merle Greene Robertson. Copyright © 1991 by the Princeton University Press.

LIBRARY OF CONGRESS CATALOGING-IN-PUBLICATION DATA

Tedlock, Dennis, 1939–
Breath on the mirror : mythic voices and visions of the living Maya / Dennis Tedlock. —University of New Mexico Press pbk. ed.
p. cm.
Originally published: San Francisco : HarperSanFrancisco, c1993.
Includes bibliographical references.
ISBN 0-8263-1823-1 (pbk.)
    1. Quiché Indians—Religion.
    2. Mayas—Religion.
    I. Title. F1465.2.Q5T45 1997
    299'. 72—dc21   97-1378
               CIP

Pa ri wixoqil

➤ Contents

➤ Preface

MYTHS, AND THE CHARACTERS whose stories they are, live in the quiet of mountains and valleys, forests and meadows, rocks and springs, until someone comes along and thinks to tell them. They have other hiding places too, inside the language we use every day, in the names of the places where they happened, or the names of trees or days on the calendar. Sometimes myths try to catch our eye, looking at us through the holes in a dancer's mask or the glass eyes in the face of a saint. In dreams they show us their scenes and characters directly, but only long enough to make us wonder, afterward, which story we were in.

Even when someone we know tells a story straight out the myth may hide itself, moving along behind the details of what happened just yesterday, right next door, and could just as well have happened to us. When the situation turns inside out and a myth is presented as a myth right on its face, the next thing we know, the teller wants us to believe it anyway, at least for the time it takes to tell.

This is a book of myths that inhabit the landscape and language, the ruined citadels and living towns, of Mayan peoples, especially the Quiché Maya in the highlands of Guatemala. I could have written it as a collection of the myths themselves and nothing more, producing something like a museum display of artifacts with a few labels attached. Instead, I wanted the reader to know how these myths came to be told and who told them, and how they go on playing their tricks after they are told, concealing and revealing themselves in memories and dreams, persons and places, stories behind stories. Some of what I recount here comes straight from my own memories of being with Mayan people and listening to them, and the rest comes from all sorts of sources that have their own ways of concealing and revealing stories. I have consulted the inscriptions on Mayan monuments from more than a thousand years ago, a Mayan hieroglyphic book written more than five centuries ago, and the Popol Vuh or "Council Book," an ancient work that Quiché writers recast in alphabetic form soon after the European invasion. And then, from the various times when Barbara Tedlock and I have carried out fieldwork among contemporary Mayans, there are stories recorded on tape and written out in notebooks, along with still others of the kind that drawings, photographs, and mementos bring to mind.

Some of the events told here go back as far as the time when the gods first made human beings, or what Mayans call by the same word they use for the number twenty, for all the fingers and toes, the same number they use as the basis of their mathematics. Others are episodes from the lives of the maiden named Blood Moon, the trickster twins named Marksman and Little Jaguar Sun, the death-dealing lords of the underworld, a red dwarf with an ax that strikes lightning, three temptresses who haunt the banks of rivers, mountains that send messages to each other, a lost ark in the form of a cloth-wrapped bundle, a stone that gets angry when its owners fail to show respect, and ordinary people who pass the night on an enchanted peak or open a trap door in the floor of an abandoned temple. Here, too, are Mayan warriors and kings, Spanish invaders and missionaries, and North American anthropologists. My versions of the Mayan past will startle readers who already know something about that subject, and they, especially, will want to consult the notes at the back to find out more about my sources and lines of reasoning.

For those of us who call the continent we live on the New World, which is to say that our families came here from the other side of the globe during recent times, Mayan myths have much to teach about being here. We have a habit of assigning stories like theirs to the past of the New World and taking the present and whatever may lie beyond it for ourselves, but in fact Mayans live in a part of the continent where most people are Mayans today, speaking Mayan languages and eating Mayan food, all the way from the flat northern shore of Yucatán to the volcanoes that mark the Pacific rim in Guatemala, and from the heart of the Mexican state of Chiapas to the edges of Belize and Honduras. If we follow Mayan ways of understanding stories, we may read them not only for the past but for signs of a possible future, a different future from the one that waits for those who ride only the currents of Old World myths. It is true that contemporary Mayans sometimes tell our own stories back to us, especially Bible stories, but they always produce revised nonstandard versions. The way they tell it, Eve helps Adam overcome his fear of her, Abel slays Cain in self-defense, Mary points out human needs to an insensitive Jesus, Jesus becomes an advocate of Earth worship, and Judas, instead of committing suicide, becomes a generous business-man with a fondness for cigars.

Wherever the stories in this book come from tape recordings, I have scored them to show changes in pacing, emphasis, and tone of voice. Short pauses are marked by changes of line (as in a poem) and longer pauses (a second and a half to two seconds) by strophe breaks with arrows ➤ ➤ ➤ . Punctuation reflects the pitch of the voice, with a dash after a thought that dangles over a pause, a comma for a slight drop of the kind that marks the parts of an ongoing thought, and a period for a steep drop of the kind that indicates completion, which may or may not come at a place that would please a gram-marian. Loud passages are set in **boldface**, soft ones in small type, decrescendos in shrinking type, and loud whispers in SMALL CAPS. Words that are pronounced slowly and precisely are s p a c e d o u t. Other vocal effects, along with gestures, are explained where they occur.

In order to move the reader more deeply into the world of these stories, I have chosen to translate many Mayan and Spanish names of persons and places. Saqi K'oxol becomes White Sparkstriker, and Nima Sab'al becomes Great Place of Proclamation. Rendering San Andrés as St. Andrew brings the Spanish and English worlds closer together, where they look like the two peas in a pod they really are. Leaving names untranslated, which is the usual practice, creates a double distortion. On the one hand, I would argue, a name whose meaning is really quite ordinary acquires an exotic effect, allowing us to keep ourselves at a greater distance from the story in which it occurs. On the other hand, a name that carries a powerful meaning, even an uncomfortable one, remains hidden behind mere foreignness. But come to think of it, my real inspiration in this matter comes from conversations with the Mayans themselves, who are so fond of interpreting names that when all else fails they simply look for a way to pun on them.

Along the way from story to story, I offer the reader an introduction to Mayan ways of praying, divining, interpreting dreams, reading omens in the movements and cries of animals, and deciphering the portents of the named and numbered days of the Mayan calendar. There is even a brief exercise in the reading of Mayan hieroglyphs, made possible by the breakthroughs of the present generation of researchers. The world of all these words, spoken and written, is a very real one where strange and wonderful (and also terrible) things happen, not only to the people in the stories but to the real people who tell them, and to myself as a seeker after myths and the mythic. Taken as a whole, this book is a story about stories, a myth about myths.

➤ Preface to the New Edition

WALKING IN THE HIGHLANDS of Guatemala, there are moments when the scent of cypress and pine gives way to a presence of another kind, the presence of a shrine. Even before a shrine can be seen, it gives itself away with an aroma that combines ashes and soot with the resins that go into the making of copal incense. This is so even when many days have passed since anyone prayed and burned offerings there. If someone paid a visit just a short while ago, the scent may be sweetened by flowers and fresh-cut pine boughs.

Mayans say that a shrine is like a book. All the names, dates, wishes, and thanks that are spoken while the smoke still rises are recorded in its pages. When I think about this now it conjures up the scent of printer's ink, though authors seldom visit the shops where their books are printed. Even so, I did take a hand in the production of the present book. After consulting with a designer I went home to my computer and formatted each and every page, just as it now appears. The hard part was juggling widow and orphan lines against the need to balance each pair of facing pages. Normally this requires making some pairs of pages one line shorter than others, which often creates new problems on later pages. But I had an advantage over designers and typesetters: as an author, I could solve some problems by adjusting the length of the text itself.

What I sent to the compositor was not hard copy but floppy disks, ready for phototypesetting. What came back was on heavy, shiny paper that left the scent of developing fluid on my hands. There were glitches, of course, mostly caused by fancy formatting codes. The surest solution was the sturdy piecework of spaces, tabs, and hard rights. I never set foot on a shop floor, but there still came that moment when my first copy of the bound book arrived. It is always wonderful to rip off the wrappings in the rush to see and grasp the new object, but what is even better is to open the pages for the first time, catching, at last, a whiff of fresh printer's ink.

The Mayans who walk and talk in the pages of this book live in a world that only seems to get better for them, at least in the past few years. The peace accord in Guatemala not only signals the end of a long civil war, but also the recognition of Mayan nations within the Guatemalan state, growing nations that have linguistic, cultural, and educational rights and desires of their own. It has taken people of European descent or persuasion a long time to get the message. The message may be getting through in Mexico as well, where the Mayans of Chiapas have added computers and the Internet to their means of communication.

Among the main characters in these pages are two Quiché Maya priest-shamans who look after shrines and keep track of the Mayan calendar. One of them, don Mateo, lives in a town called Middle, to the east of the capital of the ancient Quiché kingdom. The other, don Pedro, once lived in Altar Town, to the west of the capital. He died not long ago, but the ways that were his are honored by his wife and by his sons and their wives. They live on a footpath that begins at the Little Place of Declaration, which despite its name is the largest of all the shrines where Mayans come to burn incense in our own time. The ashes of past offerings form a mound three or four yards thick, covering several acres. Rising higher than the heads of the celebrants, stacked up like books, are potsherds the size of plates and saucers. All of these were used for burning incense in private homes before they were brought to this public place. People pray and send up smoke again when they get here. The invisible names and dates and desires of this great shrine would fill an entire library.

Today is May 27, 1997, and the Mayan calendar stands at Eleven Cane. On this date, every 260 days, the head priest-shaman of Altar Town goes up to the mountaintop shrine of Tamancu. For more on that subject turn to the chapter titled "Two Rhythms at Once," but I will tell you now that Tamancu is the sacred mountain of the sun's left hand, or what we call the south. In another chapter, "The Language of the Animals," some strange things happen on the slopes of that mountain.

➤ Breath on the Mirror

BEFORE THE MORNING STAR ROSE, before the present sun first came out of the east, a man named Jaguar Cedar walked up this mountain with a backpack. He had come from somewhere east of here himself, from where these long chains of mountains, with all their caves and canyons, climb out of the rain forest and up into oak and pine and then cypress, shedding water, making rivers that run back down to the sea from which the gods of sky and earth first raised them. He had come out of the east with his wife, Red Sea Turtle, and three other men and their wives, and among all the works, all the designs the gods had ever carried out, they were the first eight who not only wore the measure of a score on their very bodies, having toes and fingers that totaled twenty, but who knew how to act as the gods had always wanted vigesimal beings to act, who knew more than monkeys. As it says in the Popol Vuh, the "Book of Those Who Sit Together on the Mat," the Book that was written on this side of the Atlantic, this side of the Pacific, here in the very middle of the Americas:

"They talked and they made words. They looked and they listened. They walked, they worked."

And they knew how to walk to the right places on the right days, how to do the right work on the right days, how to speak the right words on the right days, from among all the days with thirteen numbers and twenty names, 260 in all, the days it takes from the time a vigesimal being first makes its presence known in the womb till the time it sees the light. The children and grandchildren of these first four couples have been counting the thirteen numbers and twenty names all the way from then until the present day, thousands of times over, and we know that today, here on this peak in the Sierra de

Chuacús, ten kilometers northeast of Holy Cross Many Trees, here in the middle of Guatemala, we've come to the day Eight Bird.

The man who brought us up here today is Mateo Uz Abaj, the eldest of three brothers, and his youngest daughter and youngest son came along. Three natives on this mountain with the three of us. Here is doña Bárbara, my wife, and I am called don Dionisio, and with us is don Tuncan, our friend. Three gringos, all three of us ethnographers, and we have been taught how to speak the thirteen numbers and twenty names.

Eight Bird. The moment the day is named, its other names speak themselves softly. *Eight Call, Eight Cry, Eight Metal, Eight Silver, Eight Money.* A good day to climb this mountain, to call, to cry out to the lord of this mountain, to ask a favor. Today also happens to be Sunday, the second Sunday in Advent, but that is not why we are here.

The flesh of the first eight vigesimal beings was made of maize, the first of all maize, maize that came from a mountain whose name in the Book is Broken Place, Bitter Water Place. It's too far away to see from here but it's not just somewhere over the horizon, it's a real enough place to the west and a little north, over near the Mexican border, north of the town of Cuilco and south of the Pan American Highway, and the people who live over there still call it by the same name, still say it's the place where maize came from. And it's true that teosinte grows on that mountain, the only wild grain that crossbreeds with maize today, the closest thing to an ancient maize that would still know how to reseed itself without any help from vigesimal beings. Whatever the Bitter Water is over there, the blood of the first eight beings was made from that. It was yellow maize and white maize that went into their flesh, ground between slabs of basalt to nine degrees of fineness by a goddess named She Who Does a Favor, the midwife who came before all motherhood, wife of He Who Puts in Order, the matchmaker who came before all marriage, the two of them so old the counting of days began with them.

And when the midwife had done her grinding, the fat for the first vigesimal beings came off her hands when she rinsed them. Around and out beyond that mountain and this one today, and countless mountains from the Rockies to the Andes, are people who keep their flesh and fat by eating maize, who grind it fine between two stones, who remember it cannot reseed itself. Down to our southeast, at the edge of a small plain there, the ripened maize was planted by don Mateo, and he knows the ways of a matchmaker, and his wife, doña Leona, is a midwife, and she shelled and ground a little of that maize, and she gave us a cloth-wrapped bundle to bring along, and in it are thick tortillas that bear fresh handprints, hers.

At the very beginning there weren't even eight beings made of maize, but only Jaguar Cedar, Jaguar Night, Not Right Now, and Dark Jaguar. Each of the four was called a "motherfather," spoken as just one word. But they had no children, no need of children, and they had no need to go on long walks that took them up in the mountains or across the plains, no need to know whether a day in their lives was Eight Bird or had some other number and name. Here are the words of the Book itself:

"Their vision came all at once. Perfectly they saw, perfectly they knew everything under the sky, whenever they looked. The moment they turned around and looked around in the sky, on the earth, everything was seen without any obstruction. They didn't have to walk around before they could see what was under the sky; they just stayed where they were." And there is more:

"Their sight passed through trees, through rocks, through lakes, through seas, through mountains, through plains." And finally:

"They sighted the four sides, the four corners in the sky, on the earth," so says the Ancient Word.

Their limits, then, were those of the world itself. The only thing such beings might miss would be something that lay outside what sky and earth could comprehend—or "skyearth" as the Book often has it written, bringing the world to a single word. Or else these beings might miss something that happened even faster than they could turn their heads to look around, or look up in the air or into the earth. Whatever space may have been for them, it was no more than turnings and twistings of their heads; there was no need for the measures of hand or foot. Whatever time may have been, it was no more than the time it took to do those twistings and turnings; there would have been no need for the measures made by celestial lights, even if the sun, moon, and stars we see today had already been there at the beginning.

But as for us today, we could not see what was on top of this mountain before we climbed up here, and we could not see around to all those other mountains before we got up high enough, or before we found a break in the trees, nor could we see this much of the sky. Even so we cannot see as far as the Caribbean, nor can we see what lies behind the next mountain, nor even inside the forest all around us, nor beneath the dirt and broken basalt we stand on. It is close to midday but Day itself is nowhere to be seen. This is the time of the solid blue-gray overcast after the rainy season, the time of the chill wind when the path of the sun, somewhere behind the clouds, has slipped almost as far to the sun's own left as it will go. We can count the days till the path will pass directly over our heads and even move from there to the sun's own right, but we cannot look that day in the face from today, from here.

According to the Book it was the gods who put us in this position. It wasn't anything we did, unless we made a mistake in just being the way we were when they made us, nor was it anything anyone persuaded us to do, unless it was the gods themselves who persuaded us. I say "we," but I don't know whether the authors of these ancient writings meant to include everybody among the twenty-digited beings whose story they were telling, or whether they thought other peoples might have their own way of accounting for their own existence, and even their own books. At the outset they wrote down a promise to account for "the beginning of the conception of vigesimal beings," seeming to mean human beings in general, but if we read far enough, the first four motherfathers begin to sound like the founding fathers of particular patrilineages, and those lineages begin to sound like a particular nation. But as far as that goes, I get the same drift when I read the Bible, the Book that comes from what we call the "Old" World. As far down the line as the three sons of Noah it sounds as though all the nations in that world might be accounted for, but by the time the Lord God cuts a special deal with Abraham I begin to feel left out. Though somehow, for reasons no one has ever been able to make me understand, I did get circumcised, even before I was baptized.

The Popol Vuh, the New World Book we've been reading here, tells us that when we still had perfect vision, it was a matter of mere conversation to talk with the gods. I say "we" again because this is at least a possible, an imaginable story about us, about a time when we had no need to cry out to the gods from a distance or over a time, but could always be just where we were and when. In the end we're no more or less able to be that way now than don Mateo, himself a descendant of one of the first four motherfathers, a member of their nation. On top of everything else I've been wearing glasses for years and he's afraid he may be getting cataracts, and his voice carries no farther beyond this little clearing on the mountaintop than mine. If we're to get any answers from anyone, up there in the sky or down in this ground, it'll have to be in our minds' ears, or we'll have to decipher an animal's ominous cry, or read an animal's sudden move, or smell the wind if it blows the smoke of our offerings back in our faces, or feel an answer in our very blood.

It was the gods who began the conversation with the first vigesimal beings, the same gods whose works and designs they were. The opening words of the makers and modelers, Heart of Sky, Heart of Earth, are written this way:

"What do you know about your being?"

Now I can't help thinking that if anyone ever asked Adam or Eve a question like this one, it certainly wasn't their maker. Think of poor Adam, hearing the wind in the Garden, then hearing these terrible words come through to the place where he hid with Eve:

"Where art thou?" And then he's made to confess with questions like this one:

"Who told thee that thou wast naked?" And the whole discussion was headed downhill from there, as we all know.

The makers of the four motherfathers also have further questions, but they're not the questions of a prosecutor:

"Don't you look, don't you listen? Isn't your speech good, and your walk? So you must look, to see out under the sky. Don't you see the mountainplain clearly? So try it."

Such words could only have been written into the Old World maker's mouth if the Lord God and the serpent had been rolled into one. Come to think of it, one of the New World gods asking these questions was Plumed Serpent, whose iridescent blue-green feathers gave light to the world when there was only a sea and an empty sky. Even Old World artists have sometimes had the grace to give wings to their serpent, though they tend to be the featherless wings of a bat. With or without something to lift him a little, lighten the weight of his scales and plates, that Old World serpent set himself against the maker when he came to Eve with an invitation to knowledge:

"Then your eyes shall be opened, and ye shall be as gods." And what was the big secret, the one that would make Eve and then Adam like gods?

"Knowing good and evil." And how did Adam and Eve react to having their eyes opened?

"They knew that they were naked." And what did Jaguar Cedar, Jaguar Night, Not Right Now, and Dark Jaguar see when they used their own eyes?

"Then they saw everything under the sky perfectly." And having taken a look around, they took their turn in the dialogue that was opened by the gods, saying:

"Truly then, double thanks, triple thanks, now we have twenty and now we have mouths, have faces, we speak, we listen, we wonder, we move, our knowledge is good and we've understood what is far and near, and we've seen what is great and small under the sky, on the earth. Thanks to thee we've been formed, we've come to be made and modeled, thou grandmother of ours, thou grandfather of ours."

The gods should've been pleased with this performance. For the first time they had succeeded at making beings who could weave the sounds of their voices into patterns of sameness and difference, who could hold some syllables constant while changing others, which is to say they could speak in paradigms. They had been disappointed in birds, who made sounds that resembled words but merely repeated the same syllables, over and over. Vigesimal beings didn't just say something like "thanks, thanks, thanks" and so on, but could say, "double thanks, triple thanks." Most of their paradigms were double, but they could also say things like, "we speak, we listen, we wonder, we move." They could even take a phrase like "now we have twenty," and instead of making a paradigm by changing "twenty" to some other word, they could weave in another, smaller paradigm, saying "now we have mouths, have faces." And all by itself, at the very head of this tapestry of sound and meaning, they formed a word the gods heard as "truly."

Yet the makers and modelers heard something in this first human speech that led them to hold a conversation among themselves, as gods in the plural seem to do whenever anything's afoot. The Book, as it comes down to us, doesn't say whether the four motherfathers could hear the discussion. Perhaps it took place behind their backs, quicker than they could turn around and lean forward to hear it. Even so, the words of the gods came to be written in the Book. Someone among them began as follows:

"What our works and designs have said is no good."

What could the gods have read as "no good" in the words of their works and designs? Was there too much variation in the patterns of sameness and difference? Should all the paradigms have been simple dual ones? Worse yet, was the paradigm consisting of "double thanks, triple thanks" an ironic comment on duality? And were triple thanks not enough? Was it some kind of sacrifice that was wanted?

Or was it rather something the works and designs omitted to say, their failure to mention feet and hands for walking and working? Did these creatures think they had nothing but mouths and faces? Should they have called the gods by proper names and glorified them with epithets, instead of calling them grandmother and grandfather? As it happens, the same god who found fault with the words of the motherfathers gives us some help here, quoting just what it was that caused concern:

" 'We've understood everything, great and small,' they say."

That's more of an interpretation than a quotation, taking the form of a summary that turns on a word that doesn't even occur in the original statement, namely, "everything." Elsewhere in the Book the same sort of thing happens to the words of the gods themselves, as their own messengers unfailingly fail to quote them exactly. The scribes who transmitted and retransmitted the Book from one manuscript to another could've made all these quotes match up with their sources, but they didn't. For that matter, they didn't make one copy of the Book itself exactly match another. The ancient scribes who only read and wrote characters of the New World kind, proceeding by word and syllable, added comments and noted recent events. So did the later scribes who read the ancient characters but rewrote them as the consonants and vowels of Old World letters, creating the version of the Book we've been reading here. We seem to be entering a world where there is no reproduction, where every act of representation is also an act of interpretation.

One thing is plain, and that is that one of the gods in the story lets the others know of his alarm at the understanding of the four motherfathers. He goes on, in the hand of the last known scribe, as follows:

"What should we do with them now? Their vision should at least reach nearby, they should at least see a small part of the face of the earth, but what they're saying isn't good. Aren't they merely 'works' and 'designs' in their very names? Yet they'll become as great as gods, unless they procreate, proliferate at the sowing, the dawning, unless they increase."

What was meant by "the sowing, the dawning" was the setting and dawning of the sun, moon, and stars, and the sowing and sprouting of yellow maize, white maize, spotted maize, all of which had yet to happen. We can already see that here, as in the Old World

Book, the downfall of humans, the beginning of increase among humans, and the beginning of the sowing of crops by humans will all be part of the same change in the design of the world. The difference is that in the New World Book we are not to blame. Or, if we were tempted to look farther into the distance than we should have, it was the gods who tempted us. Their dialogue continues:

ho chi' jea quin chic go chi'carah xa cayo-

"We'll take them apart just a little, that's what we need," and this, according to the Book, is what happened to the foursome, to Jaguar Cedar, Jaguar Night, Not Right Now, and Dark Jaguar:

ri' xuxlabix vvach lemo x moyo- x moyic guche- mo bic vbac guivach xanacah chic xe macun vi' xere chi'calah ri'e go vi'

"They were blinded as the face of a mirror is breathed upon. Their vision flickered. Now it was only when they looked nearby that things were clear."

Nowhere in this New World Book is the notion of knowledge reduced to an opposition between good and evil; from the point of view of the gods, what wasn't good was the extent, the perfection of the knowledge of the motherfathers. And once the gods had limited their vision to what was near in time and space, they made a second set of four vigesimal beings so that the eight together could procreate instead of simply remaining complete to themselves for all time. The first woman named in the Book, Red Sea Turtle, became the wife of Jaguar Cedar, and the second, Prawn House, became the wife of Jaguar Night. The wife of Not Right Now is named Water Hummingbird, after that bird with a long beak, colored green but with white breast and wingtips, found along rivers, which is to say the green kingfisher. The fourth woman, Macaw House, became the wife of Dark Jaguar. Those who had been motherfathers became fathers, and those who were newly created became mothers. Except for the fourth couple.

Macaw House and Dark Jaguar had no children, or at least no sons, but neither did they give up their vision. They became the first human diviners of the kind called "those who look into the middle," reaching beyond the time and place where they were by gazing into water.

There have been motherfathers in every generation since the time when people were divided into wives and husbands, here in these mountains and on the plains all around and between them. Don Mateo is a motherfather, the living bearer of the visible face of whichever motherfather may have stood at the beginning of his line of descent, long before the birth of his father's father's father, past the point where the memory of the names of the men and their wives blacks out. He knows what all motherfathers know: that the left side of everyone's body is female and the right side is male, though only half of this is true, for any particular vigesimal being, when people insist on thinking in strictly physical terms. He looks after the holy places on his own lands and those of his brothers, praying for the increase of their children, their animals, their crops, their land, their money. And he is a daykeeper: he knows how to investigate the unseen events of days behind and ahead of the present one, counting day numbers and names and reading their portents.

But he longs for quicker ways of seeing. On his altar at home is a glassed-in tabernacle that holds a woodcarving of the most mystical of the Twelve Apostles, gleaming in red and white enamel, and behind the pediment of the tabernacle he keeps a multifaceted mass of quartz crystals at least as big as two fists. Some people, he says, know how to use crystals as instruments for seeing, the way other people might use eyeglasses or binoculars, or perhaps they're even fortunate enough to possess crystals that simply offer themselves up as instruments for seeing without one's having to know how to use them. Perhaps the seers of ancient times, the ones who looked into water and were called "those who look into the middle," also knew how to use crystals. As for his own crystal, he's not sure whether he's ever seen anything inside it, but while he sleeps it sends him dreams.

Perhaps the ancient seers were dreamers. And perhaps their dreams were clear, shining and glittering in the darkness.

Once vigesimal beings could no longer see everything under the sky and on the earth just by turning their heads, they wandered around in darkness, in the cold before the sun first rose, somewhere in the east. They "multiplied and flowered," in the words of the Book, until there were many nations, all walking around. They prayed to the gods who had made them, naming their names, but they had never yet stood in front of objects the Book calls "tree-stones" while they prayed. They kept watching the east for Sunbringer, the great star that would rise before Sun himself was born. The only stars at that time were those of Seven Macaw and his wife, Shield, or what we call the Big and Little Dipper, and a little later came the Fistful of Boys, the Pleiades. That was all the light they had from the sky, and the only way they had of making offerings to the gods was to fast.

Jaguar Cedar, Jaguar Night, Not Right Now, and Dark Jaguar were weary of having no destination and praying in front of nothing. The Book says they spoke to one another like this:

xado ohcaba cohoh-
pu guila vego chichahin quetala
chicavie si cohfihon tachuvach
xapni gueha ohgoße mahabi
chahal que

"Let's just go. We'll look and see whether there is something to keep as our sign. We'll find out what we should burn in front of it. The way we are right now, we have nothing to keep as our own."

They heard of a great city, a city that was somehow already there, and went to it.

The Great Eastern City

PEOPLE FROM ALL THE NATIONS gathered in the city, and each group was assigned to its own district. The Book says they called the place by several different names, one of which was Tulan or Tolan. That word meant Place of Cattails in the Mexican language from which it came, but in the Mayan language spoken by the four motherfathers and their nation it has come to mean Abandoned Place, Lonely Place, Place with Only the Sounds of Insects. They also called it Zuyua, a word from a language no one understands in our own time, a word that came to mean "riddle." And they called it Seven Caves, Seven Canyons. All of these are names of great fame in the middle of the Americas, but they always seem to gather themselves around a city that has already receded into the past, a city not quite of this earth. After the Old World Book came across the Atlantic, some people thought that city was Babylon. Still later, there were people who preferred to look across the opposite ocean, toward Shambala. And still others turned the tables, declaring the true Babylon or Shambala to be here rather than shipping Tulan and Zuyua over there.

The New World Book would have us look for the abandoned city to the east of this mountain in the middle of Guatemala. Further clues are given by another document, the annals written by a member of the Cakchiquel or "Fire Tree" nation. He says his ancestors came to the city soon after the first four motherfathers. By his reckoning there were four great cities, one in each of the four directions. All the nations whose lands are now in the Guatemalan mountains went to the eastern city and paid tribute there. Then comes the best clue:

"The insignia of the royal line of Abandoned Place was a bat." So there we are. Straight east of here, just over the border in Honduras, still in the mountains but not far above the reach of the rain forest, are the ruins of a great city, the easternmost member of an ancient confederation of four Mayan cities. It is known today as Copán, but its original name is given by the heraldic emblem of its ruling line, written this way:

The large head in profile at the center is that of a leaf-nosed bat. With this bat, the mythic city becomes real.

Even while this chapter was being written it came to light that the figure at the center of the emblem is not only a picture of a bat, but a phonetic sign for the first syllable in the title of the lord of the eastern city. To say that the royal insignia was a bat, as the Fire Tree author does, is like using an initial in place of a name. The bat's head stands for the syllable *xu* (changing to *xw* before a vowel), and the rest of the emblem is read by moving to the sign at the right of the head, which reads *ku* or *uk*, and then going clockwise all around the head, with *pi* at the bottom, the complete word *ch'ul* up the left side, and the syllables *po* and *aj* across the top, these last being an abbreviation for *pop ajaw*. The result is *Xwukpi Ch'ul Pop Ajaw*, in which the first word is the proper name of the city and the last three words (in order) mean "Holy Mat Lord," which is to say the holy lord of a council whose members sat together on a woven mat.

The meaning of the name itself, *Xwukpi*, can be found among living speakers of the language of the abandoned city. They call a certain thrush, the brown-backed solitaire, by the name *xwukpik*. It's a rather plain bird, gray with brown wings and back, but it sings one of the most remarkable songs of all the birds in the world. The voice is metallic and the syllables come very rapidly, something like this:

WINK WINK. WINK WINK WINK-WINKTA-TI-TE-TA-XERKI-WERJI-XURXUR-CHE-WER-BUT-BUT-LIBA CHIP.

The Fire Tree author says that one day, at the very moment his ancestors were passing through a gate on their way out of the eastern city, they heard a solitaire sing out. In the midst of the rush of sounds, and especially in the repetitions of *i*, *k*, and *x*, someone who was good at reading signs made out this message:

KIXKAM KIXSACH IN ILAB'.

These words are easy to translate, though they no longer sound like the bird in English:

"You're dead, you're lost, I'm your omen."

What the brown-backed solitaire was telling them was that they were on the road to war.

Nothing written on paper is to be found in the great eastern city, except perhaps as thin strata of black and white specks in a spadeful of earth, but the stone monuments and buildings are covered with inscriptions. Among the monuments are stelae set up by the kings to establish their places in history, and among the readable characters in the inscriptions are these two:

They stand for the syllables *te-tun*, meaning "tree-stone," and they refer to the stelae themselves. So it is that by deciphering, in our own time, hieroglyphs that were written thirteen centuries ago, we can understand the "tree-stones" of the Book, which found their way into alphabetic writing only four centuries ago.

Numerous dates can be read on the stelae of the eastern city, running from the 1,195,200th day until the 1,437,045th day of what the Maya reckoned as the present era—or, to put that in terms of the present era of the Old World, from December 17, 159 A.D. until February 4, 822 A.D. The last fifty years before the final date brought the reign of the greatest in a long line of kings, but his name, New Sky on the Horizon, must have seemed ominous in retrospect. During the reign of his successor, Sire of the Dagger, the confederation collapsed and it wasn't long before all four cities were abandoned. The Book casts the shadow of disaster backward over the entire history of the eastern city, consigning it to the darkness before the sun first rose.

Whoever was king when the first four motherfathers arrived in that city, they got what they had come for. Along with the motherfathers of all the other nations that had flowered by then, they each received "something to keep" as a sign. That something was a *k'ab'awil,* a being with divine power, but an animate being who could live among people here on the earth—a daimon, or what those who live by the Old World Book call a demon, a particular species of daimon that slowly revealed itself to have a large appetite. In the language of the eastern city, *k'ab'a* meant "to name, praise, celebrate," and *k'ab'awil* meant "those who are named, praised, celebrated." The motherfathers took this word into their own language, and they did indeed name, praise, and celebrate their various *k'ab'awil.* But it sounded like a word they already had, *k'ab'a,* which meant "to open the mouth." They could say things like, *Kek'ab'a kichi' ri k'ab'awil,* "Those who are named open up their mouths."

Gods gape.

Divinities drink.

Deities dine.

Demons devour.

Icons consume.

Idols imbibe.

Fetishes feast.

Gods gulp, gods guzzle, gods gorge.

"Name now our names," the gods of the Book command, "praise us." Those who are named have an appetite for their own appellations. Names like to be named, and those who fail to name them make them hungry, give them a thirst.

Here in these mountains the daimons of desirous names are no longer a living species, if living the life of an animate being means keeping body and spirit together in the same place at the same time, and in fact the species had already ceased to live by the time the bearers of the Old World Book got here. The living names belonged to the darkness before the sun first rose.

The daimon given into the keeping of Jaguar Cedar was Tohil, or at least he became Tohil. The name means "having the character of Toh," and Toh is one of the twenty day names, and days of that name are characterized by painful debts.

Jaguar Night received Awilix, whose name means "Lord Swallow" in the language of the eastern city.

Not Right Now received Hacawitz, whose name means "Open Mountain" in the same eastern language, but the scribes who rewrote the ancient characters of the Book as letters, seven centuries after the city was abandoned, still remembered that Hacawitz meant "Open Mountain."

As for Dark Jaguar, his daimon is plainly Middle of the Plain, nothing eastern in the name, at least not as it comes down to us. When Dark Jaguar and his wife Macaw House carried on their practice as seers, "looking into the middle," perhaps it was Middle of the Plain they looked into.

Among all the daimons received by the first four motherfathers, only one of them, Tohil, seems to allow us to get any closer than we already have. Only Tohil seems risky, if looking for signs of life in a dead god is risky. I say dead because no one prays to him or sends him the smoke of offerings today, unless perhaps they call him by other names. Two weeks from now will be the day Nine Toh, and if we had waited till then to see this mountain, we could've called out to the lord who rules that day. Instead of saying, "Come hither, Lord Eight Bird," the words we plan to use today, we could've said, "Come hither, Lord Nine Toh." But the name Toh may have been around before there ever was a god named Tohil, and it goes on without him today. Unless the day got its character from him, rather than the other way around. There was once a time when people owed Tohil great debts, and Toh remains a day of payment.

If the name Tohil came from the same language as the names of Lord Swallow and Open Mountain, there may have been a time when it meant "having the character of clouds massing together," or even "of thunder." But when the speakers of that language carved the names of gods in stone, more than a thousand years ago, Tohil was Tahil, which gave him the character of a burning splint of fat pine and, by way of a play on words, a mirror made of obsidian. When his image was sculpted in stone or stucco he could be read either way: he had a torch in his forehead, and the forehead itself was a black mirror. Sometimes there was a stone ax head in place of the torch, and just as an ax has one handle, so Tahil was often shown with only one leg, a long handle in the form of a serpent. Tahil was small, a mere boy or even a baby in size, but his ax was a lightning-striking ax with a flaming blade. Or else Tahil himself was an ax, handle and all.

Tahil cannot be thought, cannot be looked at all at once.

Tahil the ax, Tahil the torch, Tahil the flaming blade.

Tahil the boy whose leg becomes a serpent.

Tahil the serpent who grows a leg, grows a boy.

No one knows just when Tahil became Tohil, or precisely what he looked like by that time. No likeness in wood or stone survives, or on plaster or paper, unless some object in a museum somewhere or some figure in a document is Tohil and we don't know it, at least not yet. So far we have only the words of the Book, and they tell us that Tohil, like Tahil, had his fire. When Jaguar Cedar and his people were still in the city where they received Tohil, or perhaps he was still Tahil, a great hailstorm came and put everyone's fire out. So they told him:

"Tohil, we'll be finished off by the cold," and he said,

"Well, do not grieve." He started a fire by doing a pirouette while his sandal stayed put. So there he was, standing on one leg, and his foot was the point of a fire drill and his sandal held the socket. If Tahil had the handle of an ax in place of a leg, Tohil had the shaft of a fire drill. Either way there was fire where a foot would have been.

So the people whose daimon was Tohil were warmed by Tohil's fire, and it seems that all the other people with the first four mother-fathers were also warmed by Tohil. As for the people of other nations, they just went on chattering and shivering. Finally, with "great pain in their hearts," they came to Jaguar Cedar, Jaguar Night, Not Right Now, and Dark Jaguar, saying,

"Perhaps we wouldn't make ourselves ashamed in front of you if we asked to remove a little something from your fire?" The mother-fathers then had a private conversation with Tohil, asking him what they should ask in exchange for a share in the fire he had started with his foot.

"Very well. You will tell them, ' "Don't they want to be suckled on their sides and under their arms? Isn't it their hearts' desire to embrace me? I, who am Tohil? But if there is no desire, then I'll not give them their fire," says Tohil. "When the time comes, not right now, they'll be suckled on their sides, under their arms," he says to you,' you will say," they were told.

Talking was something Tohil never did except with the four motherfathers. The nations without fire only heard his words in a quotation inside a quotation inside a quotation, as Jaguar Cedar told them that Tohil had told him to tell them that he had told them the words in the innermost quotation marks, words he said to say were said "to you," even though they were said in the third person plural. To all of which the nations replied,

"Very well. Let him suckle. And very well, we shall embrace him." As if they were consenting to the adoption of an infant. Tohil the infant, this Tohil we see in crumbling stucco relief now the color of bone, down in the ruins of the westernmost of the four great cities of the confederation, the one now known as Palenque, close to the Gulf of Mexico. Tahil, cradled in the arm of a lady in one panel, in the arm of a lord in another. One of his legs, just where his foot would begin, becomes a snake, the only part of the sculpture that still has its color, a blue snake whose head rests on the lady's or lord's other arm (see opposite page). Tahil the infant is not shown at the moment of being suckled by anyone, but Tahil's blue snake has a wide enough gape to swallow a person.

The nations without fire consented to the request of the infant Tohil without knowing that even the innermost quotation marks concealed one last layer, without knowing what it would mean, in the end, to embrace the gape named Tohil and let him suckle. What he wanted was their blood and their very hearts. The day would come when the White Dagger, a knife of chert chipped down to a fine edge, would make an incision that began below the armpit, between

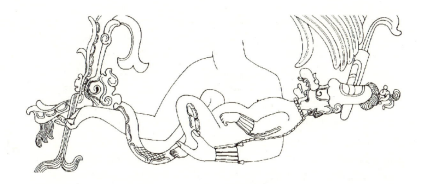

the sixth and seventh ribs, running all the way across the chest to the same spot on the opposite side, and out would come the heart in exchange for fire. Perhaps there was even a ceremony like the one in which the Mexicans let all their fires go out and then rekindled them from a single new fire, lit by a drill whose point found its socket and scattered its sparks somewhere down inside the emptiness where a man's chest had been spread open and his heart taken out.

Once the matter of fire had been settled, the first four mother-fathers left the eastern city and took their whole nation with them. All the other nations left too, making that city indeed the Place with Only the Sounds of Insects. It wasn't easy to leave, at least not for Jaguar Cedar, Jaguar Night, Not Right Now, and Dark Jaguar: the Book says "they tore themselves away from there." Tohil was the one who wanted to go. "He actually spoke to them," he was still a living member of his species, not a voice in the ear or an apparition, and he said,

"Our home is not here. Let's go on until we see where we belong." But he wanted something from them, something short of their own hearts, before they left:

"It remains for you to give thanks, since you have yet to take care of bleeding your ears and taking stitches in your elbows. You must worship. This is your way of giving thanks before your god," before your daimon, your gaping mouth. They became penitents, "users of thorns" who pierced themselves. The cord they used for their sewing had snags woven into it, thorns. And though Tohil had talked about ears and elbows, *xikin* and *ch'uk,* they knew how to read his meaning as *tz'ikin* and *ch'uq*, birds and breechclouts, and so they drew blood from birds of the particular kind known as *pich'*, the red-headed woodpeckers they hid under their breechclouts.

Now the four motherfathers and their wives and all their nation, together with other nations, set off on the long journey that would lead them westward and upward, away from the edge of the rain forest and into the forests of oak and pine that surround us here on the day Eight Bird. Jaguar Cedar, Jaguar Night, Not Right Now, and Dark Jaguar were all bent under the weight of backpacks, leaning forward on their walking sticks. Seated in their backpacks, riding high enough to look over their shoulders, were those with names, with open mouths, the daimons who did favors for vigesimal beings, who gave them advice about things that were too far away to be clear to beings whose mirror of the world had been breathed upon.

Daimons were easier to talk to in those days, the dark days when all the world was still wet and they were still a living species, though they already had an appetite for drops of blood and were looking forward to something bigger. And just as it is with the still being whose mouth gapes in the clearing at the top of this mountain today, the living gapes had to be approached on the right day, by men who had not touched a woman that day, women who had not touched a man that day, women and men who had not fought that day, not even a fight with words. Whatever "day" may have meant back then, given that the nations of vigesimal beings had yet to see Day himself. Each night they camped out on the road, whatever "night" may have meant. They must've kept track of time like people moving through an Arctic winter, watching the movements of stars. Only they had very few stars to watch.

When the nations came within several days' walk of this mountain, still on the far side of the eastern quarter of our horizon, they passed a place named Great Hollow with Fish in the Ashes, on the eastern edge of the town now known as St. Peter Fish in the Ashes. Everything under foot in that region is karst, rotten limestone full of round depressions, some of them shallow and some of them hundreds of meters deep, pools at their bottoms or else black holes that drain them down. There are long depressions that look like gulches, but this kind of gulch heads up on the side of a hill, winds its way along, and then stops dead against the side of another hill. The Great Hollow is round, but cutting through it is Painted Town River, widening into a pool that serves today as a public bath, overlooked by picnic shelters. The river leaves the hollow through a steep-sided canyon with a path along its left bank. At a long day's walk is the part of the canyon the Book calls Rumbling Intestine, where the river enters Mouth of the Change of Canyons, now known as Ravenous Cave. All the water disappears beneath a hill and then comes out on the other side.

Whatever waits inside the cave or beyond it, the Book names Spiked Rapids, Blood River, Pus River, and a tricky choice among four paths. One of those paths, the black one, goes down to the Place of Fear, the underworld whose highest-ranking rulers, named One Death and Seven Death, are lords of all the days named Death.

➤ Watching for the Great Star

IT WAS *THEM*, IT WAS the Death Lords, down beneath the world of the people who walked on by the Great Hollow: they were the ones who stood in the way of the dawning, who held it back. They were daimons of the kind who still had flesh and blood in those days. Dead at their hands were One Marksman and Seven Marksman, lords of all the days named Marksman, sons of the first matchmaker and midwife, the old couple who started the very counting of days. The dead brothers were destined to rise as evening and morning stars, but they had followed the road that leads to Mouth of the Change of Canyons, entered Ravenous Cave, shot Spiked Rapids, crossed Blood River and Pus River, and taken the Black Road to the Place of Fear. One and Seven Marksman now lay buried, except for the head of One Marksman. That was up in the fork of a tree that grew in the east, put there by order of the lords of Death. The tree had always been barren, but now it became the first calabash tree, covered with fruit whose pale and bony rind gave it the look and feel of a skull. The actual skull was still there, but it was hard to tell from the fruit.

A woman heard about the tree and went there. She was Blood Moon, daughter of Blood Gatherer, one of the lesser lords of the Place of Fear. As she stood before the tree, wondering whether to pick some fruit, the skull spoke to her. Or rather, she heard the voice of One and Seven Marksman, who were now of a single mind, speaking through the mouth of the skull.

"Why do you want a mere bone?" said the voice. "You don't want it." But Blood Moon said,

"I *do* want it." So the voice asked her to hold out her right hand, and she did. The skull spit in her palm. She saw it happen and felt it, but when she took a look there was nothing in her hand. The voice told her,

"It's just a sign I've given you, my saliva, my spittle." The spit gave its sign at the moment it vanished, pointing to Blood Moon's right hand, her male hand. She had wanted fruit, and the palm of her hand said it was hers. The right side said the fruit would be male. What she did not know was that two brothers had spoken as one. Nine moons later she gave birth to twin boys, destined to avenge the slaying of their father and uncle.

The twins were born up here on the surface of the earth. One of them was Marksman, named after One and Seven Marksman but without any number, and the other was Little Jaguar Sun, or Little Hidden Sun. In their youth they played ball near the Great Hollow, but by the time the nations came by they may well have been away on one of their adventures, down in the place their mother came from. They really went through hell, finding their way through each of the practical jokes, booby traps, fun houses, and rigged ball games devised by the lords of that place, all of which were calculated to kill. If they succeeded in only seeming to be killed, the way would be open for the dawning all the nations had been waiting for.

But the face of the earth was still dark when the four mother-fathers and their nation left the Great Hollow behind and continued in our direction. They still had three other nations with them when they climbed a mountain that came to be named Farewell, after what was about to happen there. That mountain right over there, the next high ridge northeast of the place where we now stand on the day Eight Bird. And it seems all those people knew, even before their gods told them so, that the time had come for them to divide and go their separate ways. For the first time the nations took on names. Jaguar Cedar, Jaguar Night, Not Right Now, and Dark Jaguar called themselves and all their descendants Quiché, a name that means "Many Trees." They are still called Quiché today, and their language is Quiché. When Mexicans came to these mountains from the west in later times they called this whole country Guatemala, which meant "Many Trees" in the Mexican language.

We brought tortillas and all kinds of fruit and a bottle of bootleg liquor up here with us today, but when the Quiché motherfathers and their wives went up over there on the peak named Farewell they fasted. They had only a single gourdful of atole, a gruel made of maize. Perhaps the gods, the gapes, were already getting harder to hear from. But on that mountain they did speak, saying,

"Let's just go, let's just get up, let's not stay here. Please give us places to hide. It's nearly dawn. Wouldn't you look pitiful if we became mere plunder for warriors? Construct places where we can remain yours, you penitents and sacrificers, and give one place to each of us."

And the motherfathers all went out searching from there, packing the gods on their backs again. Jaguar Night came through the valleys that separate us from Farewell and entered the forest that covers this mountain. He found a place for Lord Swallow in a canyon that heads against this very ridge, a few hours' walk east of here. We've never set foot there, but we've heard there's a small level space at the foot of a cliff, and the face of the cliff has a hollow cut into it. The Book calls this site Swallows' Place, and that's what it's called by the people who live on the slopes below it today. It sounds as though Lord Swallow was destined by his very name, his desirous name, to search for a place in a cliff, looking over the shoulder of the man who could backpack him there.

Not Right Now was the next motherfather to find a place for his god, or to have his god find it for him, but no one around here today seems to know exactly where that was. The Book gives it the same name as the god, Hacawitz or "Open Mountain," and adds that it was indeed a mountaintop that was open, not forested like this one, so again it sounds as though the name was in search of the right place. There is one further clue. To repeat the words of the Book as they appear in the only surviving manuscript, inked in watery sepia on paper long since turned yellowish brown, Not Right Now placed his god *chuvi' hun nima cal ha*. When this passage is recast by the typographic eye, with sharpened word divisions and corrected spelling, it usually comes out as *chuwi hun nima cak ha*, and it has long been taken to mean "above a great red river." Certainly there is "a great red" something here, in the second, third, and fourth words, but the first word could also mean "at the top of," and as for the last word, that could also mean "house." If the scribes really meant "river" they should've written *haa*, not *ha*, but they didn't always bother themselves with the extra *a*. So Open Mountain may have been placed "at the top of a great red house" on an open mountain—and it just so happens that in earlier times, at least, the typical Mayan temple was painted red all over, from the walls that enclosed the temple on top right on down over the terraces of the pyramid beneath.

Looking out from the mountaintop where we are today, I don't know whether there was a time when we could've seen the great red house of Open Mountain through the trees from here, on top of one of those ridges on our side of the horizon, or whether one of the rivers beyond the ridges was and still is red. How to go looking for Open Mountain's mountain?

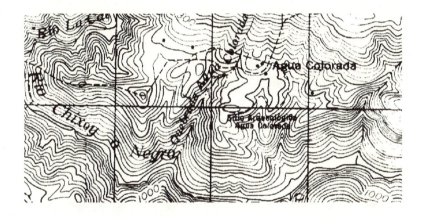

When we read our way out across the 1:50,000 quads published by the Guatemalan Geographic Institute, the first place that catches the eye is northeast of here, beyond all the ridges and valleys of the Sierra de Chuacús. Far beyond any track that even our jeep could negotiate, on the far shore of the only great river anywhere near us, the Río Chixoy, is a shelf of level land 300 steep meters above the water, surrounded by a dashed line and labeled as an archaeological site. These ruins, spotted by mapmakers on an aerial photograph, straddle the upper part of a watercourse they've labeled *Quebrada Agua Colorada*, "Red Water Ravine," in blue ink. The trouble is, the course of this "Red Water" is only a couple of kilometers long, and the blue ink that marks it is not in a solid line but in dashes and dots, meaning "intermittent." Red Water Ravine is hardly a "great red river." As for the Río Chixoy itself, Chixoy means "at the *xoy*," and *xoy* is a shrub with dark green leaves. The river has another name on the map, but that is Río Negro, Black River. Up here in the highlands it usually runs translucent turquoise, whatever may happen downstream.

If it's a red *temple* we're looking for, and if somewhere we find ourselves excavating a pyramid with traces of red paint on what's left of its coat of stucco, we could, for all we know, be looking at one of hundreds of red temples. With luck, we might find a temple with the characters for the sounds Ha-ca-witz, carved in stone or modeled in stucco, looking something like this:

But that would take us even farther from here than Red Water Ravine and back a good thousand years, to a place where the god named Open Mountain might have sat long before he got backpacked even as far as Farewell, to say nothing of the place where Not Right Now finally sat him down. To find the Open Mountain of Not Right Now, this New Open Mountain, we might have to walk the back roads and tracks of the mountains and plains that surround us here until we found some hamlet where the people still knew the name Hacawitz and could take us there. A ruin above a great red river, great and red at least in its name, or a mound strewn with the gray rubble of what was once a great red house.

But there are times when we suddenly see into the distance more clearly just by opening a book. It might even be the wrong book. The hand, instead of turning the pages of a dictionary of Quiché, turns the pages of a dictionary of another Mayan language, Cakchiquel, penned by Fray Francisco de Varea in 1699 and typed by William Gates in 1929. The eye, instead of looking something up, peruses the entries under the letter *c* . . .

```
cak
cakabah
```

```
cakar
cakbololak
cakhay
cakche
Cakchequele
caklol
```

and out jumps *cakhay,* no longer hidden by an error of alphabetization. *Cak* means "red" in Cakchiquel, just as it does in Quiché, but Cakchiquel *hay* can only mean "house," not "river." Varea, instead of translating *cakhay* literally as "red house" or "red houses," defines the term as follows:

"Small rounded mountains of stone and dry earth made by the ancients."

In other words, pyramids. Pyramids as they appeared to a friar who was writing when all of them had been in ruins for nearly two centuries, but when his parishioners still called them *cakhay.* The Quiché equivalent would be *cakha,* and when we look back at the troublesome passage in the Book we can see that *cak ha* could have been read as one word all along.

So we can give up on finding a great red river. Not Right Now placed his god "at the top of a great pyramid," whether or not pyramids were still painted red in his time, and the pyramid was on Open Mountain. Wherever that is.

As for Dark Jaguar, who ranked last among the four mother-fathers, the Book doesn't say what sort of place he found for his god, but we may guess that Middle of the Plain looked over his shoulder, or he looked right into the middle of Middle of the Plain, until the two of them saw a spot in the middle of a plain. That spot could be near the present-day town that lies down the slopes southeast of here, a town whose name means "Middle," but the name no longer tells us what it's at the middle *of.* There is a small plain down there, in fact, if no longer in the name. The man who brought us up here today has his house and his cornfields near that town, at the edge of the plain.

That leaves Jaguar Cedar, first in rank among the four mother-fathers but last to come away from Farewell and last to find a place for his god. He walked through the forest below us, came up on the ridge where we now stand, and here in this clearing he lifted Tohil from his backpack and gave him a place to sit.

The Book says there were "masses of serpents and masses of jaguars, rattlesnakes, yellowbites" all around this place when Tohil was first hidden here. And they say today that if you come to a place like this, to any high place with a hearth for offerings, a gaping mouth, and if you have touched your woman or man on that day, or quarreled or fought on that day, or let your gods go thirsty and hungry too long, then a puma will show his face here, or a jaguar, a rattler, or that viper with the yellow lower jaw, the fer-de-lance.

The Lord of the World, the lord of this earth, the lord of this mountain, the lord of this day, whatever their names, they all have mouths. In the valleys below us here live people who know how to feed them, Quiché people. The man who brought us up here today, don Mateo, knows how to feed them, and by now we've learned how to do it too. We dressed in casual clothes for this occasion, which is what ethnographers always wear when they're doing fieldwork, but he wore his blue serge suit, which is what Quiché men always wear when they're not working in a field. His shirt is Western, with bucking broncos printed all over it. His traditional touch is a wide red sash of handspun cotton, worn like a cummerbund.

For as long as the darkness lasted, Jaguar Cedar made no platform for Tohil, no terraced pyramid with a room on top, but only an arbor adorned with bromeliads and hanging mosses, picked from high branches, the same bromeliads, the same mosses that grow in the trees that hide us now. On the map this spot is marked with an ✕ (see facing page), and it is noted as being 2,589 meters above sea level, but the mark and number are both printed in sepia ink, meaning that the elevation is unconfirmed by ground observations and that we need not bother looking around in the rocks or on the ground for the brass benchmark a surveyor would have cemented in place. The nearest black ink marks the course of the road where we left our jeep, two solid and narrowly parallel lines without any red ink running along between them, meaning a one-lane road "passable in good or dry weather, loose surface." The mountaintop carries no name, but if it did the ink would be black. The only map that does

give the name was drawn by archaeologists, who first saw it written in the Book and then heard it spoken by the people who live down below here to the north. The name was Patohil, "Tohil's Place," and it still is.

Once Tohil, Lord Swallow, Open Mountain, and Middle of the Plain were all in place, the four motherfathers came back together to go on waiting for the dawn, this time on the mountain called Open Mountain, and just one nation, their own Quiché people, came up and waited with them. Jaguar Cedar, Jaguar Night, Not Right Now, and Dark Jaguar talked among themselves:

"Coming here hasn't been sweet for us. Alas! If only we could see the sun. What have we done? We all had one identity and one mountain, but we sent ourselves into exile." Out here in these mountains, they longed for the eastern city where all the nations had once been united, now the Place with Only the Sounds of Insects. It wasn't as though they could turn around and go back, but they did expect that their long journey might show them something new. As the Book has it,

"Their hearts had not yet been set to rest by the dawn."

For the gods it was just the opposite. They were feeling at home for the first time, even in the darkness—Tohil and Lord Swallow in their arbors of bromeliads and mosses, and Open Mountain on his open-topped mountain, at the top of a great red house. And it was still the case that "they actually spoke," as if they were beings of the flesh-and-blood kind. They didn't just put their voices in the ears of dreamers but spoke with hot breath, and perhaps an occasional droplet of spittle. Something like vigesimal beings, but drinkers of blood from the ears and elbows of users of thorns.

The first four motherfathers, somewhere out there on Open Mountain, went on looking eastward into the darkness, waiting for the coming of Sunbringer, but the sight of the great star didn't give itself up with ease. The Book makes the object of their quest sound more like a dream than a dawn, but a difficult dream, the kind that is sought with the waking will:

"There was no rest, no sleep for them. They cried their hearts and their guts out, there at the dawning and clearing, and so they looked terrible. Great sorrow, great anguish overcame them; they were marked by their pain." Perhaps they dreamed the star even before they saw it come out from behind the eastern horizon, catching sight of a light that does not rise but is suddenly there. It could even be that they saw the light both ways on the same morning, one way and then the other, or even sought to make the one light coincide with the other. One great star in the east, back in the same direction as the city they'd deserted. From out of the past, the light of dawn.

> The white square
> the square of white light
> is right in the center
> around it the rainbow pulses
> the white square
> is neither left nor right
> not above not below
> the white square
> the light
> is exactly at the center.

➤ The Death of Death

IF THE PEOPLE ON OPEN MOUNTAIN could have known everything that was happening during the last year before the coming of Sunbringer, they might have lost their nerve. By the end of that year Marksman and Little Jaguar Sun would meet their death, and would even seem to embrace it.

 Thirteen Wind would've been the first day of the year, and it would've given its name to the year, had there been any sun then. The daykeepers who live in these mountains now say that it is in the character of Lord Wind to get angry, have enemies, and even go mad, and that people can get possessed by him in years that bear his name, especially when the number is high. Thirteen Wind is as high as the day numbers go, and on top of that, this particular year would've opened with the dead star of evening in the west, had there been such a star, having first appeared there eleven score and four days earlier on Ten Blade, a day of lies and concealment. What was in the west instead, set up as a trophy by the lords of the Place of Fear, was the head of Marksman—or so they thought. They hadn't reckoned with the fact that Marksman's twin brother was practiced at sleight of hand. The trophy had never been anything but a carved squash, and the real head was where it belonged, on Marksman's own neck.

 Thirteen Yellow came when the year Thirteen Wind was a score and six days old. Lord Yellow has the character of ripeness, but the day Thirteen Yellow is downright rotten. That was the first day when the evening star, or rather the carved squash, could no longer be seen in the west.

Eight Sinner came eight days later, a good day to kneel on the ground and ask forgiveness before the ultimate god of sky, whose names include Dios in the present day. Back then, if there had been a great star, it would've appeared in the east on the morning of this day. Instead it was Marksman and Little Jaguar Sun who came out of the east, walking right here on the surface of the earth rather than climbing the sky. Earthquake, the last in a line of monsters, was still running around loose at that time. He boasted that he could destroy the whole earth, so Heart of Sky asked the twins to bring him to his knees. They roasted some birds, tempting him with the aroma. When he came begging they gave him a bird they'd baked inside a coat of plaster, even as they intended to put him in a coat of earth. The bird made him so weak they were able to bind his ankles to his wrists and bury him, somewhere in the east.

 Ten Tooth is a day of the good road, the straight road, the long road, coming eleven score and sixteen days after Eight Sinner. The road taken by Marksman and Little Jaguar Sun on that day would lead to their death, but it would also lead to their final victory. They started off on a descent that would take them below the surface of the earth in the east, following the same road the great star would later take. One and Seven Death were preparing one last game in the underworld, only this time it wasn't a ball game. They opened up a great fire pit for roasting the hearts of maguey plants. It was the first step in making a strong drink, the one called "sweet poison." Then they invited the twins to join them for what promised to be a party.

 Four Rain falls seven days after Ten Tooth, a good day for setting a table and getting started on an all-night drunk. But Marksman and Little Jaguar Sun never did get a drink down there in the Place of Fear. Their hosts challenged them to a contest in which everyone was supposed to jump over the fire pit, one by one. The twins cut the game short: they faced each other, locked their arms together, and leapt directly into the flames. Then came a drunken wake—or, better, the opposite of a wake—held by the lords of Death.

Five Marksman comes the day after Four Rain. All days named Marksman are good for honoring grandmother-fathers and all the other dead, all the way down to little children and even including people whose names are no longer remembered. The lords of Death merely slept it off, but exactly seventeen score days later, on another day named Marksman, would come the very dawn whose impossibility they had just celebrated.

Eight Lefthanded comes four score and one days after Five Marksman. It's a crazy day, unpredictable, but it's good for making oneself humble before the lord of the day that rules the current year, lest one become possessed by him. In years ruled by Lord Wind, one could become one's own worst enemy. As for the lords of Death, they were wondering what they should do with the remains of Marksman and Little Jaguar Sun in order to make sure they stayed dead once and for all. They considered putting them up in a tree in the west, as they had once done with the skull of the boys' father, but they rejected that idea on the advice of two diviners, the divine predecessors of "those who see into the middle" by looking into water. When they proposed dumping the remains in a river, the seers said this would be a "good death" for the boys, so long as what was left of their bones was first ground down to a fine powder.

Nine Wind comes the day after Eight Lefthanded. It would've been the last day named Wind in the year Thirteen Wind, had there been a sun, coming eighteen score days after the beginning of that year and counting as the first of the five unlucky days that ended it. The dead star of evening would've appeared in the west by now. The lords of Death sprinkled the ashes and powdered bones of the twins in the river.

Thirteen Death comes four days after Nine Wind. Such a day might signal the coming of a very great favor, but this one, counting as the fifth of the five unlucky days at the end of a year, might've seemed ambiguous. The ashes and dust of the twins germinated in the water. Marksman became a catfish and

Little Jaguar Sun became a bass, or at least that's what they looked like when the lords of Death looked into the water.

 One Deer comes one day after Thirteen Death, and it is an excellent day for a daykeeper, a motherfather, to go to a low and watery place and burn offerings. Had there been a sun, this particular One Deer would've given its name to a new year, the first in a cycle of fifty-two years. Lord Deer has a strong and even a domineering character; his years are bad for those who are ill, weak, or immoral. The twins came out of the water on One Deer, disguised as ragged vagabonds, and went around putting on minstrel shows. The lords of Death should've been able to read signs of the coming of dawn and the rising of the sun in all this, since the lords of the days that begin solar years appear precisely as wandering minstrels, but they hadn't a clue.

 Twelve Tooth comes twelve score and five days after One Deer; like Ten Tooth, the day on which the twins departed for the underworld, it's a day of the good road. The evening star, having shone in the western sky since Nine Wind, would've been dropping lower lately, staying in sight for a shorter and shorter time each dusk until finally, on Twelve Tooth, it failed to appear at all. If the lords of Death had seen this they might've read it as a sign of the death of death, but they went ahead and invited the minstrels into their own palace. The lords fell all over themselves trying to rush the two vagabonds into doing their best-known act, a sacrifice without death. So Little Jaguar Sun cut Marksman's head off and his heart out, rolling the one out the door and making a tamale out of the other. Then he brought him back to life, and the lords went wild at the sight. They even demanded to get in on the act. Happy to oblige, the twins sacrificed the lords who were first in rank, One and Seven Death. And of course they just left them that way.

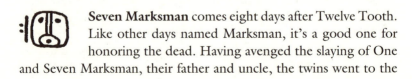 **Seven Marksman** comes eight days after Twelve Tooth. Like other days named Marksman, it's a good one for honoring the dead. Having avenged the slaying of One and Seven Marksman, their father and uncle, the twins went to the

place where One and Seven Death had buried them. One Marksman had lost his head on a bet before his body was buried, so they couldn't talk to him, but Seven Marksman's bones were complete with a skull. Not only did they try speaking to him, but they even wanted him to answer back. Their hope was that he could name all his fleshy parts back into existence, one by one, but all he managed to say was "my mouth, my nose, the eyes of my face." Thus he described the way his day name should be written, even as it is written here. The twins promised him that days named Marksman would rank first among all the days kept holy by vigesimal beings. He then rose in the east as Sunbringer, or at least his countenance did—on the day Seven Marksman, of course. On that same morning he was followed into the sky by his nephew, Marksman without any number, who rose as Sun. The solar year whose lord was One Deer was already twelve score and thirteen days old by then, but Sun had at least appeared in disguise on new year's day, even if he looked to the lords of Death like nothing but a ragged vagabond. Now, at the end of the day Seven Marksman, at the very moment Sun went down in the west, Little Jaguar Sun rose in the east as the full moon.

But perhaps the people who were watching the dawn from Open Mountain *did* know what had been going on all this time. Perhaps they had a copy of the Book with them and *read* all about it. In the days when the Book was written by words and syllables rather than by letters, and when it was amply illustrated, it was called by the same term as a crystal used for gazing, and by the same term that is used for eyeglasses and telescopes and microscopes today: *ilb'al*, "instrument for seeing." It offered a way of compensating for the damage the gods had done to the distant vision of the first vigesimal beings. Indeed, it served as a field guide to the gods themselves, describing their habitats, ranges, tracks, and identifying marks.

One complete copy of the guide to Sunbringer survives today. It covers six pages in a Mayan hieroglyphic book that went across the Atlantic in 1519, in a load of Spanish treasure, and eventually found its way to a library in Dresden. Running across five of these pages is an astronomical table that predicts both the evening and morning comings and goings of the great star, dating them by the divinatory calendar of 260 days and by the solar year as well. In a column that lists dates on which the star is due to come out of hiding and reappear in the east, written in the cramped script that packs the pages of Mayan books, is the following:

"Seven Marksman ⬤, when it falls on the thirteenth day of the month called Full Measure ⬤, brings the arrival ⬤, at the place where the sun comes out ⬤, of the great star ⬤." As it happens, there was only one occasion in all of Mayan history when a new morning star would've been expected on precisely this combination of divinatory and solar dates. We seem to have entered a world where a story that goes along sounding like a myth may suddenly make a claim on history.

The dawn the four motherfathers had long been waiting for fell on the 1,596,780th day of the New World's present era, or on June 5, 1259, of the Old World's. On that day, the great star we call the planet Venus took the role of Sunbringer, rising in the east just ahead of the sun itself. And when the sun went down in the west on that same day, the moon rose full in the east and lit the night from one end to the other, just as the sun had lit the day. For centuries afterward, the descendants of the first motherfathers would think of that time and say,

"They saw three suns in one day."

Interpreted as history, this wasn't the first of all days to have a dawn, but it did see the dawn of the Quiché kingdom, whose first capital was located at Open Mountain. The promise the other nations had made long ago, to embrace the gape named Tohil and let him suckle, was about to fall due. We don't know which of the mountains around us here today was Open Mountain. What we do know is that Tohil's Place is still Tohil's Place, and we're standing right on it.

But then, around here, a story that goes along sounding like history may turn around and make a claim on myth.

➤ White Sparkstriker

WHEN THE DAY SEVEN MARKSMAN dawned on Open Mountain, after the long darkness, Sunbringer looked really brilliant to the four motherfathers, Jaguar Cedar, Jaguar Night, Not Right Now, and Dark Jaguar. With their hearts now set at rest, they untied the wrappings of the copal incense they'd saved for this occasion, incense from all the way back at the eastern city. They held out dishes of burning copal toward the great eastern star, shaking them back and forth and side to side to keep the smoke coming. They were standing, facing the same direction they'd come from, and the Book says they were "crying sweetly." But then they called out for the birth of Sun himself.

As the moment neared, all the animals came up on the mountain peaks and looked toward the light, greeting the dawn with cries as they do now. The first sound came from a parrot, then pumas and jaguars were heard. And while eagles, white vultures, and smaller birds were spreading their wings, vigesimal beings knelt down, whether they saw the dawn from Open Mountain itself or found themselves on some other peak. In the words of the Book,

"There were countless peoples, but there was just one dawn for all nations." It was the same dawn everywhere, the same day on the calendar, even for nations the Quiché people hadn't seen since the time when they all left the city. Vigesimal beings know how to count, how to keep track of where they are in time. Even though the people on Open Mountain couldn't see the people who watched from other mountains, some of them far beyond the horizon, they could imagine just what those people might be doing at this very moment, on the damp morning of Seven Marksman. When the next day came, Eight Lefthanded, they humbled themselves before the ruler of the current year, Lord Deer, and again they could imagine what other people might be doing far away. And on and on for as long as there was light, as long as there were days to count.

All the earth was soggy when Sun himself came up, but even when he'd risen a short distance it got drier. He wasn't just a face but looked like a whole burning person, and he was every bit as hot as that. Some animals were turned into small stones, especially the ones with powerful mouths—puma, jaguar, fer-de-lance—and they remained as gapes, or gods, who need food and drink from vigesimal beings to this very day. And the daimons who still walked the earth, the ones with human form, were also turned to stone. At Swallows' Place, a little east of this peak where don Mateo has brought us, it happened to Lord Swallow. Somewhere out there on an open-topped mountain it happened to Open Mountain, perhaps within full view of the four motherfathers. Down there in the plain to our southeast, where dawn came to Middle of the Plain, he may have become a large crystal, something like the one on top of don Mateo's tabernacle, down in the town of Middle. And right up here at Tohil's Place, in this little clearing in the woods, Tohil himself was turned to some kind of stone. In other places it happened to all the other daimons. All except one.

It was White Sparkstriker who escaped, a daimon who has never been only female or only male, who has never belonged to any particular nation, who has never been brought to rest in an arbor or temple. The Book says she/he fled into the deep shade of the forest, having taken possession of all the petrified animals, and so does don Mateo. Today she/he remains as a gamekeeper, the guardian of stones with hungry mouths.

But the heat of the first dawn did leave its mark on White Sparkstriker. Whenever people catch a glimpse of her/him in a forest, in a cave, or on a back street late at night, what they see is red all over, from the hat right down to the shoes, or rather the one shoe. When she/he ran for the shade the other shoe got left behind in the sunlight, and it shrank and turned to stone. One day not so many years ago, while don Mateo was out walking, he happened to find it in a clearing. He keeps it in the bundle that holds his divining equipment, the red seeds he uses to count the days. Why there? Because White Sparkstriker is also a daykeeper—not an ordinary daykeeper, but one who once had a famous client and made a famous prediction. The client was none other than Black Butterfly Grandson of Many Hands, a prince who was ruling over the western reaches of the Quiché kingdom in the year the Old World calls 1524. Spaniards were coming his way from Mexico, and he wanted to know what would happen when they got there. White Sparkstriker goes on giving his answer to the prince even in our own time, but now he speaks from behind a mask.

Each year, in Holy Cross Many Trees, in St. Peter Fish in the Ashes, in Middle, and in forty other towns up and down these mountains, the prince and the daykeeper make a masked appearance in a play. When people happen to be talking about this play in Spanish they call it *La Conquista,* "The Conquest." Otherwise they name it *Tekum,* "Black Butterfly," or *Saq K'oxol,* "White Spark-striker," putting either the prince or the daykeeper in the title role. White Sparkstriker appears in a red mask and a nineteenth-century full-dress military uniform, red with silver and gold trim, peaked red cap with round mirrors flashing on the front and multicolored plumes on top. In Spanish $^{she}_{he}$ is called *El Brujo,* "The Sorcerer." Seen that way, the mask may look slightly demonic, but the Quiché name tells a story of a different color.

The way some towns do the play, White Sparkstriker is followed everywhere by a dwarf double, but in other towns the full-sized Sparkstriker carries a small wooden image of $^{her}_{him}$ self, tied to the belt. Either way, people say Sparkstriker has a child. So it is that $^{she}_{he}$ is neither like the first four motherfathers, who could have lived forever as four alone if the maker and modeler had not changed them, nor like the four husbands they became nor like their four wives. Not like the four who could see everything under the sky and on the earth the moment they looked, but not like the eight whose eyes were clouded either. The child is Sparkstriker's own and no one else's, and the single parent of this child can see beyond what is here and now as a daykeeper sees.

Who knows what White Sparkstriker thinks behind the red mask, but what can be heard from behind it is rhymed Spanish verse. In a town several days' walk southwest of here, not far from the ruins of the citadel where the prince once heard the answer to his question about the Spaniards in the Quiché language, the red mask tells him,

> *Never has there been such bitterness:*
> *A sign as black as it is ruinous*
> *Speaks to me of extermination,*
> *The reaper come for a whole nation,*

and the prince replies,

> *I'll hear no more of hallucinations,*
> *Fantasies, worries, preoccupations,*

and they go on speaking these lines, and many others, year after year. The lines are the same, even to the exact words, because the director of the play reads them aloud from an alphabetically written script and the actors memorize them. The same lines, that is, until someone, in this or some other town, recopies a tattered manuscript. Then, some lines might get left out. And others might be put back in, lines that survive in the writer's memory even though they got left out of the manuscript he copies from. Or a whole new speech might go in, a speech the writer picked up from some other town's version of the play, or even a speech he composed himself, after the manner of other speeches already in the play. And if people like this new speech, it might spread from one manuscript to another and from one town to another.

But one thing never changes, or at least it hasn't changed yet. Despite White Sparkstriker's forecast of bitterness and ruin, Black Butterfly takes to the field, leading an entire army to destruction at the hands of the Spaniards—or "the sons of the Sun," as they are called in the script. The suns are led by *Pedro de Alvarado,* Peter Whitish/Pallid/Motley, also known by the Aztec name he acquired in Mexico, *Tonatiuh,* or "he who goes along getting hot." But the name that sticks closest, that goes on sounding and writing itself over the top of *Alvarado*, is *el Adelantado*, the Precursor, the title held by colonial governors who exercised wide powers, also meaning "the impetuous one."

Peter Pallid rides a white horse while Black Butterfly goes on foot, but Black Butterfly has his genius with him, his spirit familiar, carved at the top of his mask. It is the male resplendent quetzal, *Pharomachrus mocino*, with shimmering green feathers that turn toward blue when the light shifts, the graceful arc of his tail three times as long as his body. A picture of the quetzal in full flight, with his tail rippling behind him as indeed it does, is printed on Guatemalan currency, on the face of the one-quetzal note. When a quetzal leaves his perch he begins by flying straight up to clear his tail, and when Black Butterfly goes into action that is what his genius does, for those who can see it.

> *Black Butterfly, armed with a mace, cuts off the head of Peter Pallid's horse.*

> *Peter Pallid runs Black Butterfly through with a lance.*

> *Black Butterfly's genius flies up over his body and then away and out of sight.*

Today the quetzal hides in the misty forests on the slopes where cypress and pine begin to give way to the lowland jungle, not far from Great Hollow with Fish in the Ashes. Perhaps he got his red belly from being so close to "him who goes along getting hot," there on the battlefield. When the one-quetzal banknote is held up to the light, a watermark appears beneath the printed bird. It takes the shape of a ghostly bust of Black Butterfly.

> *Black Butterfly's body is brought to King Quiché.*

> *King Quiché invites Peter Pallid to his court.*

> *Peter Pallid comes to the court, and King Quiché and all his subjects are baptized.*

All, that is, except one. It is White Sparkstriker who escapes, double and all, untouched by the water, unmarked by the cross. A daimon with no horns, no tail, no trident, but marked by the color red. Whenever the red daimon is not giving advice to Black Butterfly in a play, all over again, ^{she}_{he} hides in the forests of cypress and pine, in caves and canyons, and is sometimes seen on a back street late at night. One shoe is missing, the shoe don Mateo of Middle keeps inside his divining bundle.

Don Mateo brought his bundle with him today, up here on Tohil's Place on the day Eight Bird, but he doesn't need to open it and show us the shoe. We all got a good look at it long ago, at his insistence. It's a smooth, heavy, reddish stone of igneous origin, about the size of a rabbit's foot, and very much in the shape of a shoe.

All right then, but if all the rest of White Sparkstriker is red as well, why the name? And the answer:

"Sometimes, in a dream, White Sparkstriker is dressed entirely in silver. But the clothes don't quite touch the body, and the body is red." Silver is made with fire, and silver or red, this daimon stays close to the fire.

There's something right there in the name, too. Back when the New World Book was written, the word "sparkstriker" all by itself, *k'oxol,* was the term for stones that were used to strike fire. So White Sparkstriker escaped into the forest with ^{her}_{his} own kind of fire, not the distant fire of Sun, not the fire off the wooden foot of Tohil as he spins in his sandal, but fire made with sparks that fly off from stones. Today ^{she}_{he} carries a stone ax that strikes lightning. And don Mateo says a stone is left behind when lightning strikes the ground.

So here it is again, in these very mountains:

Thunderbolt

A bit of familiar folklore, this. A notion that turns up all over the world, long since spiritualized by mythologists, or psychologized. Or else traced backward through time and across continents to some anonymous and imaginary person of remote antiquity, possessed of an original mind—a person whose home, so the story always seems to go, was somewhere near the middle of the Old World.

42 ➤

thun·der·bolt A flash of lightning imagined as a bolt hurled from the heavens.

So says the desktop dictionary. Even so, there are meteorologists and geologists who know the thunderbolt as a physical object, if a troublesome object that doesn't quite belong to either of their sciences. They have a term for this object, a term that appears elsewhere in the same dictionary:

ful·gu·rite A tubular body of glassy rock produced by lightning striking exposed surfaces.

Wherever lightning strikes sandy soil it leaves behind a fulgurite, a twisting glassy mass encrusted with glassy beads.

Some neighbor of don Mateo's, watching from a distance, once saw lightning strike a small red person up in a tree, but afterward could find no body beneath the tree, nor stone. Perhaps that person had a stone ax, but who knows whether the lightning came to it, or from it, or brought the ax with it. Wherever the person went, there went the stone.

Everyone who lives in these mountains has heard of White Sparkstriker, whether or not they've ever caught a glimpse of her/him outside the play. But no one gives the name Tohil to anyone or anything they see today, much less the name Tahil, left behind a thousand years ago. These names turn up only in archives, in excavations—and yet, once we've read them, even spoken them aloud, we move a little closer to catching a glimpse of Tahil the lightning-striking ax, or hearing an echo of Tohil whose name some people once heard as Thunder. Tahil/Tohil, with one odd foot. This hard little shoe that weighs in the hand. It looks like something smelted from ore. If we read this shoe as a sign, a character recovered from a shattered inscription, it tells us Tohil got his sandal really hot.

Or else Sun got Sparkstriker's shoe really hot. Never again has Sun felt so hot as on that first day. After all, that was the only day Sun himself has ever been seen. In the words of the Book,

"Since he revealed himself only when he was born, it is only his reflection that now remains." The scribes who transposed these words from New World characters into Old World letters felt the need to add an interpretation—or, to phrase the matter more the way it is phrased in Quiché, they felt the need to tell the reader *what these words would say if we could hear what was hidden inside them*, namely,

The sun that shows itself is not the real sun.

There are people down around the Great Hollow today, people reckoned in the Book as relatives of the Quiché, who at least allow us the sight of Sun for half of each day. They say that when he reached noon on the day of his first appearance, he placed a mirror at the center of the sky and then doubled back, unseen, to the east. During the second half of that day only his reflection was seen, and so it has been on every day since.

"Reflection," those people say, and so says the Book. *Lemo'* is the word, and it's also the term for mirror. But this mirror reflects, during the second half of the day, what Sun did during the first half. Or else it reflects, during our own times, what Sun did only once, and long ago. Coming here among these Mayan nations, we seem to have entered a world where reflections are not simultaneous with the things reflected. Reading the Book, we may guess that reflections ceased to be simultaneous the moment vigesimal beings lost their perfect vision:

"They were blinded as the face of a mirror is breathed upon."

And what about the reflection in an ordinary mirror, seen close up? Leaving the land where they say *lemo'* and coming back home won't help. If any face is the true face of a vigesimal being, it's the one we all see in the mirror.

➤ Three Maidens at the Bath

AFTER SUN FIRST REVEALED HIMSELF to Jaguar Cedar, Jaguar Night, Not Right Now, and Dark Jaguar, they gave thanks before the petrified bodies of the daimons of desirous names. When they came up here on the mountain called Tohil's Place, all they had to burn before the petrified Tohil was bits of pitchy bark and wild marigolds. Tohil still spoke to them, but it wasn't the stone that spoke. It was rather his genius, appearing to them as a young man. According to the Book, he told them,

"Don't let us be hunted down, but rather hunt the creatures of the grasses and grains for us, female deer, female birds. Please come give us a little of their blood, take pity on us."

So whenever they killed deer or birds, they would anoint the mouths of the stones with the blood, and the stones, the daimons, would drink. And they drew thorny cords through their own ears and elbows, just as they had when they left the great eastern city, pouring blood by the gourdful into the gapes.

In those days the daimons would speak the moment the penitents and sacrificers arrived in their presence, even before they drank. There came a day when the genius of Tohil said,

"You must win a great many victories. Your right to do this came from over there at Abandoned Place, when you brought us here." The time had come for the nations who had begged Tohil for fire to give him their hearts and their blood, a rainstorm of blood.

Jaguar Cedar, Jaguar Night, Not Right Now, and Dark Jaguar built the first Quiché stronghold on top of Open Mountain, and from there they began to abduct the members of other nations. They would lie in wait for one or two people walking along a road and take them away, cutting them open before the stone whose genius was Tohil. From up on the peaks they gave the calls of the puma, like a woman's moaning, and the short, deep coughs of the jaguar. Once the heart and blood of their prey had been offered, they rolled the head into the middle of the road. The only tracks they left behind were those of jaguars, about the size of a fat human hand. Subtle tracks, these, with toe pads only slightly tapered and no marks at all from the claws.

When people tried to follow the tracks, the day would get cloudy and dark. All they could see in front of them was rain and mud, but they could read the name of Tohil in this. In the language of the eastern city, his name gave him the character of clouds massing together, or the character of thunder. Or Tohil now had that character because it was destined by his name. And they called the Quiché people Tohohil, "thunderers," but with the pulsation of thunder, as if to say "thunthunderers." Underneath they were calling them Tohillers, or Tohohillers, "people who utter the name Tohil repeatedly."

Sometimes Tohil, Lord Swallow, and Open Mountain went out walking, or the spirits familiar of the stones went out walking, in the forms of three adolescent boys. They did this, says the Book, "just as a way of revealing themselves," and as soon as anyone spotted them they vanished. Many times people glimpsed them bathing in a river, and that river, somewhere near Tohil's Place in the folds of these mountains, came to be known as Tohil's Bath. Perhaps someone living near enough still knows it by that name.

The enemies of the Quiché, the people who met with rain and mud every time they found someone's head in the road and tried to follow the jaguar tracks, saw an answer to their problems in this matter of the bathing. They decided to send three girls to the river.

"Let them be in full blossom, maidens who fairly radiate preciousness, so that when they go they'll be desirable," they said. It was as if they thought the three boys were of flesh and blood. Or could be tricked into becoming flesh and blood.

The women they chose were named Lust Woman, Bath Woman, and Often Married, or at least that's what they were destined to be named. They were told that if they failed to give themselves up to the boys, they would be killed. And they were to ask the boys for something that could serve as a sign that they had carried out their mission.

When the girls went off they carried laundry with them. They were on their hands and knees on the rocks beside the river, scrubbing their clothes, naked, when Tohil, Lord Swallow, and Open Mountain came along. The girls were startled, but as for the boys, they barely even stole a glance. All they asked for was an explanation, and the girls replied that they had been sent there to see them.

"We are the daughters of lords, so let a sign be forthcoming from you," they said.

"Good. Let a sign of our word go with you," the boys replied. But then they left the girls waiting by the river while they went away to plot with Jaguar Cedar, Jaguar Night, and Not Right Now.

"You must inscribe three cloaks, inscribe the signs of your being," they told them.

Jaguar Cedar was the first to write. His image, his means of showing his face, was a jaguar, and he inscribed a jaguar on his cloak.

The second was Jaguar Night. His image was an eagle, and an eagle is what he inscribed on his cloak.

And the last to write was Not Right Now. He inscribed swarms of wasps, swarms of yellow jackets on his cloak.

When the cloaks with the threefold inscriptions were finished, Jaguar Cedar, Jaguar Night, and Not Right Now went to give them to the three girls at the river, saying,

"Here is the proof of your word." They told the girls that when they got back to the lords who sent them, they should give them the cloaks to try on.

When the girls returned, the lords could see, even from a distance, that they had something hanging from their arms. They could hardly wait to get a closer look, and when they did they could do nothing but admire the cloaks, unfolding each one in turn.

One lord tried on the cloak inscribed with the jaguar, and nothing happened.

Another lord costumed himself with the eagle cloak, and he felt good inside it. He turned this way and that so the others could see. He unfurled the cloak, then gathered it back around him again.

And then the third lord tried on the last cloak, the one that was written all over with wasps and yellow jackets. The moment he got it wrapped around him they started stinging, stinging till he couldn't stand it. They looked like mere writing, but he hollered so loud he almost ripped the corners of his mouth. As the Book has it,

"It was the third inscription that defeated them."

As for Lust Woman, Bath Woman, and Often Married, it then became their profession "to bark the shins of men," as the Book puts it. They failed to seduce Tohil, Lord Swallow, and Open Mountain, but even so, they became temptresses.

Wherever Tohil's Bath may have been, these mountains are full of places to bathe, pools beside streams, below waterfalls, or fed by hot springs. And there is a woman who haunts these places, the Wailing Woman. Who knows when we first heard of her, Barbara and myself, but it was in Altar Town, to the west of Tohil's Place, that we learned anything more than what her name might suggest. It was Pedro Sabal Paja, a local motherfather, who told us her story. And it was back in May, at the beginning of the rainy season, when he had only just begun to teach us the ways of a daykeeper. He was wearing a blue serge suit, the same kind worn by Mateo Uz Abaj of the town of Middle.

"Don Pedro," I said, "last night I had a dream. I found a large jar, an earthenware jar, on the floor of a room. It appeared to be whole, but when I picked it up, it came apart in two halves, one in each hand."

"This jar, well," he said, "perhaps it's our work together, and someone is coming to screw it up. Because—and take careful note of this—the jar is secure. But when it is taken up, it comes apart in halves. So there are persons who are coming to destroy your work. A woman is coming."

"Why a woman?"

"Because yesterday was Four Foredawn, and days named Foredawn have a feminine character."

"I don't know why, but when I woke up from that dream, the day Thirteen Snake came into my head."

Now don Pedro drew back inside himself and whispered the names of days, holding his hands in front of him and moving his fingers slightly as he counted.

"Six Snake," he said out loud, "tomorrow is Six Snake. Twenty days after that comes Thirteen Snake. And you simply thought of that day?"

"Yes."

Now he whispered the name Thirteen Snake several times, then the day after that, One Death, and just as he was moving from the one to the other he suddenly looked down at his left leg. Then he looked up at me and spoke aloud again:

"This jar broke, then you thought of Thirteen Snake because that day brings an enemy. And One Death," he said with a laugh of recognition, "means a woman, even by itself. But when I came to it, I felt the lightning move this way up the road," and here he moved his finger up the center line of his left calf. "What it said was, 'The woman comes.' Lightning on the right side would've said, 'The man comes.' So, Thirteen Snake is an enemy, or envy, and One Death, a woman. After that, Two Deer means that you're learning all the days now, you're already something of a daykeeper. Three Yellow says,

"'It's ripening. You're giving the food, the drink to the mountain,' is what it says," and again he was chuckling to himself. "This is what it all means: the work is going well, but an enemy, or envy, can come and destroy it. That's why you thought, 'Thirteen Snake, One Death,'" he said, as if peering around the corner of what I had remembered thinking.

The food and drink don Pedro spoke of were not flesh and blood but copal incense, candles, and a little liquor, offered by him on our behalf, and the mountain was not Tohil's Place but stood for all mountains with names and even the whole earthly world. Whenever he burned these offerings he named our names and prayed that the Holy World would allow us to go on walking the path of novice daykeepers.

"It's like registering your names in a book," was his way of explaining it. So far he had done this four days ago, on One Marksman, and thirteen days before that, on One Deer, walking down to a shrine near a small spring in the bottom of a canyon. The shrine has two names, One's Place and Water's Place, but when he invoked it he said,

"Cloudy Pool, Clear Pool, Cloudy Lake, Clear Lake, Cloudy Sea, Clear Sea, Cloudy Depths, Clear Depths," turning a quiet puddle into all the waters of the world. The cloudy waters, he said, were like sickness, and the clear waters washed us clean. He also invoked the sheet lightning that flickers and flashes in distant clouds and casts its reflection in distant lakes, saying,

"May the yellow lightning, white lightning stir at the place where the sun comes out, at the place where the sun goes down, four corners of sky, four corners of earth," and asking that it stir beneath our own skins, casting its reflections in our blood, giving us signs of past or faraway events. He had also been invoking the help of the ancestors, saying,

"All grandmotherfathers, all motherfathers, powdered clay, powdered pumice, powdered bone," not just the dead whose names and resting places are still remembered, but the thousands who have been forgotten, whose remains might be mixed, for all we know, with any handful of earth we might pick up.

But we were in a delicate position just now, since he had asked the waters for permission to ascend to the mountains but had yet to make the climb. In three more days, on Eight Deer, he would go up on the rim of the canyon to Eight's Place, also known as Small Place of Proclamation, saying,

"Great Hill, Small Hill, Great Mountain, Small Mountain, Great Volcano, Small Volcano, Great Flat, Little Flat, Great Plain, Small Plain," turning the slopes of a mound and the level spot where he stood into all the features of the face of the earth. And forty days after that, on Nine Deer, he would climb to Nine's Place, the Great Place of Proclamation, again invoking the mountains and plains, all the way to the ends of the earth.

It happens that there are broken jars around the shrines of One's Place and Nine's Place, and that Eight's Place is crowned with scores of stacks of countless shards that reach higher than a person's head, but don Pedro said nothing about that. What concerned him was the news that we had invited a rival ethnographer, let us call him George, and his girlfriend Betty, visiting from the States, to come to dinner, and that tomorrow was the day we had picked. Tomorrow was Sunday, and what we had in mind was a proper Sunday dinner. Ah, but tomorrow was also Six Snake.

"If you show them what you've been learning," he said, "and this woman doesn't like it, then that's where the trouble will start. Or if he comes to know this work, he can destroy it. His own work isn't going well. These two things go together."

From here our conversation wandered off into illnesses, some of them "hot" in character and others "cold," the hot ones requiring cold remedies and the cold ones hot.

"The illness we call 'twisted stomach' is cold," he said. "For this, pieces of cotton cloth, rags, are put in hot water with a little salt, which is hot in character, and soaked, then wrung till all the water is out. Now the salt is carried by this rag, and put there on the middle of the belly, over the umbilicus. This heats up the stomach."

And then, with conversation about a broken jar, an envy, a female enemy, dangerous dinner guests, and a cold and twisted stomach behind us, we wandered into asking don Pedro what the Wailing Woman might be like.

"Does she appear in dreams?" asked Barbara. And here begins the answer we recorded on tape, translated according to the measure of don Pedro's voice, lines for his unbroken phrases and hard right returns for his pauses:

> No, she's not in a dream.
> She appears **in person.**
> During Lent.
> When Lent comes,
> that's her proper time.
> When there's
> bright moonlight
> and everything is clear, clear.
> One can even go out to bathe
> at night.
> Right now
> to get dry

we have to bathe during the day,
but when it's clear we can get up at night
at 1:00 or 2:00 in the morning
to go to the baths.

Now the stage is almost set for her, and when she first appears she gets a line all to herself:

It happens when
a person is
thinking about too many things
that's when
she represents herself:
the Wailing Woman.

Yes, she *re*appears, and who knows what or who she is between her representations?

She might be going along ahead of one,
or she might come
to meet one.
And she
sings songs,
and cries.

He laughs a little as he speaks that last line, the sort of laughter that seeps out around the edges of horror.

She has a white dress,
white, white.
We've heard her before, it was when we
went to the bath at the Thistles.

Now he leaves his lines dangling, one after the other, and he even raises his voice at the ends of some of them, as if asking questions:

We went out there over the top of Big Mountain—
since there's a river on the other side of Big Mountain
then, when we came through there—
where the cross is

on top of Big Mountain—
then
when we came through there—
we heard
around 3:00 in the morning,
that people were bathing in the river on the other side,
singing, crying, doing things there in the canyon,
but there was nothing there.
It was the Wailing Woman.
➢ ➢ ➢

He pauses a couple of seconds here to let her have her space, then
starts out again, slowly:

And if one is
➢ ➢ ➢
twisted,

which is another way of saying out of luck,

then she comes out,
comes out on the road,
she comes to meet a person.
One is left unconscious then,
no longer speaking, no longer
➢ ➢ ➢

and he leaves this sentence unfinished, unless a fade is a finish. The
next voice is Barbara's, asking, "Can this be cured?"

Yes indeed, with kerosene.

"Kerosene?" she asks.

Yes, with kerosene.
But not
a lot.
Just one little drink, nothing more.
When the Wailing Woman frightens a person,
then one no longer speaks,

one is left prostrate,
the body is stiff, it doesn't move.
Then,
the mouth has to be pried open with an iron tool,
to pour in the kerosene.
The person doesn't drink it.
Since kerosene is like oil,
it seeps in,
little by little it seeps in
goes on heating the person.
➤ ➤ ➤
Because the Wailing Woman is—
she's **cold.**

Now don Pedro puts a little distance between himself and her:

So we've heard, but none of us
has come to this extreme.
They say that a mere touch
feels like ice, ice, through the whole hand.
It seems that a person who touches her
ends up flattened out, thrown down
by the cold she carries.
➤ ➤ ➤

"Where does she come from?" asks Barbara.

This one comes
from the rivers.
And from the sea as well.
Because
they say that
this woman
it seems that
one day,

don Pedro is slipping a story into the conversation, telling us what
"they say" the Wailing Woman did one day—he's passing the story
on to us, not inventing it himself,

on Holy Friday
just like this last Holy Week—
on Friday—
she went to bathe
on this day, they say,
in the river.

So she wasn't among the women who watched the crucifixion.

But when God
gave the benediction
she went into the river.

That's a strange way of saying it, "benediction." What the Old World Book says is, "The veil of the temple was rent in twain from the top to the bottom; and the earth did quake, and the rocks rent; and the graves were opened; and many bodies of the saints which slept arose." As for the woman in don Pedro's story,

She didn't just die, but rather
she fell into the river
and she remained there
once and for all.
So that's when she comes out,
it's in the time of Lent that she comes out.
She deceives people.

With these last words comes a trace of laughter again. Now don Pedro has finished the story he started with "it seems that one day," but he moves right into another story, the kind that happens closer to here and closer to now.

It happened to someone there in St. Christopher Hot
Springs.

That's a town not so very far from where we're sitting. During the next lines don Pedro rolls his eyes upward, as if searching his own head:

What's his name?
I d o n 't remember

as if he were s t r e t c h i n g his memory and giving up on it at one and the same time

what surname the boy had,

but we had better believe that if he could remember the name, we'd be a little uncomfortable recognizing which family it was—why, they could almost be our next-door neighbors,

he was around twenty years old, they say,
then, he already had a fiancée.
Then
he spoke
with his fiancée, they say,

and here he speaks both their parts with a shy, delicate voice,

"Let's go to the bath at such-and-such a time."
And the fiancée said, *"That's fine.*
Come by to get me."
"Very well."
And so it resulted that
the man, they say, had
the intention of going
there
with his fiancée.
Then the fiancée came, they say,
not the real one
but the Wailing Woman.
She came to get the man up,
she knocked at the door, they say.
"The hour has come, let's go."
And the man **got up.**

He should've been surprised, as don Pedro pointed out later, since *he* was the one who was supposed to get *her* up. But never mind.

He put on his clothes and
he got his
towel, everything, soap

he was pleased to be going to the bath with his fiancée
and on arriving at the bath, they say, the man took off
    his clothes
but
she vanished
that Wailing Woman.

Now don Pedro stutters, as if he were the one who'd just seen an
apparition, then speaks rapidly, as if he were the one in a hurry:

Yet it was his fiancée that he'd, that he'd he'd seen.
Andtheboylefthisclothesthereatthebath,
andhecamenaked, wearing only his shorts
to his house
threw himself in his bed
he bolted the door, they say
and there he remained.
Around this time

which is to say around 10:00 in the morning

they went to see,
he had the room closed tight
they knocked and now he didn't, didn't answer
and so then, "What happened?"
And the fiancée
came there.
To the boy's father.
Then
"What happened to———"
I don't know what the boy's name was, *"What
    happened to him?*
I was expecting him.
We were going to the bath, but
he didn't come."
Then
they went to open the door, they say,
right away
they broke the door open,

they entered, his corpse was stiff in the bed,
naked,
and his clothes were at the bath.
This was on account of the Wailing Woman.
Oh yes.
She deceives people.

Again, laughter wells up under these words. "Only boys?" asks
Barbara.

Yes, yes.
When one is not married
and loves one's fiancée,
the Wailing Woman is ready
to screw things up.

Even before this last line is over, all three of us burst out with pained
laughter, and then we fall quiet. Don Pedro repeats his closing line
at this point, but then he almost goes back where he started:

➤ ➤ ➤

She deceives people.
She sings in the streets, in the rivers, she makes an
uproar.

This same woman, always dressed in white and always appearing at
night, is known all the way from here to northern New Mexico, and
some even say she's kin to the Siren of ancient Greece. In Mexico
City, she shows up in streets that follow or cross the buried canals of
Tenochtitlán, the city under the city. In Santa Fe, she haunts the
banks of the stream that runs through the middle of town or walks
the streets by the main irrigation canal, the Mother Ditch. But in
those faraway places she wails for her lost children, and some say she
killed them herself, perhaps by drowning. No one down here in these
mountains talks about her children, and it's only here, it seems, that
she haunts the baths and has such a clear preference for younger
men. So perhaps she's Lust Woman, Bath Woman, or Often Married,
come from out of the New World Book, still waiting for Tohil, Lord
Swallow, or Open Mountain to join her down at the river.

➤ Jealous Seeds and Crystals

THE NEXT DAY, SIX SNAKE, George and his girlfriend Betty came to Sunday dinner. He must have told her something about us, about our apprenticeship with don Pedro and the offerings he was making to the mountain gods, but they never brought this up and neither did we. What happened instead was that Betty's eye fell on one of the few books we had with us, a book on the art of William Blake. On the cover, in color, was *The Judgment of Adam,* with God the Father berobed and seated within a circle of fire, scowling and pointing down at the bowed head of a naked man.

"Blake was *crazy,* you know," she said, looking at us, and she picked up the book and started leafing through it. She said nothing more until she came to *Satan Smiting Job with Sore Boils,* in which a powerful male figure with bat wings stands on the prostrate Job, splattering some vile liquid across his chest and face while his wife kneels at his feet, wailing.

"Well, look at *this,*" she said. "I thought it was God who had smitten Job. But then, maybe for Blake, the devil *was* God." What could we say? And when she came, near the end of the book, to *Behold Now Behemoth Which I Made with Thee,* in which God and the angels look down from heaven, in complete calm, at a fanged hippopotamus standing on the land and a scaly leviathan writhing in the sea, she couldn't think quite what to say, either.

The rest of the conversation with George and Betty stayed on completely forgettable topics, and two days later, when we saw don Pedro again, we told him the whole story and showed him *Satan Smiting Job.*

"Job was a man who believed in God," he commented, "and then the evil one asked permission of God to touch this Job." So don Pedro, for his part, remembered perfectly well that the Satan he was looking at had made a deal with God. That Satan and God could enter into dialogue with one another.

"Well, we think she was talking about our work here, not about Blake," I ventured.

"That's it," he replied. "She was looking for a way of translating. Just as I told you, a woman would come, and that woman would be an enemy."

It was now Eight Deer, and early that morning, before he came over to see us, don Pedro had gone up to Eight's Place to begin the mountain offerings that would counterpoint his continuing visits to Water's Place, naming our names and asking permission of the Holy World that we might one day come to such places on our own, as daykeepers.

"When are we going to begin practicing divination?" we asked, wondering whether he might have his bundle in the breast pocket of his jacket.

"If you'd like, right now," he answered. Barbara gave him the same kind of cloth we knew he used at home, a cotton brocade made locally. This one was orange with bands of frets, diamonds, and birds running across it in black, white, green, yellow, and red. He arranged it so that the bands ran across in front of him, then reached into his vest pocket and pulled out his bundle, a cloth pouch a little smaller than a fist, and set it down in front of him. No sooner did he let go of it than he began to pray over it in a low, muttering voice—it would be some time before he taught us the words. Then, without stopping his prayer, he picked up the bundle, untied the string that closed it, and poured the contents out on the cloth: well over a hundred seeds of the flute tree, about the size of dried pinto beans but orange-red, blood-red, and sometimes the color of dried blood, mixed with ten small crystals and a pebble of opaque quartz. While these things were still spilling out he turned with a jerk to look down at his left thigh. In the same instant he stopped praying, then said, in a voice we could barely hear,

"The grandmotherfathers." He set his cloth bag aside, now empty, and pulled back his chair to show us precisely what had made him stop. He had felt the lightning in his blood, the same sheet lightning that moves over distant horizons, just beneath the skin on the back of his thigh.

"It's the ones who have died," he told us. "It's the ancestors who are giving the light for your study. And it's women, because it happened on my left thigh. Now, if the blood had moved on the front of my thigh, it would've been a sign that your living kin were in accord."

Now don Pedro set to mixing the pile of seeds and crystals by running his right hand over them, still praying in a low voice. At this stage he could've stopped to ask us what question we wanted to ask him—or rather, to ask the seeds and crystals—but he didn't. And where we might've expected to hear him inserting our question into his prayer, we heard instead the words "their study," referring to us. Then he stopped mixing and began picking the crystals out from among the seeds and putting them in a row on the far side of the pile, with their points away from him and toward us. The largest one, he explained, was the mayor, and then came a pair of aldermen. He stopped to study the crystals remaining among the seeds and then picked one out and held it vertically between his thumb and middle finger, turning it in the light.

"Look, here it is. This one has a light in it." He let us handle this crystal, the only part of his paraphernalia he ever let us touch. We turned it till we saw a small gold speck glinting inside it, then handed it back.

"If it is one's destiny, then one looks for the facet where this light can be seen. Then, if it moves up, the person who is sick will get well, or whatever it is one is asking about. If there is some trap, or if there is some enemy, then the light moves crosswise. Now, if the person is dying, the light goes up, then it almost falls on the earth. But it's not moving now. We're just practicing." Putting this crystal with the mayor and aldermen, he said,

"This one is the secretary, the scribe. And the scribe writes down what one owes, writes whether it's been paid, whether one is to be freed, writes the decree." Then he lined up the rest of the crystals, explaining that they were minor officials. When he put the pebble in the row, he said nothing.

"And what is this?" one of us asked, pointing at the pebble.

"I found it after I already had the crystals. It was in my path, at a shrine. I saw that it was a fine stone, so I put it among my seeds. I don't know what its destiny is, so I have it here. I found another one about the same size, black, but I didn't like it, so I left it in its place." Then he went back to mixing and praying, this time with nothing but seeds in the pile, and we caught the words when he said,

"Come hither, Great Place of Proclamation, come hither, Small Place of Proclamation, Cloudy Pool, Clear Pool," and later, "may the yellow lightning, white lightning stir over the Cloudy Sea, Clear Sea, Cloudy Lake, Clear Lake, Cloudy Depths, Clear Depths," and then his voice was drowned out by the rattling of the seeds until we heard him speak of ourselves, saying, "the requests have begun already, asking permission for their work, their service, their mixing, their pointing," and then he stopped his mixing of the seeds and his praying at the same moment. He blew into the palm of his hand, grabbed a fistful of seeds, and put them down to his left, saying,

"These are apart, whatever one's hand can accommodate. It's a test, like taking a pulse." Then he moved the remaining seeds off to his right, leaving a clear space in front of him, and began arranging the seeds from the handful in groups of four in rows, from left to right, between the crystals and himself. "It's not like cards, which are counted out; it's random," he said. When all the clusters of four were arranged he had one left over, which he put in position as if it were a full additional cluster. Then he pointed to the upper left cluster of four seeds and said,

"Now here, today, is Eight Deer," then he began counting, one day per cluster, pointing with his middle finger, until he reached the end, "Thirteen Snake," then he went back to the upper left and counted through again from where he left off, coming to "Six Net. So the one who spoke first, Thirteen Snake, is the enemy, and Six Net says 'the debt.' One owes by netsful, one has missed some number of days of offerings. This is the way it's done, and one mixes again."

So then he scooped all the seeds together in one pile and mixed them again, and we heard, "They are going to receive the dark beans, light beans, cloudy crystals, clear crystals," and the word "study" again, and "let the answer be given into my head." The answer to what? Was it our *study* he was putting into question? He grabbed a new handful of the seeds and began arranging them, saying to us,

"So it goes, like the first time. Sometimes it comes out on the same day again and sometimes it changes." When he had three seeds left at the end, he said,

"When there are three, one puts out two in one group and the last one by itself." Then, pointing at the upper left cluster, he said "Eight Deer" again, and at the end, when he came to the solitary seed, "One Death, 'the woman.'" On the second count through he came to "Eight Death, this means 'the woman, the woman,' whether it be a human woman or else a shrine, the place one mustn't touch. A shrine is a woman, and the work, the bundle, is also a woman. As I said the first time, Thirteen Snake says that one has made an enemy of someone, and then came Six Net, saying that one is in debt to someone. For example, suppose I asked you for money, ten or fifteen quetzals, and after a fortnight I wanted another fifteen or twenty, and you were bothered by this. Now you wouldn't want to pay, and you would no longer be in accord with me. So it is with the bundle, and the shrine."

Did don Pedro *mean* something by this "example"? Was he worried that we might tire of paying for the candles and incense he was burning for us whenever he went to a shrine, to a "woman"? If so, he never came closer than this to saying so. The costs seemed quite low to us, and in fact they didn't run anywhere near ten or fifteen quetzals.

"That completes two questions," he said, "but we have to ask four times." He mixed the seeds again, and this time we heard, "Come hither, grandmotherfathers, all motherfathers in common, the blessed departed." As he lifted his fistful and started to move it aside, a few seeds fell between his fingers. He put them all back, mixed again, and took a new handful, saying,

"Yes, when one drops some of them, one must get a handful over again." Never before had we seen him drop any seeds, and we have never seen it since. Looking back, what happened on this one occasion seems like an act put on for our benefit, but it didn't look that way then.

When don Pedro finished his arrangement of the third handful of seeds, he came out with one at the end again.

"This is a test," he commented. "It's a study, and for this reason it never comes out even. It's as if we were deceiving the seeds." He didn't say, "Oh well, this is only a rehearsal," but instead spoke of deception. It was as if there could be no such thing as a "practice" divination, not unless the practice "answer" came in a form that pointed to the practitioners.

"Now, when one is posing a real question," don Pedro continued, "it comes out with four at the end and sometimes two. At other times it comes out with one, like this, which means that a sick person will not get well. It means evil because there is only one. Now if there were four or two, the person would get well, but not with one, or with three, arranged as two and then one. The offering would not be accepted, the sick one would not get well."

Now don Pedro started from Eight Deer again, arriving at "Three Yellow. Now the day has changed. Or Two Deer, Three Yellow," he said, naming the last two days. "The day Yellow means,

"'One goes to burn incense, candles, sugar.' And Deer means,

"'The motherfather gives the food, the drink.'" On the second time through he came to "Eleven Dog, it means 'jealous words.' It's as if the two of you were jealous. You are jealous of her, and you are jealous of him, that's what the day Dog means here."

Again we thought he might *mean* something, but he went right on to a fourth handful of seeds. This time we heard him mention us by name, and we wondered more than ever where practice might end and the real thing begin. But when he came out with one seed at the end yet again, he said,

"If we were asking a true question, this would've come out even by now. The bundle knows very well that we're merely practicing." Then he counted to One Death and said, "This is the same as the second handful: it came out One Death and then Eight Death." Next, he moved his finger back and forth between the end of the arrangement and the beginning, saying "One Death, Two Deer. One Death, Two Deer," but instead of going on with the second count he said, chuckling, "It's as if you two were now walking the road of the work, and One Death said,

"'It belongs to the woman.' And Two Deer said,

"'It belongs to the man,' Deer is a male day. This is about the bundle, which is like a husband to a woman: he is hers. And like a wife to a man: she is his. And the bundle is jealous of a person's real spouse. That is why, whenever one divines or goes to the shrines, one must keep the day, one must not touch one's spouse."

After a few more practice runs don Pedro began putting his seeds and crystals back in their bag, saying,

"On another day we'll try again. You should buy some beans in the market, and try counting them out for yourselves." The beans he meant are a little larger than pintos, and they come in a mixture of colors, some of them spotted and others solid.

"What days would be good to practice?" we asked.

"The same days I'm burning offerings for you. If someone came to me right now and said,

"'Do me the favor of posing a question,' then I would answer,

"'With great pleasure,' because I'm clean today. But tomorrow or the day after, perhaps I couldn't do it. Then I would answer,

"'Wait till tomorrow,' so I could keep the day. Now, if one didn't have a spouse, or a lover, then one could say yes on whatever day a person came with a question." Which means that White Sparkstriker, who is complete to her/him self, is the perfect daykeeper, able to pose a question on any day, all thirteen-times-twenty days.

"But are some days better than others?" we asked.

"Yes, such as Deer, Death, Sinner, Thought, Foredawn, Tooth, Cane. Right now it's Eight Deer, but if we wanted to ask about something we thought might be wrong right here in the house, then Cane would be a better day. But we could say,

"'Eight Deer, what's going on here? Eight Deer, lend me the day One Cane for my question about my house, to search for something in my house, this place of mine, this shelter of mine.' One would call on One Cane because it's the next day named Cane after Eight Deer, one would ask today to lend that day. If the question were urgent, that is. Otherwise, one would have to wait."

It was time for don Pedro to go home to lunch, but we had one more question for him, a question prompted by the thought that we'd be without crystals when we practiced with beans:

"What is it that the crystals do?"

"They are authorities, and one goes before them. They are the ones who determine what days come out when questions are asked."

"They have an effect on the seeds?"

"Yes, the seeds are tuned in to the crystals, like a radio. If the crystals sent letters, they'd take a long time to get there."

That afternoon Barbara and I went for a walk, going eastward past the Altar Town cemetery and on into the countryside, among tall yellow pines and scrub oaks, past a cliff of volcanic tuff wearing down into slender pinnacles and deep crevices. Some people said they'd caught sight of White Sparkstriker around this place, so don Pedro had told us. In my mind's eye, just walking along the road and looking at nothing in particular, I saw a small figure dashing across a dark opening between two bright masses of tuff, showing his redness in the moment he cut through a shaft of sunlight, and I can see this again even as I tell about it. But when I turned and looked into the cliffs and crevices above the road, nothing moved but a few pine boughs in the breeze.

Lower down, here and there in the grit of the talus slopes, something glinted in the sun, just as it does in the mountains and canyons of New Mexico, west of Santa Fe. We stopped to gather some of these glints, each of them a topaz, clear or less often yellow or blue, octahedrons that sometimes had all their facets intact. Not one of them even reached the size of a match head, but we were wondering whether they might be suitable for the bundles we'd be receiving in a few months.

Back on the road again, scattered in the gravel, we started seeing bright spots of red. They were seeds of the flute tree, and we couldn't resist picking up a few of them. Don Pedro had warned us that these seeds were not to be handled casually, but we put them in our pockets.

➤ The Language of the Animals

"I WAS DIVING IN THE OCEAN off Catalina Island," Barbara told me, "passing through some dark plants, and then I saw light coming down through the water ahead, showing me a cave whose floor was covered with sea shells. Suddenly, a large fish came out of the cave—at first I thought it was a shark, but then I realized it was a dolphin. Then I went up to the surface, and so did the dolphin."

"Well, I was walking a path through a pine forest," I told her, "and a deer with big antlers was following me at a distance. And then, lying beside the path on the right, I saw another deer, with big antlers again, facing in the same direction I was going. When I walked past him he got up and followed right behind me. But when I looked he had split into two deer, walking side by side so close they touched, and the left deer had the left antler and the right the right."

Such was our breakfast conversation on the morning of Nine Yellow, the day after Eight Deer. When don Pedro came over we didn't tell him our dreams right away, but rather showed him the topazes we'd found when we went out walking.

"These are almost the same as crystals," he said. "But they don't have any use. Or maybe for earrings or something." Then we showed him the red seeds.

"Where did you find these?"

"In the road beyond the cemetery."

"And are there flute trees there?"

"Yes."

"Good. That means they weren't lost out of someone else's bundle. We can keep these. When I get the rest for your bundles, I can add these. But I'll keep them apart, according to which of you found them, so they won't be confused. It's a matter of their destiny."

Now we came to the matter of our dreams. When Barbara told hers, don Pedro questioned the days in a low voice, starting with Nine Yellow. When he got to Thirteen Tooth, the day of the road, he looked down at his left leg, and again when he reached Tooth, Seven Tooth this time.

"It seems this has to do with the family. The lightning moved here, on the inside of my calf, so it's inside the family. But this is the ancestors, they are the ones who are giving this sign: that the work you are accomplishing, and the permissions I am asking, are going to come out well, come out in the light. It was a woman who has already died who came out to give this news, this sign. The dream is a sign: the dolphin came out to the surface of the water, which means that the work will come out well. And the light came down into the water."

"Yes, the dolphin came up when I came up," said Barbara.

"And the work is going to mate with you, to come out in the light. But I don't know if it was your mother or your grandmother who came to give the sign."

"What about the cave?"

"The cave is the tomb of the mother or grandmother who has already died. Is your mother still living?"

"Yes, but my grandmothers are both dead."

"Then it's your grandmother who came."

"And the shells in the cave?"

"The shells are not shells, but—all kinds were found there?"

"Yes."

"Then these are the red seeds, the crystals."

"And the dark plants?"

"The plants are like the shade. When one is in the shade, the ground seems somewhat dark. When one comes out into the sun, then everything is clear."

So then I told don Pedro my dream. He looked off into space and said,

"Nine Yellow, what is this?" After a long silence, he looked at me and said,

"What this dream means, what these deer are, is the Holy World. Yes, it's the World. Water's Place and the Small Place of Proclamation. And the Great Place of Proclamation too, the three of them. And these three places are already following the two of you. If you leave here, they will go with you, they won't let you go without them, they'll go on appearing to you. Two of the deer are already united, since I've already been going to One's Place and I started going to Eight's Place yesterday. The third deer is farther away because I still haven't gone to Nine's Place. That will come on Nine Deer."

When don Pedro finished I suddenly remembered that when I had awakened from this dream, but was still sleepy, I had seen two yellow sparks in front of me, in quick succession.

"These sparks," said don Pedro, "are the light of the World. The World already knows that you two are going to accept what you're hearing. The sparks, the light is now being given to you. Right now it's tinged with yellow, but as we go along it will clarify."

At the limits of the lands of Altar Town the number eleven has four mountains higher than Eight's Place and Nine's Place, mountains whose names are so old no one thinks about what they might mean. Names that mean nothing except the four mountains whose names they are. Each mountain has a shrine on top, but these shrines are not for the scores of motherfathers like don Pedro, who serve the needs of people who live on the lands of particular lineages. The motherfather who walks to these four untouchable places is the one who looks after the entire town. He goes out to Quilaha in the east, then Socob in the west. Tamancu in the south, then Pipil in the north. The four stand for the mountains at the very limits of the earth, wherever they are, and where his two paths cross is the center of the earth.

The main road out of Altar Town climbs up to a broad sheep meadow on the shoulder of Tamancu, the southern mountain, then descends through a tall stand of cypress and pine and comes out in the town of St. Francis the High. One day, when Barbara and I were driving through this forest on the way to Altar Town, a coyote ran across the road just in front of us and was quickly out of sight. When we told don Pedro about this he said,

"That's appalling!"

And that is the sum total of what he said. But there did come a day when he happened to tell us that just as people have dogs, so mountains have coyotes. He was talking about the shrines on the lands of his lineage at the time, the shrines called "the resting place of the house," which is to say the foundation.

"When someone hasn't given the motherfather offerings for the resting place, then a coyote comes to the house, enters the yard to take away the chickens, or the pigs, or sheep, whatever people have at their houses. He grabs them and eats them. Then one has to divine, asking,

" 'Why did this dog of the World enter, why did this dog of the mountain penetrate the house?' Then the seeds say,

" 'Because of the untouchable place, the untouchable place.' One can divine that they haven't complied with the requirements of the resting place of the house, which serves to prevent the animals of the World from entering their house." Then don Pedro looked away from us and off into the distance, and we could see a story coming even before he spoke the opening words:

It h a p p e n e d one time,

he's taking us s o m e distance back,

> I don't know what year,
> this was told to us by our
> grandfather,
> who said
> there was a lord
> who had a lot of **lucre,** they say.

There are the words "they say" again, it was already that kind of story when his grandfather heard it, the whole thing is embedded inside an indefinite number of quotation marks.

> So, he paid servants
> who came to work in his house
> I don't know how many servants
> he had under contract.
> Then

there came a day
in the course of the work, they say,
when the lord didn't want to spend his money?

Don Pedro intones these last words as if he were the lord himself,
asking, "Why should I spend my money?"

Then he said,

and he's going to sound a little close-mouthed, as if he were talking
to himself,

"Better I go out hunting."
For the meals
of the servants.

During his next line don Pedro, who sits with the south to his right,
turns his head a little toward that direction and tilts it back slightly,
as if to glance at the skyline out of sight beyond the wall:

Then he went up here on Tamancu.
On Tamango,

the same name twice, pronounced as if in Spanish the second time,

they say.
He went until he came upon a
a **deer,** they say,
a buck.
But he had, what's it called,
silk in his
his antlers
they were adorned with silk.

"Silk?" we ask.

Yes, silk.
Threads,
threads of silk.

"Ah," we say, we've decided the buck he's talking about is "in the
velvet," as we would say. And when a Zuni tells a hunting story up

north in New Mexico, or a Maya tells one down in the lowlands of Yucatán, a buck in the velvet is not to be treated as if he were just any deer.

> Yes.
> Then
> the lord
> was able to kill this
> this deer.
> Yes.
> And then
> he brought it into the house, they say.
> For them to butcher, divide, everything.
> Then
> all of a s u d d e n he got sleepy.

Getting sleepy, even suddenly, still has a s l i d e to it.

> At about
> 3:00 in the afternoon, they say
> he went to bed.

And now don Pedro sighs as if he were the one falling asleep,

> A a a a a h, he slept—
> then he **dreamed** during these hours, they say.
> Then Tamancu **spoke**
> with **Mines**
> in spirit.
> Tamancu has contact with Mines.

"With where?" we ask, not having heard of a place named Mines.

> A **world,**
> a mountain of the Gathered Range
> named Mines.
> Of the Andean Cordillera.

The Gathered Range, which people around here think of as an extension of the Andes, rises some distance north of Altar Town. It is indeed massive, and it supports a high, cold plateau with open grasslands. At a town named Drinking Water, at the foot of the steep slope on the south side, there were silver mines in the time of Spanish rule.

> Then
> Tamancu
> spoke with Mines.
> "Mines, do me a favor
> send me the
> little dog
> the bobbed one."
> It doesn't have a tail—
> or the tail is small,
> bobbed.

Who knows what dog this is. All the wild members of the dog family have very long tails. The only small native dog from anywhere near would be the chihuahua—which does have a rather short tail, if not a bobbed one.

> Then the lord woke up, they say.
> "What is this?
> Tamancu spoke with Mines—
> the dog is going to come—
> the bobbed one,"
> said the lord,
> ➤ ➤ ➤
> then
> he paid his servants not to go to their houses,
> since he had sheep,
> I don't know how many hundreds of sheep he had.
> He told the servants to stay around the corral
> with fires going.

Now don Pedro goes on describing the instructions to the servants, but he sounds insistent, as if taking the part of the lord:

> And he ordered them to bring a **lot** of **fire**wood.

Here follows a silence of a few seconds, as time goes by in the story:

> ➤ ➤ ➤

The servants were awake in the middle of the night.
All of a s u d d e n they got sleepy.
By around 1:00 or 2:00 in the morning, when they
        woke up—
all of the sheep

and here don Pedro just keeps us waiting, waiting for the inevitable

> ➤ ➤ ➤

had been **killed.**
Because, how to say it,
that **deer** was the **horse**
of Tamancu.

So mountains have their own kind of dog, and they also have their
own kind of horse. So watch out for bucks in the velvet.

> Yes.
And since the lord killed it,
Tamancu spoke to another
another mountain—
one that has more power—
and then it came to do justice.
How many leagues is it
from Mines
to here?

Yes, they still speak of leagues in these mountains, about three miles
to one league.

> It seems there are
eight leagues from here to Deep Pool.

That's a big town northwest of here.

> And one league to Drinking Water
makes nine,
and more
beyond there

it comes to about **fifteen** leagues.
And the animal came in a **moment**
to do ^{jus}tice here—

With his sheer words don Pedro makes a declaration, "to do justice here," but at the very same time he sounds like a second person expressing amazement at this declaration, intoning the words almost as if he were asking a question—"to do justice all the way over here?"—but not quite to the point of crossing the fine line between amazement and disbelief.

> Then, such is, what to call it,
> such is the coyote.

We looked a little puzzled at hearing this little bob-tailed dog called a coyote, so don Pedro explained that there are three kinds of coyote:

"Coyotes proper are a lot like ordinary dogs," he said, "and they are found nearby. Then there are the hide coyotes, they only have hides, no hair on their hides, just hides. And then the bobbed ones, they have no tails, as if the tails had been cut, the 'bobbed little ones,' as we say." The "hide coyotes" sound like the Mexican hairless, and they in turn make the "bobbed little ones" sound as though they might indeed be the chihuahua, the only other New World dog that seems at all odd. But don Pedro summed the matter up this way:

"Such are the coyotes, and they come around houses to snatch the chickens." As for old man Coyote himself, who's always getting in trouble in stories they tell up north, perhaps he deserves this picture of himself, sometimes hairless and sometimes a bob-tailed runt.

On another day we learned that mountains not only have their own horses and dogs, but their own chickens as well.

"The quail is the chicken of the World," said don Pedro.

"And do people hunt them?" we asked.

"Yes, and their flesh is rich, the same as chickens, but they eat the corn one sows in the field. They come onto the bare ground and scratch out the corn that's buried."

"What if one comes across quail in the woods?" we asked.

"It could mean good luck. But if a quail crosses one's path it could be bad, according to which way it goes, or whether it dives into a canyon, which signifies evil. A movement to the right is good, to the left is evil. The World is the one who sends it, sends it as an announcement. Since animals don't talk, they cross one's path." And then don Pedro got that storytelling look in his eye again, saying,

> It's like the squirrel.
> It happened to a fellow from just above here,
> he's almost a neighbor of ours.

So it's someone from nearby again, like that young man who was taken to the baths by the Wailing Woman. Someone whose name don Pedro might almost remember.

> Now this fellow
> in the time of Ubico
> in '36 or
> '37

General Ubico was a dictator, the old-fashioned kind who got a lot of construction done and didn't just fill graves

> when all kinds of papers were asked for—
> certificate, identification
> summons, I don't know
> how many papers—

our protagonist might've had to show that he had already put in two weeks of conscript labor on public road projects that year, or to make a case that he shouldn't be arrested for vagrancy and shipped off to a plantation on the hot south coast

> now this fellow
> didn't take his papers with him.
> He didn't remember.
> When he took the road to St. Francis the High, he went
> to sell
> his blankets.

so he's a merchant, selling the wool blankets people weave in Altar
Town, and his path will take him near Tamancu, where all sorts of
things seem to happen

> But
> when he left his house, he was now about a
> league and a half, or two leagues
> from his house,

that would put him very close to the place where the coyote crossed
our path

> then a squirrel came out—
> it crossed the road,
> to the left,
> it went inside a tree.
> Since there are trunks of massive trees
> that have holes,
> and the squirrel went inside there—
> l o o k i n g at this fellow as he came along,

the squirrel doesn't just make a leftward mark, the legible mark of
evil, but s t a r e s at the person who ought to be reading it

> but the fellow didn't think about what it announced, this
> this animal—
> then, when
> he went on down to St. Francis,
> he just handed himself over—
> they were looking at

don Pedro pauses just a moment as he chooses the right word

> the tickets,

and there it is, the kind of paper that gets you somewhere, but

> the poor fellow went for a stay in jail,
> now he didn't sell
> his goods.
> He just handed himself over.

"Sell" becomes "just handed over" at the same time "his goods" become "himself," and don Pedro, who chuckles at the thought, states it in fewer words than a structural analysis would've taken to reveal the hidden workings of the mythic mind. Now he looks back over the story:

> This was the announcement the animal gave
> looking at him here as if he were already in jail there.

So in case we missed it, just as the poor fellow who forgot his papers missed it, that's the way he should've read the squirrel that not only ran leftward across his path but went for a stay in a hollow in a tree, staring out at him. The squirrel said as much as a squirrel could without speaking, writing in the way that squirrels write, and it was up to the man to put words to this writing.

> Such are all the animals.
> The quail, rabbits,
> and the jays—
> the **jays,**
> when one goes on the road,

here we go again, don Pedro closes off the story of the squirrel, but he lights up the moment he speaks of jays, dark Steller's jays they are, black on the head and crest and dark blue for the rest, and sometimes

> they suddenly whistle:

First comes a loud cry, but with the second cry don Pedro cuts to a voiceless whisper that almost whistles, meanwhile shifting his vowels from the back and middle of the mouth (*ao*) to the front (*ie*):

> "S H A O W W W W s h i e w w w w,"
> then, there is
> evil
> in the road.
> Since the jays are **whistling.**
> And when they just sing,
> "S H A O W W W W S H A O W W W W
>   S H A O W W W w,"

it doesn't mean anything.
But when it's, "S H A O W W W W s h i e w w w w,"
then, there is
a problem in the road.
Yes.

So when these jays just repeat themselves, singing the same thing several times, there's nothing to read in their sounds—except that we know there are jays around even if we can't see them. But when they sing and then cut to a whistle, keeping some sounds the same (*sh* and *w*) while changing others (*ao* to *ie*), they almost sound as if they might be conjugating a verb, something like saying "befall, befell" in English. There are no such words as "shaow" or "shiew" in Quiché, but the word for this jay is *xar* (pronounced "shar") and the word for cricket is *xir* ("shir"), so there's a hint, a resonance at the back of the head, of a transformation in the jay itself. Even without that resonance we would still have the fact of the change in the jay's cry, the difference between the two parts, and that difference invites us, or invites a person who is alert to omens, to look for something more than the mere presence of jays in the pines that shade the road. But "animals don't talk," so it's up to us to put words to the difference, to think what change might befall us in our easy walk along this road.

"What about that coyote we saw on the road, up near the pass?" we asked don Pedro.

"Which way did he go?"

"To the left."

"But what did he do then?"

"He jumped up the embankment."

"And let's say he went on up the mountain after that. Then this would be good. Now, if he had gone down, even if it were to the right, but down, then that's where the evil would be. But he jumped up after crossing the road."

"The other night we saw a possum walking along the road. And he was moving very slowly," I ventured.

"That's the custom of the possum. It doesn't walk rapidly but scarcely moves," said don Pedro, and then he added, laughing, "as if it were about to die."

"But what does it—"

"It doesn't mean anything."

"What if he'd crossed the road?"

"No, not even then. Only the fox, armadillo, jay, they're the ones who give announcements, and the quail."

And, of course, the squirrel.

There came a day, perhaps it was a year or so later, when I found myself in a big hurry to negotiate a series of twisting parkways and dog-eat-dog rotaries to get from Arlington Heights to an office in downtown Boston, pick up an auto insurance policy, and then reach my campus in Back Bay in time to teach a class about the Maya. As I neared the Charles River in Cambridge a squirrel ran to the right directly in front of me, then leapt the curb and shot straight up the trunk of a tree to a high branch. After that I encountered not a single road crew patching a pothole, nor was this one of those days when a truck driver strays onto Storrow Drive and wedges his rig under a low bridge. The traffic fairly parted in front of me, the light at the end of my exit ramp was green, there was a legal parking place on the street directly in front of the building, the elevator door was standing open, I was the only passenger to the fortieth floor, a sign pointed directly to the right office, and the receptionist had my papers waiting for me. What could I do but tell my students the whole story?

➤ Two Rhythms at Once

DAYKEEPERS LEARN to *speak* the thirteen times twenty days, backward and forward. Some of them write important dates in the squares of printed wall calendars, the kind that chart one week per line and one month per page, or in the margins of printed almanacs, the kind that keep track of saints' days and the phases of the moon. But the count they've been keeping for the last two and a half millennia would continue even if no one ever wrote anything down again.

"What about a lapse of memory?" you may ask. Well, let's suppose we didn't think about the calendar for a few days, and when we thought of it again, counting from the most recent date we could remember, we slipped in one day too many, thinking it was now Eight Deer when it was really only Seven Death. Up the path to Eight's Place we would go, only to find the hilltop abandoned when we got there. We could've saved ourselves the trouble by checking on the plans of our neighbors.

Reciting the thirteen day numbers is no problem, at least not by itself. Memorizing the twenty day names in correct order isn't all that difficult, though it's a little harder to learn them well enough to begin and end just anywhere, rather than starting from some fixed point. The trick is to remember to keep turning back to one again whenever the numbers reach thirteen, while

Jun Kej
Kib' Q'anil
Oxib' Toj
Kajib' Tz'i'
Job' B'atz'
Waqib' E
Wuqub' Aj
Wajxaqib' Ix
B'elejeb' Tz'ikin
Lajuj Ajmak
Julajuj No'j
Kab'lajuj Tijax
Oxlajuj Kawuq
Jun Junajpu
Kib' Imox
Oxib' Iq'
Kajib' Aq'ab'al
Job' K'at
Waqib' Kan
Wuqub' Kame
Wajxaqib' Kej
B'elejeb' Q'anil
Lajuj Toj
Julajuj Tz'i'
Kab'lajuj B'atz'
Oxlajuj E
Jun Aj
Kib' Ix
Oxib' Tz'ikin

at the same time letting the names repeat themselves only every twentieth time. When you can keep both these rhythms rolling for a while it creates an odd tingle in the back of the mind, feels like singing two different songs at once, something like counterpoint, but the two songs differ in length, and they don't come out even till you've sung the thirteen numbers twenty times and the twenty names thirteen times. Or it's something like harmonic progression, but it takes you thirteen score chords, all of them different from one another, to get where you're going.

Suppose we start from One Deer, the day when people who already qualify as daykeepers begin their work, making their first visit to Water's Place, and the day when the names of daykeepers in training are first announced at Water's Place. If we start with One Deer, we'll keep noticing the number one as it comes up:

> One Deer, Two Yellow, Three Thunder, Four Dog, Five Monkey, Six Tooth, Seven Cane, Eight Jaguar, Nine Bird, Ten Sinner, Eleven Thought, Twelve Blade, Thirteen Rain;
> One Marksman, Two Lefthanded, Three Wind, Four Foredawn, Five Net, Six Snake, Seven Death, Eight Deer, Nine Yellow, Ten Thunder, Eleven Dog, Twelve Monkey, Thirteen Tooth;
> One Cane, Two Jaguar . . .

and so on. Meanwhile we'll be noticing the name Deer whenever it returns, at a different pace:

> One Deer, Two Yellow, Three Thunder, Four Dog, Five Monkey, Six Tooth, Seven Cane, Eight Jaguar, Nine Bird, Ten Sinner, Eleven Thought, Twelve Blade, Thirteen Rain, One Marksman, Two Lefthanded, Three Wind, Four Foredawn, Five Net, Six Snake, Seven Death;
> Eight Deer, Nine Yellow, Ten Thunder, Eleven Dog, Twelve Monkey, Thirteen Tooth, One Cane, Two Jaguar, Three Bird, Four Sinner, Five Thought, Six Blade, Seven Rain, Eight Marksman, Nine Lefthanded, Ten Wind, Eleven Foredawn, Twelve Net, Thirteen Snake, One Death;
> Two Deer, Three Yellow . . .

and so forth. If we were to start our count with One Marksman instead of One Deer, we would notice Marksman whenever it came up again, and the sequence of its numbers would be the same as for Deer. The full sequence of numbers, relative to names, creates a double series, with One through Seven alternating with Eight through Thirteen:

One, **Eight,** Two, **Nine,** Three, **Ten,** Four, **Eleven,** Five, **Twelve,** Six, **Thirteen,** Seven

and back to One again. This means that the rites at One's Place and Eight's Place are so timed that the set of day names for one shrine is repeated, in the same order, for the other, with the rites at the second shrine running as closely as possible (twenty days) behind those of the first:

One Deer, One Marksman, **Eight Deer,** One Cane, **Eight Marksman,** One Death, **Eight Cane,** One Rain, **Eight Death,**

at which point Nine's Place and days numbered nine are added to the alternation of one and eight, repeating the same set of day names for the third time but running forty days later than eight, which is still running twenty days later than one:

Nine Deer, One Tooth, **Eight Rain,** *Nine Marksman,* One Snake, **Eight Tooth,** *Nine Cane,* One Blade, **Eight Snake,** *Nine Death,* One Monkey, **Eight Blade,** *Nine Rain,* One Net, **Eight Monkey,**

and on the eve of Eight Monkey, which comes closer than any other day in the series to halving the distance between the first of all visits to One's Place and the last of all visits to Nine's Place, apprentice daykeepers are visited by their teachers. Each apprentice is ready with a large earthenware jar and a small calabash, or some other small vessel, neither of which has ever been used before. The teacher picks up the jar with both hands and breaks it. *I found a large jar, an earthenware jar, on the floor of a room. It appeared to be whole, but when I picked it up. . . .* The shards of the jar are used as dishes for the burning of copal incense, and the name of the initiate is spoken into the smoke. The calabash receives water from Cloudy Lake, Clear Lake, Cloudy Sea, Clear Sea, and the ashes from the burning of the incense are emptied into it. *I was diving in the ocean, passing through some dark plants, and then I saw light coming down through the water ahead. . . .*

The next morning, on Eight Monkey, initiates accompany their teachers to Eight's Place, the Small Place of Proclamation. The shards and calabashes find their places among the stacks upon stacks that are already there, each and every item left in someone's name, a vast public registry with no writing in it. Then the initiates receive their divining bundles, which they have never seen or touched before, and cast their own offerings into the fires. After that, as the days move along, both the old and new daykeepers go to the three shrines:

Nine Tooth, One Thought, **Eight Net,** *Nine Snake* . . .

after which a new number comes into play, the number eleven, with Eleven Deer coming eighty days after Nine Deer, which came forty days after Eight Deer, which came twenty days after One Deer. But eleven is too great a number for ordinary daykeepers, and too great even for their teachers. While they all continue with one, eight, and nine, the number eleven is taken up by the motherfather who says prayers and burns offerings for the whole of Altar Town, going where those of lower rank cannot see him, to the four high mountains that mark the limits of the town's lands. His purpose is to moor the town, to make it ride steady on the moveable earth. He goes east to Quilaha on the first day numbered eleven and west to Socob on the second:

Eleven Deer, One Dog, **Eight Thought,** *Nine Blade,* Eleven Marksman, One Foredawn, **Eight Dog,** *Nine Monkey,*

and on Nine Monkey, when the town's motherfather is halfway through his task of stabilization, the bundles of the new daykeepers become truly their own at the Great Place of Proclamation. After this, they can go on visiting the shrines for the numbers one, eight, and nine with or without their teachers. Meanwhile, on the next two days numbered eleven, the town motherfather completes his task, going south to Tamancu and north to Pipil:

ELEVEN CANE, One Sinner, **Eight Foredawn,** *Nine Net,* ELEVEN DEATH, One Thunder,

and Thunder is the day whose name in Quiché is Toh, once the day of Tohil who demanded payment, Tohil who had a taste for blood. Daykeepers finish their business at Water's Place on One Thunder, paying up on any debts of words or candles or incense or liquor that may have accumulated since One Deer. They need not come back to One's Place for six times thirteen days, when One Deer comes again. By now the number eleven has dropped out as well, leaving only eight and nine still in play:

Eight Sinner, *Nine Thought,* **Eight Thunder,**

and here is Toh again, when daykeepers pay their debts at the Small Place of Proclamation. They need not return there for six times thirteen days, when Eight Deer comes again. Ordinary daykeepers can leave the number nine aside as well, waiting for the return of Nine Deer, but motherfathers who work on behalf of lineages will continue to worry about nine for four score days past Eight Thunder:

Nine Dog, Nine Foredawn, Nine Sinner, Nine Thunder,

and so they reach the final day of payment. They don't name Tohil himself on this day, and they don't stand in front of a stone with a mouth, but at least they call upon the lord of the day Toh and burn heaps and piles of offerings for him, sending up a column of black copal smoke from the mountaintop of the Great Place of Proclamation. The hearths up there are on two grassy mounds that may well hide the fragments of ancient temples. And the mountain rises a short distance west of the plaza of Altar Town, just as the pyramid dedicated to Tohil rises on the west side of the plaza in the town where King Quiché met Peter Pallid.

Nine Thunder leaves only eighteen days to go before One Deer, when everything starts over again. But the quiet time for ordinary daykeepers, from Eight Thunder to One Deer, lasts two score and eighteen days, which is to say two moons. For Barbara and myself, the first Eight Thunder happened to fall three days after a full moon, and the moon was one day short of rising full again when we found ourselves and our new bundles far from don Pedro and far outside of Altar Town, in the small clearing on top of Tohil's Place with don Mateo.

➢ On the Road to Ruin

FOUR LAKES REFLECT THE LIGHTNING that moves over distant horizons, but they mark out a much larger world than the four mountains that mark the limits of Altar Town. Even so, the western lake coincides with Altar Town's western mountain. According to don Pedro, this lake is a small pool in the rocks on top of Socob, and come to think of it, there is an old Quiché word for water jar that sounds the same as Socob. He said that when the sky lights up in the direction of Socob, or Water Jar, it means that rain is on the way. The same is true for lightning over the southern lake, only that one is the largest and deepest lake in all these mountains, spreading wide between tall volcanoes. It is known by the same name as a town whose southern limit it marks, a name that means Puppet Trees.

When lightning is seen in the clouds above the other two lakes, to the north and east, it shows that rainy weather is on the way out. The northern lake is near a mountain called Landslide Place, on the northern boundary of a town called Sweatbath House. It is only about eight inches deep, don Pedro said, and about the size of the room we were sitting in when he told us about it, which was not very large. The eastern lake is located at Dripping Place, but he didn't know just where that might be. Even so, knowing the locations of the other three lakes makes it possible to plot a likely place for it.

The western lake is equidistant from the northern and southern lakes. If we assume that the eastern lake at Dripping Place is at the fourth corner of a quadrangle of four equal sides, and if we plot it that way on a map, it falls near the eastern limit of a town called Among the Rocks. Now, it so happens that Among the Rocks is the last town toward the east whose people speak the Quiché language. Not only that, but Sweatbath House, bounded by the northern lake, and Altar Town, bounded by the western one, are the last Quiché towns toward the north and west.

As for the southern lake, it marks the southern limit of the last towns in that direction whose people belong to the Fire Tree nation. They are not speakers of Quiché, but their language is more closely related to Quiché than any other, and there was a time when they were ruled by the Quiché kings.

What, then, might we find where the east-west line from Dripping Place to Water Jar crosses the north-south line from Landslide Place to Puppet Trees?

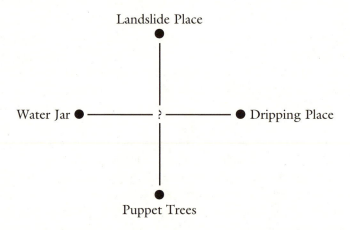

The answer is: the town of Quiché itself, *K'iche'*, the place whose name means "Many Trees," founded by the fourth and fifth generations of Quiché kings.

And, in the rural reaches of Many Trees, a little southwest of the town center, is a fifth lake, much smaller than the lake at Puppet Trees but unsurpassed among all the bodies of water that lie within the limits marked by the other four lakes. The name of this middle lake is *Lemoa'*, which means "Mirror Water."

Also within the limits of Many Trees, a little northwest of its center, is the mountaintop known as Tohil's Place.

The imaginary lines that cross at Many Trees are not the same as the imaginary lines of latitude and longitude that tell us the town is 15° 2′ north of the equator and 91° 9′ west of the observatory at

Greenwich, but they have their own way of telling us where we are, or where we once set foot without knowing it at the time.

Much of the land around Many Trees was once a plain, now dissected by a maze of canyons. Fragments of the plain remain in the form of tablelands, each one about 2,000 meters above sea level. The largest single fragment runs eight kilometers from north to south and gets almost as wide as four kilometers from east to west. From the cuts on its long eastern edge the streams turn south and then east to form the Great River, also called the Motagua, which runs east through a widening valley to the Gulf of Honduras. On the way there the Motagua gathers up the small river that flows through the ruins of the eastern city where Jaguar Cedar first loaded Tohil in his backpack.

Where the tableland falls off to the west the streams turn north and east and then north again, first becoming the Black River and then emerging from the mountains as the great Usumacinta, the River of Revered Monkeys, running all the way through the northern rain forests and savannahs to the Gulf of Mexico. At the northern end of the table the headwaters of the Motagua and Usumacinta cut their canyons to within less than a kilometer of one another.

The canyons that border the southern end of the table belong to the Motagua, but thirteen kilometers farther south, where the Pan American Highway follows an east-west ridge, streams find their way south through the row of volcanoes that marks the Pacific rim, some of them headed for the lake of the south and others going all the way to the ocean.

On this high tableland in the middle of the Americas, at the heart of the Mayan highlands, at the uppermost reaches of rivers that run to three seas, equidistant from four lakes and near the fifth and middle lake, is the center of the town called Many Trees.

There are two sides to Many Trees, one of them full of people and the other full of ghosts. On the east side is Holy Cross Many Trees, founded soon after the arrival of Peter Pallid. It stands in the open, away from any canyon rims, with streets laid out in a grid plan around a central plaza. There was a time when travelers approaching Holy Cross could see a single stone bell tower in the distance, rising over the red tile roofs of whitewashed houses. It looked like the single tower of an unfinished cathedral, but seen close up it turned out to rise, as if by mistake, from the middle of the palace that houses the office of the regional governor. Perhaps there was once a cathedral on the site of the palace and the tower was the only surviving part of it, or perhaps a new cathedral was once projected and the tower was the only part that ever got built. However that may be, there is an actual cathedral, without any tower, on the left flank of the palace. The facade has three tiers of simple columns, cornices, and pediments, topped with pinnacles and entirely covered with white stucco. There are multiple niches, but all except one is empty. The dome over the crossing has no tile on it, just white stucco.

Much of the stone in the older buildings on the east side of town was taken from the still older buildings on the west side, leaving nothing but mounds and rubble behind. The streets that lead toward the ruins pass through the walled compounds of an army base that seems intended to protect the modern Guatemalan state from the ghost of the ancient Quiché kingdom. Or at least that's what the base looks like in peaceful times; at other times it reveals its character as the stronghold of an army of occupation. Speeches are made in which the word "reconquest" is heard, and lists of selected local civilians are written in red on public walls by nameless midnight scribes. The Quiché leader of a rural hamlet is called to the palace, where the governor, who is not a Quiché, threatens him with jail if he continues to make speeches with words like "poverty," "injustice," and "freedom" in them.

"Blessed are the poor, for theirs is the kingdom of heaven," says the governor.

One day, a Quiché who organized a rural savings and loan cooperative is shot while walking home by two men in black masks and army boots. Then the director of Radio Quiché disappears and is found the next day with his hands tied and his skull crushed. Next, the first Quiché to serve as mayor of Holy Cross in two centuries, a Christian Democrat who opposes the use of violence, is machine-gunned while hoeing corn by two masked men who are seen driving away in an army jeep. The Guerrilla Army of the Poor blows the tower off the governor's palace, killing two pedestrians. In the next town north, Quiché men armed with old hunting rifles kill a wealthy landowner and fire shots at military conscription officers. To the south, near Mirror Water, three Quichés are arrested for carrying bundles full of food; they deny that the food is for guerrillas, but they are taken away and never seen again. In the west, beyond the ruins, the families of a farming community awake to find themselves surrounded by soldiers armed with Galil rifles from Israel, and when they attempt to flee they are showered with grenades from Bell helicopters supplied by the U.S. Department of Commerce. To the east, as don Mateo and his neighbors walk home from market in a group, they step aside to let a personnel carrier full of soldiers speed by in the opposite direction, toward Holy Cross. As they continue walking they see a large bonfire beside the road up ahead, and as they get closer they realize that what is burning is a pile of bodies. It's the people who started home from market not long before they did.

In the course of two years, the mortuary in Holy Cross handles 2,020 bodies of civilians who died (as a matter of official record) from unnatural causes, and the newspapers report twice that many deaths. A billboard on the main highway into town says,

"The army carries out its mission." Things quiet down again, except of course for those whose names turn up on lists of selected local civilians. There are no official inquiries into the recent past, but people all around the countryside know the locations of mass graves. They speak the word "justice" in prayers and private conversations, and they keep alive all the names of the dead and missing.

Heading west out of Holy Cross, walls give way suddenly to cornfields and the pavement to gravel, and then, to the left of the road, a solitary knoll rises from the flat, covered with brush. The practiced eye can see that it sits on an artificial earthen platform, grown over with corn plants. "Guard Post" is the name the European imagination has given this site, but the knoll is a pyramid, the temple gone from the top. West of it, still on the platform and hard to make out among the rows of corn, is a courtyard flanked by the long foundations of two palaces, and at the western end is a ball court with corn plants growing up and over its banked sides and spilling out its open ends. Below the platform, in every direction, lies the main residential district for the commoners of the old town of Many Trees, completely invisible from anywhere farther away than the eyes of people who look at the ground in front of their own feet. In roads and paths, in weeded fields, and in the bare yards of scattered farmhouses the traces of the old town come to the surface. Here is a shard from the rim of a cooking pot, there a fragment from a flint knife or obsidian blade. The broken-off end of a lava grinding stone, flecks of charcoal or smears of ash from kitchen hearths. Or some fragment that clearly betrays the human hand but gives no picture of what the whole object was.

No one remembers what the Guard Post was called by the people who built it, but the people who own and plant the place today are named Rojas. According to the New World Book, the first-ranking noble house of Many Trees took the name Rojas when Holy Cross was built, its previous name having been Kaweq. The baptismal name of the man who would have ruled at that time, had there still been a Quiché kingdom, was Juan, and the last time we stopped at the Guard Post, the man who allowed us to enter the cornfields there bore the name Juan Rojas. He didn't care at all to talk about the past and soon went back to weaving a hat out of palm fibers, but for what it's worth, his ancestors retained the right to hold serfs until 1801, when reforms began to sweep the Spanish empire.

Not far beyond the Guard Post the tableland falls away three hundred feet into canyons, but just a little farther west, beyond a ragged isthmus, lies a high island of flat land about five hundred yards across. The main district of the old side of Many Trees was there, the citadel named Rotten Cane. Across the canyon to the south, on a similar island, are the mounds of Bearded Place, settled one generation before Rotten Cane. And across the canyon to the north, on a third island, are the mounds of Ilok Place, founded by a noble house named Ilok. After four and a half centuries of abandonment the woods have come up over the canyon rims and grown around and even inside these ruins, leaving very little to be seen from a distance.

The Book gives the names of the founders of Rotten Cane as Lord Plumed Serpent and Lord Holy Sweatbath, who ruled jointly in the fifth generation of Quiché kings. That was seven generations before the invasion led by Peter Pallid, which took place, by Christian reckoning, in 1524. With a total of twelve generations to span the distance between that date and 1259, when the kingdom dawned at Open Mountain on the 1,596,780th day of New World reckoning, the average reign comes out at about twenty-two years and the founding of Rotten Cane falls close to the middle of the fourteenth century. It was Lord Plumed Serpent's line that later took the name Rojas, while Lord Holy Sweatbath's line chose the name Cortés. No one around the town of Many Trees bears the name Cortés today; the last man in that line was dead by 1788.

The present road to Rotten Cane drops about fifty feet to cross the neck that connects it to the main plain and then regains that much to reach the level of the site. Built to accommodate motor vehicles, this road all but obliterates what was once a causeway for pedestrians, higher and narrower than the present approach. The slope on the left side of the causeway was steep enough to please the ancient builders as it was, but they cut away the gentler right-hand slope to make it steeper. At the narrowest point of the isthmus they left a break in their roadbed, bridged by a removable structure of wood and lashings. When Peter Pallid saw this causeway, he thought the break and the bridge might be a trap constructed especially for him. On the far side, he could see a rampart that gave a good shot at anyone making the crossing. Today, the rubble of that rampart is scattered down a steep slope and sometimes rolls out onto the motor road, just where it starts the climb to the citadel.

All the way round the limits of Rotten Cane are fragments of stone walls, perched on canyon rims or fallen over the edge. The only obvious entrances, other than over the causeway, were near the western end of the site, where the remains of two stairways ascend the northern and southern slopes. The two paths that led to the stairs came in from Ilok Place, across the canyon on one side, and from Bearded Place, across the canyon on the other.

As for the motor road, it cuts into the site a little north of the end of the causeway and winds its way over mounds and across court-yards, never once following the lines of the original streets and buildings, then comes to an end on the north side of the main plaza. Back in the times when people walked into the citadel from the causeway, all they had to do was bear slightly left to find themselves on a straight street that ran past various residential compounds and private temples and then opened directly into the southern end of the plaza. When Peter Pallid looked down this street he didn't see enough room for horses to go abreast or turn around quickly, and it seemed to him there were too many stacks of firewood along the way. He imagined himself suffocating in the smoke of a burning town, or else falling headlong over a cliff in the attempt to escape.

The plaza is paved, clear across, with cement, three layers of it, hard even after four and a half centuries, softened only by patches of encroaching grass. Or at least that's the way the pavement was the last time we walked across it. Several years later the commander of the army base at Holy Cross celebrated the annual Day of the Indian by driving armored personnel carriers into the plaza, so it may look different now.

In the middle of the plaza is the outline of a small round structure, entirely leveled, said by some to have been the temple dedicated to Plumed Serpent, a god unknown in the days when Jaguar Cedar, Jaguar Night, and Not Right Now built their first citadel on top of Open Mountain, somewhere between here and the great eastern city. In the center of the circle, marked out by a few loose stones, is the black smudge of a hearth, and perched on one of the stones is a stick, ready for stirring the fire. Scattered around the hearth are the leaf wrappings of packets of copal incense. Sometimes the government caretaker sweeps away the traces of this shrine, all except the smudge, but it has a way of reappearing.

On the east, west, and south sides of the plaza are pyramids, or rough shapes suggesting pyramids. Each is a worn-down mass of rubble, earth, and weeds, without any trace of temple foundations on top. According to the Book,

"These were the locations of the stones whose days were kept by the Quiché lords." In those times the homes of Tohil, Lord Swallow, and Open Mountain were no longer scattered in the mountains east of here, but stood within shouting distance of one another on the tops of three artificial mountains, ranged around a paved-over plain at the center of a single citadel. The Book doesn't tell us whether the spirit familiars of the stones could still be seen taking a walk on a wooded slope or bathing in a canyon river, or whether their voices could still be heard whenever the stones got a taste of blood. Nor does it mention whether backpackers might have carried them to their old homes from time to time, there to see the light of the great eastern star and be burned by the sun once again. Or whether they might at least have seen their new homes decorated with bromeliads and hanging mosses, brought down here from the eastern mountains.

It seems to be in the way of Open Mountain not to let his place be known. He had rested on a pyramid before, a "great red house," but that was in the lost citadel of Open Mountain. As for his pyramid here in Rotten Cane, no one is certain precisely which one it was. It could have been the one on the south side of the plaza, to the left of a person entering from the street that comes from the causeway. The axis of that pyramid is rotated a little away from the cardinal points, so that the east side would've been favored by the sun of winter mornings and the west by the sun of summer afternoons, but it's not at all clear which side was the front.

On the east side of the plaza, facing directly west, is the pyramid that may have been dedicated to Lord Swallow. The traces of a broad stairway ascend the front side, and near the top is a wide terrace with a pit in it, dug by looters and presently serving as a hearth for the burning of incense. Directly across the plaza is the western pyramid, turned slightly north of east to face the sun of summer mornings, the same sun faced by the daimons when they turned to stone at the first dawn. This is the one pyramid everyone seems agreed about, the one whose name is given in the Book as Great Monument of Tohil.

When the first North American traveler saw Tohil's pyramid a century and a half ago, it was terraced at the corners, and the north, east, and south sides were ascended by steep stairways, flanked by wide balustrades. Each step was seventeen inches high and the treads only eight inches deep, giving an angle of ascent more than twice as steep as that of a standard modern stairway. Above the nineteenth step there was nothing but rubble, but a century and a half earlier a Spanish visitor had seen twice that many steps.

The surface of the pyramid was covered with plaster, gray but still showing traces of color when the North American saw it. When he peeled a corner away he could see that there were several layers of plaster, all of them covered with polychrome paintings, and he exposed enough of a fresh surface to make out the figure of a finely drawn jaguar.

The Spanish visitor, a priest, found it frightening to ascend Tohil's steep stairway, and the North American, a lawyer, found it necessary to exercise caution when descending. Both of them, when they stood at the top, imagined scenes of human sacrifice. The priest saw the victim with his back to a cement wall, bound to the wall itself with thongs that passed through holes made for the purpose, while the lawyer saw the victim lying face up on an altar, his arms and legs held down by four priests. As for the making of the supreme offering to the idol, the lawyer saw the heart still palpitating, while the priest imagined the celebrants preserving its natural warmth.

As for the Book, it tells us that the Quiché lords sanctified the temples of Tohil and the other daimons by going on long retreats inside them. The lords burned offerings and let blood by day and slept apart from their women at night. They ate nothing but the fruits of trees of the forest, abstaining even from fare made of maize. Sometimes they did this for nine score days, five days short of half a year; at other times they did it for thirteen score, running through all the numbers and names of the days. And there were even times when they did it for seventeen score, beginning when the great star was leaving its eastern role as Sunbringer and ending when it was almost ready to return. All this while, says the Book,

"They just cried their hearts and their guts out when they asked for light and life for their vassals and their domain." So it was that they relived the lives of the first four motherfathers, who had cried out for the light of Sunbringer in the long darkness before the first of all dawns, or the dawn of the Quiché kingdom.

Today the Great Monument of Tohil still shows its steepness, but only thirty feet of its height remain. Every single bit of plaster and all the facing stones beneath it have disappeared, exposing a core of uncut stones whose sides are nearly vertical. A pile of rubble ascends to the middle of the east side, where looters have opened a sort of grotto that reaches several yards into the body of the pyramid. The inside of this hole is as black as black can be, as only the soot of copal could make it, and the stain runs outside onto the stones above the entrance. The Book says that when the subjects of the Quiché lords came to pay tribute at Rotten Cane, the first thing they did was burn offerings before Tohil. The last time we walked by his pyramid, we saw two motherfathers from a nearby town standing in the entrance to the grotto, swinging an incense burner and saying prayers. Among the names they invoked we caught King Quiché.

South of the Great Monument and still on the west side of the plaza are the ruins of a ball court, with its long axis running east-west at about the same angle as the pyramid. The **I**-shaped playing field measures about forty yards from end to end and fifteen across, widening to twenty yards at the ends. This is the same kind of court as the one where Marksman and Little Hidden Sun played against One Death and Seven Death, down in the Place of Fear. As the ball went back and forth, the fate of the great star and even the sun itself was at stake. The playing surface of the court at Rotten Cane is cut below the general level of the ground, bringing it just a little closer to the underworld. It is covered with grass and weeds now, but there is probably pavement underneath. The ends of the court are relatively open and the sides are bordered by high structures with sloping inner walls that kept the ball in play. A short tunnel has been cut into the northern structure from its outer side, and once again the black stains of copal incense have followed the looters.

The plaza is bounded on the north by a long mound that served as the platform for a palace, and another pair of palace mounds runs north and south from the eastern pyramid. Along the front of each palace was an open terrace, reached by a stairway at the center. Perhaps it was at the top of such a stairway that the two kings displayed the emblems that gave them the right to rule. The Book says there were eight pairs of emblems:

Canopy, four-tiered for the first king and three-tiered for the second.	Throne.
Bone flute.	*Ch'amch'am*, with the sound of birds warbling, perhaps an ocarina.

Sparkling powder, a face paint that may have had bits of mica in it.	Yellow ocher, another face paint.
Puma's paw.	Jaguar's paw.
Deer head.	Deer hoof.
Leather arm band.	Snail-shell shaker, perhaps a leg band with a row of clinking shells.
Tobacco gourd, a vessel for ground tobacco.	Food bowl.
Parrot feathers.	Egret feathers.

When the palace that runs south from the eastern pyramid was excavated a few years ago, what came to light was a single long room with a plastered bench against the back wall and a hearth at each end. The bench was wider at the middle, perhaps providing the platform for a throne. Underneath the platform was an urn burial, and it could be that the remains were those of a lord who once sat at the middle of the bench above. With the bones were the pieces of three necklaces, two made up of assorted jade beads and the third of forty-four round gold beads, interspersed with twenty-three thin-necked flower buds of gold.

The Book says there were twenty-three palaces in all, serving as the official residences of twenty-four holders of noble titles. Indeed, long mounds that mark the sites of palaces, most of them grouped into compounds, lie in every direction beyond the plaza. The largest compound contains more than a dozen buildings, including five palaces and a small pyramid, arranged around courtyards and raised above the general level of the ground by an earthen platform that runs west and south from the ball court to the edge of the citadel. Visible in two of the courtyards are the round foundations of cement-walled cisterns, holding only shallow puddles today.

Excavations in the great compound have revealed murals. Fifty years ago, in the palace nearest the ball court, an archaeologist found a painting with yellow shells in a blue lake. Above the lake was an ornamented canopy, and above that a winding serpent covered with green feathers. The painted plaster came loose from the wall even as it was uncovered, so he stopped short of exposing the whole wall. All that remains today is his written description.

A generation later another archaeologist, working in the same palace, found a warrior in profile, performing what the Book calls the Shield Dance. The wall was broken off at the level of his forehead, but a couple of feathers hung down behind him from what was clearly a large headdress. His face was painted blue everywhere except his temples and around his eyes, his mouth was open with the teeth showing, his nose had an ornament stuck through the septum, and a heavy jade pendant hung from his neck. Before him, with his left hand, he held a small shield bordered by tassels, and behind him, with the other hand, a rattle with a tasseled handle. He wore sandals, fringed leg bands, and a kilt with the decorated end of a long loincloth hanging down in front of it. Behind him were the traces of a second dancer, with kilt, loincloth, sashes, and, apparently held in his hand, an elegant but unknown object. Near that dancer and in a band running beneath the feet of both figures were multicolored curvilinear shapes that seemed to be freehand abstractions of leaves, buds, and tendrils, rather like the ornamental bands and details in lowland painting from the time before the dawn of the Quiché kingdom. Once this mural was recorded, it was covered with plastic and reburied.

On a wall uncovered elsewhere in the same compound, a monkey with a fringed sash, knobby knees, richly tasseled leg bands, and slender toes sticking out of jeweled sandals took a long stride with his tail curving out behind him, everything gone above his sagging belly. In the Book, twin monkeys became the divine patrons of flautists, singers, jewelers, painters, and writers. When the two of them put on a dance, people could see the "things below their bellies," and so it was with this painted monkey.

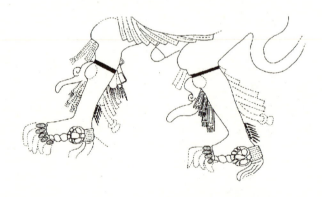

Anywhere in the citadel, wherever a plastered wall comes to light with some part of its surface intact, whether it weathers out or someone digs it out, there always seem to be at least traces of polychrome painting. Since no walls stand higher than a few feet above the original floors, what comes to light is always the lower part of some larger composition, more often than not the band of vegetal lines and shapes that marked the ground where dancing figures once trod. Even surfaces exposed to the weather were covered with paintings; nowhere is there evidence of the vast expanses of solid red that covered the walls of large buildings in the time before the dawn of the present sun. And these were all paintings with fine details; from any distance at all a pyramid or palace might have looked as if it had been covered with colorful tapestries. Figured tapestries, yes, but needing a closer reading to find out what the figures were.

Somewhere among all these painted buildings, Lord Plumed Serpent "blazed with power," as the writers of the Book have it, and he did so by means of his genius, his guardian spirit.

"On one occasion he would climb up to the sky; on another he would go down the road to the Place of Fear," they say, and we see the shaman-king entranced inside his palace, we see his spirit leaving his body.

"On another occasion he would be serpentine," they say, and we see him possessed by a serpent's writhing, but then they add, "becoming an *actual* serpent," and we find ourselves inside his dream.

"On yet another occasion he would make himself aquiline, and on another feline," they say, and we see him spreading his arms and hands or baring his teeth and nails. "He would become *like* an actual eagle or a jaguar in his *appearance,*" they go on, and we see him masked, dancing where the public can see him.

"On another occasion it would be a pool of blood; he would become nothing but a pool of blood," they say, and now we see a great magician, complete with stage trappings and hidden assistants. Now we see him and now we don't.

"All the other lords were fearful before him," they say. "He didn't do these things just so there would be one single lord, a being of genius, but they had the effect of humbling all the nations when he did them," they go on, and we see the lords of provincial towns brought in to watch him perform.

The Book says nothing about what happened to Lord Holy Sweatbath, the second in command under Lord Plumed Serpent when Rotten Cane was founded, but it does mention that there was a period when Plumed Serpent held both of the top-ranking positions. After his reign was over, there was a pair of kings again. They "merely served out their reign," but genius appeared again in the two who succeeded them. First in rank, with four tiers to his canopy, was Many Hands, and the lord with three tiers had the Mexican-sounding name Cauizimah, hard to understand but possibly from *cauitzmina,* meaning something like "memorable maker of wounds with an obsidian knife." They spent a good deal of time away from Rotten Cane on military campaigns, expanding the Quiché kingdom all the way southwestward to the point where the border between Guatemala and Mexico now meets the Pacific. Each time a new citadel was conquered, they replaced its rulers with warriors chosen from among their own loyal vassals.

"Let them be like a palisade to us," they said, "and like a stockade, a fortress to us." It was as if they were expanding the walls of the citadel of Rotten Cane all the way out to the frontiers of the kingdom. And there was more:

"Let them now become our anger, our manliness." These weren't just border guards, but were ready to make war. They were the very "point of the arrow, angle of the bowstring," as the Book has it, out there on the front lines. When they did their work the lords of Rotten Cane, back here in the center of the kingdom, received the prisoners and spoils of war.

And then there came a day when Many Hands, Cauizimah, and the other Quiché lords bestowed titles of nobility upon those who were foremost among the warriors. They didn't perform the induction among the palaces and courtyards of Rotten Cane itself, but rather sought a place that befitted the status of the candidates as keepers of borders, and as "points" and "angles." They chose a mountaintop to the south, near Mirror Water, on the boundary between the lands they ruled directly and the lands overseen by the warriors. Under the Twine, Under the Cord is the name of the mountain, taken from the fact that a boundary passes over the top of it. In the present day, as in that one, boundaries are measured by stretching cords from point to point to point, making angles even as a bowstring does.

Three generations after Many Hands came another lord of that name, only the new Many Hands held the second-ranking position. It was his grandson, the warrior known today as Black Butterfly Grandson of Many Hands, who took to the battlefield when the kingdom was invaded by the combined Spanish and Mexican forces under Peter Pallid. That happened during the reign of Three Deer and Nine Dog, who took their names from their days of birth. They put Black Butterfly in command of an army that included warriors in twenty companies of four hundred men each, drawn from all over the kingdom. By that time the guardians of the frontiers had lost three battles with the enemy, whose forces included cavalry and artillery. They had entered the kingdom from the west, by way of the Pacific coastal plain, and then turned inland and upward, passing through the row of volcanoes by way of a steep valley and reaching the high plateau of the citadel of Under Ten Deer. That put them less than a three-days' march southwest of Rotten Cane.

The Hanging of the Kings

JUST BEFORE HE WENT OFF TO WAR, Black Butterfly was carried through the streets of Rotten Cane on the shoulders of his men. As he approached the tune of the bone flute and the warble of the clay ocarina could be heard, and as his men moved forward they danced. He was crowned with masses of blue-green quetzal feathers, encrusted with drops of turquoise and jade, and painted with the yellow ocher and sparkling powder of royalty. Starting on the day One Bird, which is good for crying and calling out to the gods, he came out every day for the next seven days, reaching Eight Wind, when anger grows into fury. The solar calendar was meanwhile running through its thirteenth score of days, the one named Third Stick of Firewood. The ruler of the current year was Lord Tooth, who had brought it in on the day Five Tooth. His years are for staying on the good road, or else for losing track of it.

Six days after the dance, with the thirteenth division of the year nearing its end, the great battle took place. Black Butterfly, with his feet on the ground and his green and red guardian spirit in the air, met Peter Pallid, who rode a white horse. The date was One Yellow, when good things ripen and bad things turn rotten. The site was a rolling plain a little east of Under Ten Deer, on the banks of Blood River—not the Blood River that crosses the road to the underworld, but a river up here on the surface of the earth, one that got its name from the way it ran that day. Even the sun turned red that day, or so people used to say. Perhaps they were thinking of Peter Pallid, whose Mexican name means "he who goes along getting hot," or else of the "sons of the Sun," which is what the Spanish invaders are called in the script for the play about Black Butterfly. Even with the battle won, these sons of the sun and their Mexican allies kept on spilling the blood of those who attempted retreat. By Peter Pallid's own account,

"They made the greatest destruction in the world." When Three Deer and Nine Dog received the bad news they sent a messenger to Peter Pallid, offering peace and inviting him to come as their guest to Rotten Cane. He arrived two weeks after the battle.

If we follow the play at this point, we see King Quiché (or Three Deer) holding court. When Peter Pallid enters, the king embraces him, requesting baptism for himself and his courtiers. Exit all, making their way to church. All except for White Sparkstriker, the daykeeper who told Black Butterfly not to go to war in the first place. And so ends the play.

If we follow Peter Pallid's account, he suspects his hosts of planning to destroy him by setting fire to the town and removing the bridge from the gap in the causeway on their way out. He escapes before the plot can be carried out, somehow managing to take Three Deer and Nine Dog along as prisoners. Having secured a position on the plain to the east of the citadel, he questions them, and after a time they confess that his suspicions were correct. He has both of them burned at the stake. Since the citadel is "a strong and danger-ous place," he orders that it be burned as well.

As for the writers of the alphabetic version of the Book, they state that Three Deer and Nine Dog "were hanged by the Castilian people." Neither they nor any other native Guatemalan authors of their generation make any mention of a plot to burn Rotten Cane with Peter Pallid trapped inside it, nor do they say that in the end, Peter Pallid burned the place himself. Early authors from the other side of the Atlantic, for their part, content themselves with embellish-ments of Peter Pallid's account. In more recent times, authors who call themselves historians have been consistent in their judgment of early sources, settling disagreements in favor of accounts written by Spaniards. Peter Pallid discovered a plot against him, escaped, burned the conspirators, and then burned the citadel. These are now well-established "facts," so much so that they have found their way into ordinary schoolbooks—always written, of course, in a European language.

No one seems to remember that when Peter Pallid came to Rotten Cane, he had already been through the experience of finding himself trapped inside a town. He was with the Spaniards in the Mexican town of Cholula when they discovered that their hosts were setting up blockades in the streets around their quarters, and that an army was closing off the only roads out of town. And he was there when the same thing happened again on the island of Mexico City itself, only it turned out much worse. The Spanish forces were under heavy siege for a long time before they fought their way out of their quarters, and half of them never got out of the city alive. Perhaps the worst moment came when they were fleeing down a long causeway on their way to the mainland. There was a water gap in this causeway, and when they got there the bridge had been removed and canoes full of warriors were in the water. Of those who managed to get past the gap, Peter Pallid was among the last. When it was all over, a story went around that he had used the shaft of a spear to catapult himself across.

Rotten Cane is surrounded by cliffs, not by a lake, but it's not hard to imagine what Peter Pallid might've thought about when he saw the causeway, complete with removable bridge. The plot against him could easily have taken shape in his own mind, whether or not it also took shape in the minds of Three Deer and Nine Dog. If they had heard an account of the events in Mexico City, then they might indeed have thought precisely what Peter Pallid thought they were thinking. But in that case, why wouldn't they also be thinking about what happened when the Spaniards first arrived in Mexico City? Montezuma received them as guests but ended up as their prisoner, and whether this possibility crossed the minds of Three Deer and Nine Dog or not, they were to suffer the same fate. Whichever way we construct the motives, the actors on both sides seem to be playing out a variation on what was, even in their own time, an old story.

What we do know is that the New World Book says the Quiché kings were hanged by the Castilian people, while Peter Pallid says he burned them and historians say he had them burned. If we go back and read the Book in the original Quiché, what it says about Three Deer and Nine Dog is *xejitz'axik,* which can indeed mean "they were hanged." But if, instead of jumping to conclusions, we look at the more general sense of this verb, it means something like, "they were suspended with a rope." And there is more than one way to suspend a person by means of a rope. In those times, a favorite European method for extracting a confession from a suspect was to tie his hands together, tie weights to his feet, and then hoist him by the wrists till the weights were dangling free. This method was as common then as the use of electricity is in our own day.

To pursue the matter of the interrogation of the Quiché kings any further we must turn from the Book to another native Guatemalan account, this one written by former lords of the Fire Tree nation who lived near Puppet Trees after the invasion. Calling Peter Pallid by his Mexican name, they say that the Quiché kings "were tortured by Tonatiuh." And yes, after that, the kings "were burned by Tonatiuh."

Now, on the plain outside the citadel of Rotten Cane, we see Peter Pallid questioning the kings about their plot against him, and we hear him giving the order to hoist them off the ground by ropes. If he has to go any further to get their confession, custom will demand the lash as the next step, followed by a broad array of choices. In the end, we see the confessed criminals burning at the stake.

Would historians have evaluated Peter Pallid's account of these events any differently if they had considered his methods of interrogation? For an answer, we can look at how they sort out the story of the Holy Inquisition among the Maya of Yucatán. There are two sets of testimony in the Spanish records, one obtained by means of torture and the other without it. In the first set, the defendants reveal all sorts of religious crimes, ranging from the possession of idols to the clandestine sacrifice of the hearts of small children. In the second, the same defendants say they made these stories up because it was the only way to satisfy their tormentors, and they reveal that earlier witnesses coached later ones on what to say. Nevertheless, historians have always preferred the testimony that was taken under torture, even including a social historian writing in 1984. They disapprove of the actions of the inquisitors, of course, but they share with them the notion that truth and method can be separated from one another.

If we follow the Fire Tree account a little further, we learn what other questions Peter Pallid might have had for the hanging Quiché kings, there on the plain outside the citadel of Rotten Cane. What most impressed these authors, judging from the amount of space they devote to it, was his demand for money, for metal, for gold, a demand which he never ceased repeating when he came to their citadel.

"Why haven't you brought me the gold? If you don't bring me all the gold from all your towns, I'll hang you, I'll burn you," they have him saying, and on another occasion,

"I'm telling you that I want the gold here within five days. Woe to you if you fail to bring it, for I know my own heart." The Fire Tree lords, unlike their counterparts at Rotten Cane, managed to leave town ahead of Peter Pallid.

As for the date of the events at Rotten Cane, it is something of an embarrassment for historians that Peter Pallid seldom bothers to supply such information. To find the date on their calendar, the one they share with him, they must look between the nearest two dates he does happen to give. That leaves them with several months to slide around in, and the only way they can make the date stop somewhere is to resort to a native account. The Fire Tree authors note that the burning of the Quiché kings fell on Four Net, and indeed a day of that name and number comes within the gap left by Peter Pallid, falling on March 9, 1524. Days named Net or *K'at* are for paying debts, even to the extent of filling up a net bag of the kind that serves as a backpack. Daykeepers sometimes look for a further meaning in this day by playing on the sound of it, saying *kak'atik*, "it is burning." As for the solar year, it was in its fourteenth division by then, the one named *Che'*, meaning trees, logs, poles, and stakes.

There remains the question of the burning of Rotten Cane, mentioned only in the accounts of Peter Pallid and those who take him at his word. In this case we have only to consult the reports of specialists in hard evidence, which is to say archaeologists. It turns out that just as native Guatemalan accounts are silent about this event, so is the dirt that fills the ruined buildings and streets of the citadel. The digging of pits and trenches has failed to reveal anything that looks like a stratum of charcoal and ashes from Peter Pallid's fire.

➤ Eyes and Ears to the Book

WHEN THE TOWN OF HOLY CROSS was still new, in the first generation after its founding, a few residents who had been born in Rotten Cane learned how to write their native language in the script of the invaders. It was missionaries who taught this skill, as always seems to be the case wherever Roman letters are introduced for the first time, and their long-range goal was the production of the literature of indoctrination: catechisms and sermons, together with questionnaires for use in eliciting confessions, all in the language of those who were to be indoctrinated. As for writings in the native script, the missionaries saw nothing in them that did not contain "superstitions and falsehoods of the devil." They were unable to read the script, of course, but the pictures were enough. Nothing but false gods and sinister rites, page after page. Whenever they got their hands on books, or copies of the Book, they burned them in public the same way the Inquisition would burn the worst of heretics.

In a house somewhere in Holy Cross, thirty years after the fall of the Quiché kingdom, the knowledge of the native New World script and that of the Old World invaders came together in the same room. Whoever was in that room, their purpose was to produce a new version of the Book, using the alphabetic script for the Quiché language. In what they spelled out on paper they only call themselves *oj*, "we," and they are especially careful when they touch on the source of their knowledge.

"There is the original Book and ancient writing," they say, "but he who sees and counts by it hides his identity." They could be talking about themselves, or someone who collaborated with them.

It seems there were two ways to read the old version of the Book. One was to look something up, an event of some kind, exploring its place among the deeds of gods, finding a date in the pages about the character of the thirteen-times-twenty days, and finding it again in the pages about the moon and eclipses, then the great star, the seasons and years, the thirteen houses that divided the road of light, and finally in the pages about the deeds of past kings and the fate of past kingdoms. It might be a date proposed for the installation of a new king, the start of work on a new palace, or an attack on an enemy town. Or it might be the date of something that had just happened, something that seemed to be a sign of things to come, the appearance of a comet, or the news that strangers had come over the sea in large boats and landed on the east coast of Mexico. It wasn't that events were expected to repeat themselves exactly, but rather that they had similarities of character. The Book had no circles in it, no cycles, no spinning wheels of fortune, but rather lists, charts, and tables with the qualities of a richly brocaded textile, one whose overlapping patterns could be projected backward or forward from the sections that were actually shown. And since the whole text was on a single long sheet of paper, folded back and forth like a screen to make pages, it was possible to compare two widely separated patterns by bringing them side by side, folding under all the intervening pages.

The other way to read the Book was to move from one page to the next, starting from the beginning. On the same pages with the tables were pictures of the actors in the events tabulated, and the pictures had captions naming the actors and their actions. Any one picture and its caption, read simply as an event and a sentence, covered only a moment in time, but there were clues to the larger story in the characters of the actors, as revealed by their features and costumes and the meanings of their names. Taken together and traced from one page to the next, actions and characters provided the means for reading across time rather than into it. This was the path chosen by the writers of the alphabetic version of the Book, and they tell us what to expect at the outset:

"It takes a long performance and account to complete the lighting of all the skyearth, the fourfold siding, fourfold cornering, measuring, fourfold staking, halving the cord, stretching the cord, in the sky, on the earth." Theirs was not to dwell on the measurements themselves, as the charts and tables did, but to give an account of how the canonical intervals of time and space were traversed for the very first time, and by whom.

Anonymous though the writers may be, their loyalties are clear enough. Once they are done with telling the deeds of Marksman and Little Jaguar Sun, and once they have brought the great star and the sun and moon out of the underworld and into the sky, the royal story is the only one they follow. They start with Jaguar Cedar, Jaguar Night, and Not Right Now and come all the way down to the living descendants of their own present time. At the same time, they trace a path from the great eastern city, the Place with Only the Sounds of Insects, all the way to the new town of Holy Cross. They linger when they reach Rotten Cane, abandoned within their own memories, and tell of the Quiché kings in their day of glory.

The king who was first in rank headed a council of lords, and the second directed the collection of tribute. The members of the council sat in a row, each assigned a seat and cushion by his rank, in one of those long palace rooms in Rotten Cane. Their affairs were woven together like a mat created from the folds and tucks of leaves from a cattail plant, which itself has a mat of roots beneath the water. When they met,

"They knew whether war would occur; everything they saw was clear to them." So they were something like those first four vigesimal beings, who "saw everything under the sky perfectly" until the gods became alarmed and clouded the mirror of their vision. The members of the council had a way of correcting this human defect:

"Whether there would be death, or whether there would be famine, or whether quarrels would occur, they knew it for certain, since there was an instrument for seeing, there was the Book. Council Book was their name for it." So there it is again, as it was at the dawn of the kingdom. With this instrument before their eyes, the members of the council returned to the condition of the first four humans, who "didn't have to walk around before they could see what was under the sky; they just stayed where they were." But where those four had "turned around and looked around in the sky, on the earth," all these latter-day seers had to do was sit in one place and unfold the pages of the Book. And it wasn't just anyplace they sat, but in the citadel at the center of the Quiché people and their subjects, equidistant from the four outer lakes and near the fifth and middle lake, the one called Mirror Water.

Those who wrote in Holy Cross thought of their work as a successor of the original Book, but they never once called it "an instrument for seeing." They left out all the pictures, for one thing. Pictures would tell a prying missionary what little he needed to know at a glance, even a missionary who didn't know the language of the text that went with the pictures. And then there was the problem of the script itself. To write with clarity in the old way was to produce

<table>
<tr><td>lemo tzij</td><td>mirror words</td></tr>
<tr><td>cholo tzij</td><td>ordered words</td></tr>
<tr><td>ajilan tzij</td><td>counted words</td></tr>
</table>

but once a page was reduced to alphabetic script the mirror was gone. Each sign became a sound the moment it was recognized. The assembled sounds formed words and the words might then call pictures to mind, but there weren't any pictures that called up sounds and words, not even sketches made with just a few strokes.

Even in the original script there were signs that seemed to make no picture, or at least not a picture that anyone still recognized.

Seeing a sign like this , especially if it appeared with a number written in front of it this way , called up the name of one of the twenty days, *Aj* or "Cane," in this case *Wuqub' Aj* or "Seven Cane." The reader had no need to ponder whether the lines inside the sign for Cane sketched some kind of object, or did so at some time in the past. But it still wasn't like a letter of the alphabet, since it could mean something all by itself, standing for a whole word and not just a fragment of a word. It could be combined with other signs to make bigger words, in which case it only stood for the sound of the syllable *aj,* but knowing the day name *Aj* helped the reader remember what sound to pronounce. Written right beside *aj* might be this , which happens to be a sign whose key lay in reading it as a picture rather than going straight to a word. Seen as a seed pushed into the ground, it pointed to the word *awex* or "sowing" and then, if it was to be read only as a sound, the syllable *aw*. When the two signs were combined like this , as they often were, they yielded the word *ajaw*, meaning "lord" or "king."

Now of course, a reader who was familiar with the usual spelling of *ajaw*, perhaps a reader who wanted to get on with the story rather than lingering like a poet, could perfectly well pronounce this word without giving a thought to a day named *Aj*, or to seeds or sowing. Well and good, but the other meanings were still there for a reader who could see and hear them—even the same reader perhaps, but in a different mood. Seen and sounded out more slowly, the word might seem to begin with the suffix *aj-*, meaning "master of," suggesting that *ajaw* might once have meant "master of sowing." Whether that was a proper etymology or not, our poet might remember that pictures of kings often showed them in the act of sowing. They could be casting seeds on the ground, or else casting pieces of copal into a fire. Indeed, the sign could be read as a piece of copal in the dish of an incense burner rather than a seed stuck in the ground, in which case it gave the word *pom*, "copal," or else the syllable *po*. With such a reading, our poet could get *ajpo* out of . That's not a word as it stands, but when it is sounded side by side with *ajaw* or "lord," it points straight to *ajpop*, which happens to be the highest title a lord can possess. *Ajpop* means "master of the mat," referring to the interwoven strands that pull the council of lords together.

But then, not wishing to lose sight of what was in the dish of the second sign, the poet might remind us that the master *(aj)* of the mat *(pop)*, like all proper heads of lineages, should burn copal *(pom)* and pray for all his kin on the day Seven Cane *(Aj)*. And if he still wanted to keep a sense of sowing *(aw)* alive in the second sign, he might make a pun on the first one, pronouncing it as the word for an ear of green corn *(äj)* instead of the word for a cane plant *(aj)*. Ah, but no one plants a whole ear of corn, you may say, much less a green ear. But that is just what Marksman and Little Jaguar Sun once did, and it so happens that they did it on a day named *Aj*. First they said to their grandmother,

"Here is a sign of our word," which makes it sound as if they were about to write something.

"Each of us will plant an *äj,*" they said next, and when they said it they were holding two ears of corn they had passed through the smoke of burning *pom*.

"We'll plant them in the center of our house," they went on. But instead of sticking the ears in the earthen floor they did just the opposite, hanging them up in the middle of the attic. When the time came to store ripe ears of corn in the attic, the two smoked ears would serve as the living heart of the harvest, just like the hearts people have in their attics today.

At this point our storyteller might turn poet again, pointing back at the sign for the day *Aj* and saying,

"Here indeed is the sign of their word: it shows two supporting posts for their house, with a crosspiece resting on them , and these two little marks at the top are the two ears of corn." And whether this was a true account of the appearance of the sign or not, we would never forget how to write it.

Much was lost to vision when the Book went the way of a script that dissolved into sound as fast as the eye could see it, but the eye's loss was the ear's gain. If the writers of Holy Cross had limited themselves to a word-by-word or syllable-by-syllable transcription of the signs they saw in the ancient Book, they would have produced a brief and cryptic work that cried for illustrations and footnotes. Instead, they wrote what they might say in their persons as orators and storytellers, speaking to an audience.

At the very end of their work, where other Quiché writers of those times would have signed their names, they describe three lesser lords who have played no role in their story. These lords were "mothers of the word, fathers of the word," and there was one for each of the three lineages descended from Jaguar Cedar, Jaguar Night, and Not Right Now. Their noble title was *nim chokoj*, "great convener of banquets," specifically wedding banquets. One of the things people did at such banquets was to *chokola'j*, "drink chocolate together," chocolate being a beverage made from *kakow*, "cacao." In "chocolate" and "cacao" (or "cocoa"), the sounds of Quiché meet the sounds of English by way of a long route that goes through Spanish, and this very page meets a page from the Book.

Cacao came to Europe as an exotic and expensive import, and in the beginning the proper drinking vessel was imported along with it. That was a hollowed-out calabash, misnamed as a gourd *(calabaza)* in Spanish. A calabash does look something like a gourd, but it grows on trees, taking the shape of a human head. We were served a cacao beverage in a calabash just this past year, in a Mayan village in Belize, but Europeans and their New World cousins have long since dropped this custom. As for the great convener of banquets in the Book, we may be sure that when he offered chocolate to wedding guests, he passed them a calabash full.

It is on this point of drinking from a calabash that the anonymous authors of Holy Cross tip their hand, or at least the hand of someone who was telling them what to write down. When they begin the story of the gods who once lived on the face of the earth and established the customs now followed by humans, they say,

"And now we shall name the name of the father of Marksman and Little Jaguar Sun. Let's drink to him, and let's just drink to the telling and accounting of the begetting of Marksman and Little Jaguar Sun." In other words, they speak like a great convener of banquets about to pass a calabash around, and the reader becomes a guest at a wedding. The father they mention is One Marksman, and when they get to the point where his head is cut off and put in a barren tree, they say,

"When his head was put in the fork of the tree, the tree bore fruit. It would not have had any fruit, had not the head of One Marksman been put in the fork." As time went on, they explain, it was impossible to tell his skull from the fruit, and so,

"This is the calabash, as we call it today, or 'the head of One Marksman,' so to speak." In other words, dear wedding guests, you are now drinking from the skull of the very person whose story we are telling.

What happens next in the story is that Blood Moon comes to look at the tree and the skull tells her,

"Stretch out your right hand here, so I can see it." When she does so, the skull spits in the palm of her hand, making her pregnant with Marksman and Little Jaguar Sun. If the calabash happened to come to the hand of the bride at this moment, perhaps her eye fell on the froth of the chocolate. As for Blood Moon, when she looks at the palm of her hand, there is nothing there. The skull says,

"It's just a sign I've given you."

No one from the Old World seems to have known about the alphabetic version of the Book until a century and a half after it was written. All through those same years the last independent Mayan kingdom held out in the lowland rain forest of what is now northern Guatemala, falling to Spain in 1697. It was just a few years later that someone in the highlands happened to show a Spanish friar the Book, or a copy of the Book, and he made his own copy. His Christian name was Francisco, though he was a Dominican, and his surname was Ximénez, of Moorish origin. When he happened to see the Book he was the parish priest in St. Thomas above the Nettles, the next town south of Holy Cross. He was a linguist, in the process of writing a grammar of Quiché, and just as the linguists of our own day include "native texts" as appendices to their grammars, so he treated the text of the Book as an appendix to his. It might seem strange to put texts after grammars, since grammars cannot be written unless texts already exist, but how else could grammars take command of languages, claiming to set forth laws that somehow existed before anyone said or wrote anything?

Between his grammar and his native text, Brother Francis inserted a lengthy "treatise on everything a minister should know for the proper administration of these natives." In this he included a confessionary and catechism, translated into Quiché so that a priest could read them aloud to his parishioners. Next comes a page headed this way:

"Here begin the stories of the origin of the Indians of this province of Guatemala, translated from the Quiché language into Castilian for the greater convenience of the ministers of the Holy

Gospel." Soon after that comes the Quiché text of the Book with a parallel translation, but not before Brother Francis prepares his readers for the dangerous road ahead. They might fall into the temptation of comparing One Marksman with God, or his son Marksman with the Son of God, or Blood Moon with Most Holy Mary. Lest they see these or any other points of comparison with Holy Scripture whatsoever, he issues a general warning:

"Since these things are found wrapped in a thousand lies and tales, they should be given no more credence than the Father of lies, Satan, who was their Author, no doubt for the purpose of deceiving and confusing these miserable people, the catholic truths coming out as impure as what fairy tales might produce, the sorts of things he succeeded in sending through the mouths of Arius, Luther, Calvin, Mohammed, and other arch-heretics."

For all that, Brother Francis himself succumbed to temptation a few years later. It was a tale about a mysterious sacred object that caught him, the one called *pisom q'aq'al,* meaning "Bundle of Flames," or else "Bundle of Glory." When the Quiché people were still living at Open Mountain, Jaguar Cedar left this object to his descendants, saying,

"This is for making requests of me. I shall leave it with you. Here is your fiery splendor," and then he left them. They never saw him die; he just left. The bundle became his memorial, and his descendants burned offerings before it. According to the authors of the Book,

"It wasn't clear just what it was; it was wound about with coverings. It was never unwrapped. Its sewing wasn't clear because no one looked on while it was being wrapped." They make it sound as if it no longer existed in their own time, but perhaps they meant to protect it.

The Bundle of Glory came into the mind of Brother Francis while he was putting the finishing touches on a Quiché-Spanish dictionary. For the opening pages of this work he composed a dedication in the form of a long letter addressed to the Most Holy Virgin Mary. When he spoke to her of "Indians," he said this:

"Where they didst venerate thee most appropriately and have thee in mind, was in that bundle they called *pisom q'aq'al."* Then he explained his reasoning to her, saying, "Since the Indians said that they did not know what it was made of and that it was hidden from them—which is what the sacred text says about the ark of the covenant, that after the prophet Jeremiah put it in a cave, when Jerusalem was destroyed, nothing more was known of it—then it was a symbol of thyself, my lady, since after thy sons the apostles placed thy most holy body in the sepulchre in Gethsemane, and on the third day the apostle St. Thomas came there wishing to adore and venerate this greater ark of the covenant, not knowing of thy most felicitous transit, when he opened the sepulchre he did not by any means find it."

It is true, at least, that the Bundle of Flames has vanished. No missionary claims to have burned it, no archaeologist claims to have dug it up, no private collector or public museum claims to own it, and no antiquities dealer claims to have it for sale. The authors of the Book list the temples that housed the gods at Rotten Cane, but they say nothing of where the bundle was kept.

➤   The Trap Door

THERE IS A SECRET BENEATH the citadel of Rotten Cane. Well, it's not exactly a secret, since nearly everyone who takes a good look at the place finds out about it, but nearly everyone who has ever written about Rotten Cane has forgotten to mention it, archaeologists included. And when descriptions do appear they are never precise, partly because it's hard to see in the dark with nothing but a lit match. No one ever seems to remember to bring a flashlight, not even on a second or third visit.

The secret hides northwest of the main plaza and down over the canyon rim, where a cliff of volcanic tuff is pierced by a tall doorway. It's about twice as high as a person and just wide enough to clear broad shoulders. The sides are vertical and the top is cut in the ▲ shape of a corbeled arch. To the right of the opening, loose rocks have been arranged to make a hearth for the burning of copal.

The door begins a tunnel, cut to the same shape. The walls are blackened with the soot of copal, and those who go in are likely to come out with oily black stains on their sleeves and smudges on their hands. Several short tunnels—no one seems to remember how many there are when they write about them later—branch off from the main passage, which goes back about ninety yards through solid rock and reaches its end below the middle of the main plaza. If there was a project to make a connection with one of the buildings there, by way of a trap door, it was never completed. Perhaps Lord Plumed Serpent was thinking of a great act of magicianship. He would let himself be seen disappearing over the edge of the western canyon, even as the great star of evening disappears into the realm of the Lords of Death, and then have the spectators gather in the plaza while he stole his way to the secret tunnel in the cliff. When the moment came he would rise right out of the platform, even as the great star rises in the east at morning.

Part way along, the tunnel turns, as if there had been an argument about whether it was heading in the right direction to reach some particular spot. As it turns, the entrance goes out of sight and the daylight goes with it. A little farther into the darkness a warm glow appears up ahead, then becomes two points of light, then the flames of two tallow candles planted in the floor at the end of the tunnel, moments away from burning out.

That's the way it was the last time we were in the tunnel, anyway. Probably the candles had been left there by the same two mother-fathers we'd seen up above, standing in the grotto of the Great Monument of Tohil.

The next time we saw don Mateo, over in the town of Middle, we asked him about the tunnel. He knew that some people went inside to burn offerings, but as far as he was concerned there was nothing there. Now, the little cave right there on the plaza, in the face of the pyramid, was another matter. Indeed, he had a whole story about that. He didn't say when it happened, and I don't remember everything he said, but it goes something like this.

Once a very poor man went inside the pyramid with small candles and a little incense. While he was praying he suddenly saw a trap door at his feet, made of pure silver. When he got hold of the edge and pulled it came open, and there was a stairway descending into the ruins. He went down, down, down about sixty feet, until he came to a door. Hanging just inside were clothes just like the ones worn by characters in the play named after White Sparkstriker and Black Butterfly, with buttons and braid that shone like gold and silver. He passed through that room, and another, and another, and then came out into a whole town. Seeing no one, he went on until he came to what looked like the basin of a fountain, two basins in fact, only they were corrals, filled with tiny goats, tiny cows, all kinds of tiny animals.

There, by the corrals, the man tried to enter a house, and the moment he did a little boy met him at the door. It was White Sparkstriker, or the child of White Sparkstriker. His clothing was made of pure silver, but it wasn't touching his body.

"Who sent you? What did you come here for?" he said. Only he said it all in signs, since his kind can't talk.

"Nothing. It's just that I'm very poor, I have nothing."

"What were you saying just before you came down here?"

"I was asking for luck, up there at the hearth." At that moment he noticed big bags of money all along the wall, silver and gold coins, pieces of twenty, a hundred, every bag full up.

"Well, who's going to know?" said the poor man.

"Well, no one. But don't say anything. Everyone is sleeping."

"I'll just take a little bit. But I'm a little sad, because the truth is, I'm poor." The poor man didn't even have pockets, since he was wearing those plain white pants of coarse cotton cloth, the old kind that ties at the waist. So he said,

"What I'd like to take is just a fistful of money, like this."

"Don't you have a little bag? Nothing to put it in?"

"No."

"You could take some in a hat." But the man didn't have a hat. So he came away with his hands as full as he could get them. There was a lot more, but he couldn't take it with him because he had nothing to put it in.

And so he made his way out of there. He tried to go back for another load, but the silver trap door was gone.

Now, this man was just an ordinary fool, someone from right around here, but he came out rich with just his hands full. He put the money in a small strongbox, and it multiplied. Next he put it in a chest, and the morning after that the chest was full.

The man lived for twenty years on this money and then, when his time of life came he died. Just before the end he began to talk about what had happened to him, and the very moment he finished his story, he died.

Since then many people have gone to Rotten Cane to look for the hidden town, but they haven't been able to find it. One man went there thinking only of the money. He didn't burn his candles and incense, or he didn't think about what he said when he did it. He went inside the pyramid at 6:00 in the morning, and at 6:00 in the evening he still hadn't come out. When people came to look for him, they could see that he'd gone down below.

There's a great animal down there, they say, bigger than a house, with a mouth more than four yards wide, and then—people fall into it! The man who disappeared wanted to take the money, but the mountain, the World, wouldn't allow it. As for the people who went looking for him, they stayed in the cave only five minutes.

"We'd better go, or else that animal will eat us," they said, and they got out. There's money there, but one must give presents of candles and incense four times. Only then is it possible to go down inside and speak with White Sparkstriker. If one has no fear.

And there is a day for this. One has to go on Eight Wind, or if not, Nine Wind. Or else Eight Jaguar.

Leaving Altar Town, in the west, and coming over here to the middle of the old kingdom, it wasn't only the places that were new to us, but the times. None of the days don Mateo suggested for trying to open the door to the secret of Rotten Cane is on the regular calendar followed by daykeepers. Eight Wind is the next day numbered eight after Eight Thunder, coming at a time when ordinary daykeepers are free of obligations of any number and motherfathers have nothing left but days numbered nine. Nine Wind follows Nine Thunder, coming when even motherfathers have finished their work. Eight Jaguar, the day don Mateo added as an afterthought, falls between One and Eight Deer, when the number one is back in play again but eight has yet to return.

On Eight Wind we weren't anywhere near Rotten Cane, but on a mountain named Stone Voice, overlooking the battlefield where Black Butterfly's body fell to the earth and his guardian spirit took flight. It's a small mountain but a hard one—so hard, they say, that when the Pan American Highway was under construction, the machinery couldn't break it and the roadbed had to be rerouted. Water is what the mountain wants; whenever a hurricane comes anywhere near, the mountain pulls the rain the way a magnet pulls iron. At night it speaks with all the other mountains in view, and when this happens people in the valleys can see burning rocks flying over their heads and trailing sparks, back and forth among the peaks. Near the top of Stone Voice itself are two large rocks with a black crevice between them, something like a keyhole. Whatever may be inside, what comes out is the sound of a bell.

As for the secret beneath the citadel of Rotten Cane, there is nothing more to report. By the time Nine Wind and Eight Jaguar came around, we would be out of the country.

➤ Too Steep a Slope

DAWNING POINT IS THE NAME of the mountain where don Mateo really wanted to go, Sakiribal. That's an old name, one that appears in the Book, but the problem is that there's more than one Dawning Point. When the first four motherfathers burned copal for the great eastern star at Open Mountain, that became the Dawning Point for themselves and their branch of the Quiché people. But two other branches saw the great star on their own two mountains, not far away, both of them called Dawning Point.

For don Mateo there was only one Dawning Point, and he would rather have taken us there on the day Eight Bird than to Tohil's Place. People go over there to spend the night, to see what dreams they might have and then greet the dawn; he had been there years ago, with his father. He thought we could get there in a jeep, and when we came for a visit a week before Eight Bird he persuaded us, solely by means of his own passion for Dawning Point, to head there without giving the least consideration as to whether the date on the ancient calendar might be auspicious or not. It was, in fact, One Yellow, a good day for a visit to a shrine all right, but a shrine in a low and watery place and not on top of a mountain.

We didn't even take food and blankets with us. Don Mateo guided us eastward out of the town of Middle on a gravel road, then had us angle left onto a muddy track whose center was so high I had to straddle first one rut and then the other. At the edge of the plain, with a steep mountain directly ahead of us, the track dived into a stream and I went into four-wheel drive; we crawled over an assortment of boulders, pitching, tossing, and splashing, and slithered up the opposite bank. From then on our general direction was northward, directly up the slope of a foothill—no switchbacks here—then down the side of a ravine, steeply up again across a saddle between two higher foothills, down across a canyon with a small stream at the bottom, and then up a slope of mountainous size with the top clear out of view.

At this point even people out walking would've had difficulty believing they were on any sort of trail that might lead somewhere. It was only the openness of the floor of the pine forest that permitted us to proceed at all. When the grade began to move ever closer to 45°, the kind of angle at which our shoes might have begun slipping on pine needles had we been walking, and when it was still not apparent when we might be able to rest on a ridge, I had a sudden horror at the thought of the jeep's center of gravity, at the thought of how we might get back down at the point where it stalled out even in its lowest gear, and, yes, at the thought that the jeep had been borrowed from a friend. Even right where we were, turning the jeep around without turning it over was going to be tricky.

Don Mateo seemed surprised that even a jeep might have its limits, or that we might, but all right, we could just leave it here, on a tilt, and continue, right now, on foot. Well, how far was it, anyway? And which way? Yes it was going to be far, and it could only be the way we were already going. No plan beyond that, no descriptions of the landmarks we should watch for, only this passion to go to Dawning Point, a place he hadn't seen since he was a child. With a shrug he started up the slope without us, and we pleaded with him to come back. Where was any sign of the trail other than our being there, and what did we really know beyond the fact that we needed to head north and a little eastward, and that after a very long walk in that direction, a day's walk over a whole mountain range and down again, we might finally come out somewhere near the town whose double name means St. Andrew Plaster House? With luck, perhaps someone in a remote farmhouse, or someone out gathering wood, or someone as crazy as we were might know something, might tell us to head off in some other direction, might even send us doubling back part way to a turn we missed, before we got all the way over to Plaster House, but right here in these pines there wasn't a soul in sight, any more than there was a trail.

Finally, inch by inch, low low and reverse, low low and reverse, I got the jeep turned around. Don Mateo got back in, quiet now that he had nothing to urge us on about, saying all he needed to say with a fixed dark look.

➤ Don't Tell Anyone

ON THE EVE OF OUR TRIP to Tohil's Place, while the day Seven Jaguar was going out and Eight Bird was coming in, don Mateo talked about Dawning Point again, his Dawning Point, while we sat in his house on the outskirts of Middle. He brought it up even though we had already settled on going to Tohil's Place. Sometimes, he said, people made overnight trips to Dawning Point in groups, and even hired a marimba band to go along and help them get past midnight. Musicians walking a mountain trail, one on either end of a hand-carved marimba, holding it high enough to clear the graduated rows of gourd resonators, and perhaps a third man with a battered cornet, and a fourth leaning forward with a tumpline across his forehead, the other end of the rope passing around the load on his back, a homemade bass fiddle with a fresh coat of red enamel. And someone else in the party might carry a bagful of fireworks, skyrockets, and he'd light some while the band was playing—blares, plunks, and the trills and warbles of long ranks of wooden keys, cut through with whooshes and blasts.

Don Mateo told the story of his own visit to Dawning Point—not for the first time, but this time we got it on tape. The voice that comes out of the machine now, into my wallpapered room with rugs and upholstered furniture, carries the resonance of the room where he spoke, with ceiling of planks across bare beams, walls of stuccoed adobe bricks, floor of packed earth. Nothing to soften the sound, just a few double strips of crepe paper, twisted together and hung in scallops over our heads. Just the small pine table with his tabernacle on it, as far from the outside door as possible, and a few pieces of pine furniture: a fragile folding chair, a bench without a back, a couple of low stools, a cleanly sawed-off stump. And the sound behind the voice is a night sound, a cold and dry December night with everything closed up, no chickens outside, no one walking or driving past on the gravel road out front, the rest of the family already off in the kitchen and quiet, staying close to the fire while we hunch ourselves against the chill, sitting still on bare wood for don Mateo, who talks a lot.

And he mostly talks Spanish tonight, he's too hot for what he has to say to let himself be led into a conversation that might go down the slow and halting path of a language lesson, once his gringo guests ran out of things they'd already learned to say in Quiché. But he doesn't translate the name of the place he's talking about, it's always Sakiribal, not "El Sitio del Alba" or something of the sort. He's already spoken the name by the time the sound starts coming off the tape, but I can hear his voice in my mind's ear. He speaks a highly clipped dialect of Quiché, so Sakiribal comes out as "Skribal," sounds almost like "Scribble." He's been showing us some of the stones he keeps on the lower shelf of his altar, close to the earthen floor, stones that have mouths, stones that like strong drink and the light and scent of burning offerings, stones that like the sound of words. He's told us that one of them came from Scribble. Here are the first lines heard from the tape, the first strings of sound separated by short silences, after the double jump to English and ink on paper:

> We went to sleep just a little above there.
> There's no—SSSSSSSHHHHHHHH!
> GET DOWN!

He doesn't want to be bothered by his dog just now.

> There's nothing there.
> There's just a little farm there
> and in the middle of the n i g h t cars were coming
> we suddenly heard cars and we all woke up
> but there's no highway there, there's nothing
>
> but cars came $_{rrr}r^{rr^{r^{r^{rr^{rrrr}}rr}r}}_{rrrr}$ another one, another
>   one, a$^{nother one, a}$nother one.
> **After**ward airplanes came, well

they came down where that hearth is.

He's talking about a hearth for burning offerings, *porob'al,* a shrine, *awas,* a spot you mustn't touch with your hand.

> They all came down there.
> And they all went away, some went up, some down,
>   they all left
> and we were watching to see what—
> what they were doing, well—
> whether **people** would get out of the **cars,** but we
>   didn't see **any**thing
> just noises, nothing more.
> Then
> we were w i d e awake, well, we were a bit startled.

Now a car is approaching on the road outside, late at night in this lonely place—but this is the kind of car that leaves its sound on a tape. Someone in the story (perhaps don Mateo is quoting himself) says,

> "What could this be?"
> Then my papa said, since he
> knew about such things

and here don Mateo changes voices, sounds like a kindly father reassuring his children while the car comes nearer,

> "Don't worry about this.
> This is the Holy World, . . .

it's the Santo Mundo, Saint Earth, Diosmundo, the Earth Deity, and at this point the car goes roaring right past the house,

> . . . these are
> the **chiefs** . . .

earth angels, terrestrial saints, distant mountain peaks, taking the forms of vigesimal beings

> . . . who come to
> see the customs being done, . . .

who come to see orange flames of copal incense, yellow flames of tallow candles, to smell smoke of resin, smoke of fat, ringed with pine needles and petals of red and white roses, who come to taste strong liquor, to hear their names spoken,

> . . . they are
> presenting themselves to the people.
> Don't worry.
> It's as if we offered them a meal and they came to try it.
> Don't worry.
> It's as if they liked the table we set."

These are the words that come out of the speaker when the tape slides across the head, or the words I hear in my mind's ear, spoken by an inner voice that sounds the way don Mateo would sound if he could speak English, as he himself gives voice in Spanish to the words his father once spoke in Quiché, words he can still hear in his own mind's ear, spoken by an inner voice that sounds like his father. Then another voice (perhaps don Mateo's own again) answers,

> "That's good."
> And we were only there a l i t t l e while when a woman
> a woman who went there with us, my brother's woman

and now he tells us something he must've heard her say later, but this time, instead of giving voice to her, he gives voice to the Narrator who stands within all of us, that third person who only speaks of what others sense, what others do, saying,

> she saw a fire like so
> of this size

and here he holds his hands, or Narrator's hands, with the palms facing each other, one about two feet above the other, and

> a **fire** came out, it was about
> ten yards from where we were

"we," he says, he's almost taking the story away from Narrator, but he's not giving it back to the woman who saw the fire, but to himself and all the others who were "we" that night, and

> the fire came out and
> rose up, a flame like so:
> Ee! it went.

He raises his right fist in front of him, keeping the folded fingers in front, and when it reaches higher than his head he bursts it open on "Ee!" Fingers slowly close, hand comes back down, then

> Ee! it went again
> but it wasn't like the
> glow of

and here the resonance of his voice changes as he turns aside to look at the only light in the room,

> a candle—what it was, was a fire somewhat
> the color of
> what's it called?

Here he pauses longer than usual, waiting for an answer that might come from someone in his audience, but then he finds it on his own:

> ➤ ➤ ➤
> Corundum.

Aluminum oxide with iron in it, the same stuff rubies are made of.

> Yes indeed,
> it **came up high**
> it was seen clear overhead.

With that he shifts to another voice—not back to his own, nor to that of the woman who saw the fire that night, but to the voice of all of "us" who speak to all of "you" about what we should all know and do, the voice of collective wisdom:

> It's good when you see the fire
> you shouldn't tell anyone about it, not even a
>   companion
> whether it be your brother, your papa, whether it be
> your woman, whoever it might be.
> You mustn't talk with anyone, just keep it to yourself.

"Let's see what happens," as the saying goes.

Then comes another voice, as he tells us what he sees right now but we can't see, something he should keep to himself if he really sees it, and he does indeed fade out:

> Well, little by little this fire is going out, going out,
> going out, . . .

as he holds his hand out in front of him, palm down, and lowers it little by little, leaning forward to have a better look, to follow the fire going out, going out as it floats toward the earth, then he stops with his face as low as his knees, staring straight down at the back of his hand, palm almost touching the floor, right on top of

> . . . this
> here, and when there's a—

whatever it is, a "—," a silence, the white of the page, something that can't be named, waiting to be caught on the floor under his palm,

> you grab it . . .

he closes his fist around the thing on the floor,

> . . . and there's nothing there.
> Then you look at the place where it went out—
> and it left you a sign there.

The fire left a sign by letting you see where it went out, like an animal crossing your path in the woods and then disappearing again. Like the spit that vanished in the palm of Blood Moon's hand.

> And if you have a hat, you leave a hat there, or if you're
>   · a woman
> you leave a scarf or something else there.
> Then, when dawn comes, there it is—

you make the sign stand still—or perhaps it's more like giving it a way to hide itself. You're a dreamer marking the spot where something just happened, planning to find it again in the morning, and

> there's the sign—well, the place to dig, there's a fortune.

He's whispering those last words, almost choking off the final syllable, and if something like this should ever happen to you, keep it at least that quiet.

Yes, oh yes.

With "yes" he hints at an opening, hints at the hope of some response. The tape has my own voice saying, "Where it went out?" and don Mateo says,

Yes, where the little fire went out.

Then I say, "You have to cover it," and don Mateo, motioning toward the invisible spot on the floor, says,

There, with a hat.
If it weren't for the hat it'd all be for nothing.
It's to see, later, where to dig.

Then he offers some wisdom he left out the first time through:

You mustn't talk about it with anyone
until another day, then
you can talk.
And you have to do a custom there like the other
customs
that we have:
you have to put a
c a n d l e . . .

he often speaks of little candles, but here he says "candle" in a little voice. He holds this unseen candle between his right thumb and forefinger and stands it on the floor at the right spot, now a hole where the treasure once was,

. . . like so

and doña Bárbara's voice comes in here, "Incense," she suggests, and don Mateo says,

Incense,
e v e r y t h i n g .

Then it'll still
still be there, the fortune won't go away.

The treasure is in danger, even after it's been taken home. The Holy World has one more hungry mouth than before, the mouth that gave up the treasure.

Yes.
And if not, it'll turn into
turn into cinders.

And here I say, "Aha," and then, having already heard a few things about the proper care of treasure, I add, "If it weren't valued, it would decay."

Yes.
And when you went to see it, money is not what it'd be.
It'd be cinders.

"Money" is the quick gloss the translator inside me puts on Spanish *dinero,* but "dinero" is already the quick gloss the translator inside don Mateo has put on Quiché *pwaq,* and *pwaq* rings with metal in the Quiché ear even quicker than money might ring in ours. *Pwaq* is metal, especially precious metal, and *pwaq* of the greatest value is the kind that gives itself away, letting itself be noticed on the ground right in front of you, or pointing to its hiding place with a sudden sign. It could be an old silver coin or a ring, but there are other things that have a ring to them, or bear the marks of great heat— meteorites, fulgurites, volcanic concretions, things in the shape of small animals, ears of corn, squashes, or White Sparkstriker's lost shoe, smelted on that morning when Sun came up in person. Such *pwaq* is kept hidden at home and never spent. It is *uk'ux pwaq,* the very "heart of metal."

Now don Mateo pauses longer than usual, but instead of tying off the end of his story he comes back round to speaking of the place where it happened:

➤ ➤ ➤

This is in the township of St. Andrew Plaster House.

Then he speaks as "we" again, only this time it's "we" who are seated in his front room, we who were headed for the place he's been talking about until I thought our jeep might turn over:

> It's higher up than we were
> last week
> ➤ ➤ ➤
> and the lady who saw this—
> I don't know where she is.
> She doesn't have her family here . . .

and the tape we made when the day Seven Jaguar was on its way out and Eight Bird was coming in goes on a little longer, but something's buzzing inside the darkening room where I listen to don Mateo's voice, where I tap away at my keyboard. A wasp climbs the screen of my monitor, headed for the place where I've lit up the words **St. Andrew Plaster House,** bright amber on dark gray. I stop it before it gets there.

➤ Thanks Be to the World

OUTLINES OF MOUNDS can be traced on the peak called Tohil's Place, beneath the trees and in the clearing, and strewn about are slabs of gray basalt quarried nearby, and silvery schist from somewhere to the north. After the first dawn, after Tohil became stone, his arbor of bromeliads and hanging mosses was replaced by a temple, and a few houses were built for people who came up here on retreats, burners of copal and users of thorns.

By now the very ruins have been ruined, the stones so disturbed it's hard to trace out the line of a single wall, much less a room. On the cloudy day Eight Bird, the three ethnographers and the three Quichés approach the rim of a dynamite crater, blasted by treasure hunters. The crater itself has been disturbed; it takes a practiced eye to recognize it for what it is. After the adventurers came archaeologists, out here on a surface survey. All we have from them is a report that they took away several artifacts, carved out of cream-colored volcanic tuff. Four of these were square-headed tenons, 40 cm. long and 20 cm. in diameter, apparently used to hold masonry veneer in place on a building. Another was a relief panel, 30 cm. on a side and 5 cm. thick, showing a face with a mouthful of large teeth, a nose marked by a hole, and square eyes with round pupils. The effect of this piece, the only known example of figurative art from Tohil's Place, is reported to be that of a skull.

Here and there around Tohil's Place today we see discarded wrappers from packets of copal incense, and even as we enter the sacred precinct of the crater we can smell the untouchable place at its center, the heavy scent of the damp ashes and resinous soot of old offerings. The hearth, reconstructed since the blast was set off in the old one, is open to the west and bordered on the other three sides by rubble, piled up in some places and stood on end in others. The sides are blackened with the smoke of copal, and the stones and bare earth of the floor within are smudged with ashes and caked with candle drippings. A long stick is handy, left at the edge of this hearth by previous visitors, and at every other hearth in all these mountains, good for stirring pieces of incense to make sure they burn completely.

Looters looking for a priceless idol would never know which of the stones in this shrine might be the one haunted by the daimon of the place, the stone with a gape, with lips that like to be wet with strong liquor and sometimes get a taste of hot blood from a hen with her head cut off. Gapes of the present day, or at least the ones that remain in places like this, are heavy pieces of dark gray basalt, hard and dense enough to clink.

An archaeologist, after examining one of these stones, would have to say, "It looks unworked to me."

An art historian might say, if somewhat grudgingly, "That's an example of found art."

A gape might look slightly like the head of a snake, tapered toward the mouth, and where there was once a bubble in the molten rock there might be a cavity in the right place for an eye. Or a gape might look a little like a human head, tapered toward the chin, with parallel ridges across its face at the right levels for a brow ridge, cheekbones, and lower lip. The one thing all gapes have in common, other than the fact that they are difficult to describe in words, is an edge or crease or cavity that could be called a mouth.

As for the stones here at Tohil's Place, don Mateo points out the one with the mouth as if it were completely obvious. While we unwrap our offerings and lay them out along the open side of the hearth, the two children go off to explore the rocks and woods nearby. When everything is in place it looks as though a buffet had been set for the Holy World, with the courses laid out in the order in which they should be eaten. On a flat rock, raised above the level of the food, we place four cloth bundles, each tied shut with a string and each containing all the paraphernalia needed to read the auguries of the thirteen-times-twenty days of the ancient calendar. Hidden here are hundreds of bright red seeds the size and hardness of dried beans, seeds of the flute tree. One bundle, far larger than the others, has all sorts of ancient artifacts inside as well—spindle whorls, stone knives, figurines, things don Mateo has found in his path and seen fit to keep over the years. On top of his bundle he gently rests the heavy cluster of crystals from his altar at home, together with a single red seed, an unusually large one, that he picked up off the ground just the other day. The other three bundles are those of novices. They belong to the three ethnographers.

Don Mateo starts talking even while he puts a few last things in place and checks for matches in his pocket. He prays fast and long, breathlessly as can be, he leaves a silence only, breathes in only when he comes to the very end of his breath, it's as if he were writing a long run of prose with hardly ever an indentation. What he says when he prays takes its shape from the little rise in pitch that begins each phrase and the little fall that ends it, but everything in between returns to his monotone, the level he keeps all the way from beginning to end, it's all one single sentence that never seems to end, it's all one long soft mutter unless we tune in when he gets a little louder, or slows down slightly, or the breeze shifts and carries the words our way, or else we lean and strain one ear in his direction. We try to hear at least a little of what he says in the long pauses that break up our own attempts at a few lines of prayer, and then again in that longest pause that comes when we've run out of lines, the lines we've memorized, words he himself and other motherfathers have given us to speak for ourselves.

We try to hear don Mateo, but after all, we're not the ones he's talking to right now, he looks like he's talking to nothing but thin air on an empty mountaintop, but he names, he calls upon an unseen host, and we catch a few of the names, or something sounds so familiar we don't even need to hear each syllable clearly, or he says it exactly when and where we'd expect to hear it, near the beginning he says *pardon my trespass,* pardon a mere vigesimal being for presuming to stand on this holy ground, *on this holy, this beloved day, this day of the Lord Eight Bird, this fifth of December,* and he takes a pair of long wax candles and holds them up never stopping, *here is my stake, my present,* here is the thing I'll stand on the ground *before you,* and now he begins to name his Holy Quaternity, *Holy King of the World,* his head is tilted a little skyward, *Holy Savior of the World,* he looks out level here, *Holy Creator of the World,* his gaze includes the ground before him here, *Holy Martin of the World,* we don't know which St. Martin this is but he says it's St. Martin who holds us all from below, who can cause the earth to tremble by moving his little finger, and he holds two candles in one hand, one crossing the other to make an X, the same two candles he held this morning, touching the glass of the door where the semblance of St. John looks out from inside the tabernacle on top of his altar at home, and now he touches this cross of wax to the face of the stone that has the mouth, and talking on and on he lights these candles, softening the end of one with the flame of the other, and stands them up on a slab of stone that rests on the holy earthen hearth before the mouth, the ground he must not touch with his hand, between the thighs of the World, and we set out our candles too, he's ending this part of his prayer but not his one long sentence by raising his voice, not bringing it down, using the word for the one we call Our Father for the first time, using the word the only way he'll ever use it, God becomes the one to mark off paragraphs, God becomes the cry of affliction, God comes just before we catch our breath, we hear the short stretch of silence that comes when don Mateo says, *O God—*

And then he says *and furthermore,* and here he takes up candles of tallow, not smooth and innocent candles made of wax but sticky candles made of the fat of slaughtered pigs, *Come hither, Mary Black Butterfly,* he summons a mountain west of here, or the lady who rules that mountain, she's Mary Black Butterfly, half her name from the one we call the Virgin, the other half she shares with Black Butterfly Grandson of Many Hands, the man who cut off the head of Peter Pallid's white horse, and another mountain, *World of Don Manuel,* every mountain a microcosm, *World of Don Juan,* and all along don Mateo lights whole bunches of tallow candles, he lets them burn lying down on the holy ground and we put down our candles too, *World of Don Pascual,* a mountain whose summit shrine has the Pascual Rock, carved with eyes and nose and mouth, arms crossed like a pair of candles, *World of Don Diego,* wherever that may be, and a giant, *Golden Earthquake, Shining Earthquake,* the lord within another mountain, the one who had his ankles tied to his wrists by Marksman and Little Jaguar Sun, and on with the names of every mountain, every world in Guatemala if don Mateo only knew them, and *Red Sparkstriker, White Sparkstriker,* whose ax of flint strikes lightning that moves in the blood of daykeepers, who predicted Black Butterfly's defeat by Peter Pallid, who never got baptized any more than he ever got petrified, red daimon who gives riches in dreams and dark places, who reveals the locations of stones with mouths—we hear a blast from the horn of a truck.

"What's that?" says don Mateo in his normal voice, turning his head toward the road where we left the jeep. Now we all hear that the truck did not stop but is still on its way over the ridge from Holy Cross to St. Andrew, from Many Trees to Plaster House, and don Mateo continues as if he'd never been interrupted, his mood is the same as if he'd never wondered whether someone might get curious about what the people from the jeep might be doing, he names the Two Archangels, *Thunderbolt St. Gabriel, Thunderbolt St. Michael, lightning, storm, the entering darkness, O God*—

And again he says *and furthermore, here are my little tamales, here are my gourds of gruel,* and begins to unfold the leaves that wrap the copal in packets, *King Quiché,* the last Quiché king to rule the mountains and plains around us, and he takes the small round cakes of incense one by one, *King Black Butterfly,* whose spirit familiar, whose genius was a quetzal, last seen flying over the battlefield where Peter Pallid killed him, and he tosses a piece of copal on the hearth for the flames of the tallow candles to feed on, *King Monarch, King Montezuma,* the man who was king in faraway Mexico, we smell the incense, smoke of the blood of trees, we untie our own copal, *eight hundred churches,* churches with graves beneath their floors, *eight hundred cemeteries,* each on its own holy hill, *eight hundred angels of glory,* angels who once had flesh and blood, and here come the Four Apostles, *St. Peter,* by his key he's the patron of all who divine, *St. John, St. Paul, St. Bartholomew,* all of these were once vigesimal beings, *First Lord Mayor, Second Lord Mayor of the blessed souls in the place of fleas,* "pulgatorio," it's purgatory he means, he salutes the sparks in the dripping caves below, sparks that may one day sprout from the earth, stars on the rise, *First Prison, Second Prison, First Key, Second Key, on the First Table, the Second Table,* and all the names of the dead are recorded somewhere, *in the First Book, in the Second Book, on the First Shelf, on the Second Shelf,* the deep orange flames from the resin reach up high, who knows how high the soot-black smoke ascends, *and all grandmotherfathers in common, all mother-fathers in common, however many souls of the dead there may be,* the smoke stains our clothes, *O God*—

And again he says *and furthermore,* and here he brings out a bottle of bootleg liquor, *hear our request,* he sprinkles the open-mouthed stone that stands in the shrine, *do me a favor,* he turns to each of us in turn, *along with our companions here, our neighbors here,* and he cuts to his normal voice, turns to one of the three ethnographers, "your name?"

He knows our names but asks us anyway, gives us each a place in his prayer, *Tuncan Er-le,* "and your name?" *Bárbara Tet-lok,* "and yours?" *Dionisio Tet-lok,* as if he were entering our names in a form, then he sprinkles our divining bundles, *give us our house, our land, our animals, our business, our car, our airplane, our clothes,* and a long list of coins and bills in ascending denominations, and sums that would add up to stacks of big ones, *O God*—

And yet again he says, *and furthermore, perhaps some neighbor, some companion piled up words behind our legs, behind our arms, made thirteen prayers, thirteen words, thirteen speeches, spoke through the breeze, spoke through the chill, spoke through the clouds, set up stakes, handed out presents, asked that pain come into us, asked that my animals die, asked that my animals disappear, the pig I had, O God*—

So he's got something on his mind. A few days ago he found the corpse of his prize pig, his perfectly healthy pig, and again he says *and furthermore,* and here he must've used the words he gave me as a gift, told me to write in my notebook, words to ask for justice, *may my neighbor, may my companion be delivered into the hands of St. Peter and St. Paul and St. Bartholomew, and the Holy King of the World, and the Holy Savior of the World, and the Holy Creator of the World, and Holy Martin of the World, and Mary Black Butterfly, don Manuel, don Juan, don Pascual, don Diego, I give a present before you all, I remember the thunderbolt, flash, storm, entering night, come St. Gabriel, come St. Michael, raymasters, O God*—

And the way don Mateo ends a prayer is easy to remember, he says, *and furthermore, may this confession be received, this petition, in the day, in the light, let it be done at 6:00 in the morning, at 7:00, at*

8:00, at 9:00, at 10:00, at 11:00, at 12:00 noon, at 1:00 in the afternoon, at 2:00, at 3:00, at 4:00, at 5:00, at 6:00, at 7:00 in the evening, at 8:00, at 9:00, at 10:00, and at 11:00, and midnight, the very center of darkness, and at 1:00 in the morning, and at 2:00 in the morning, at 3:00, at 4:00, at 5:00, at 6:00 in the morning, the sum total of twenty-four hours, in the World, the earth, the chill, the breeze, all worlds together, and thanks be to the World, and here he says **kintoj,** *I'm making payment,* **toj,** "to pay," **Toj,** the name of the day the ancient daimon of this mountain was named for, **Tojil,** "he who has the quality of **Toj,**" whose resonant name is Thunderer, **Tojojil,** and now don Mateo drops his voice, ends his one long sentence, *I'm making payment to all the mouths of the World together, one word, one speech.*

➤ The Story of Evenadam

NOW WE HEAR THE VOICES of two children, don Mateo's youngest daughter and son, running out of the forest, bringing us something that looks about the size of a fist.

"We found another gape! We found another gape! Look!" Don Mateo turns their stone in his hands. He finds the mouth and says, "That's a gape, all right."

There's nothing more to be said by way of prayer, but the tall wax candles still make an offering of light, the coals of copal still make black smoke, the rocks are still wet with liquor. We settle down on the rubble that rims the shrine, chunks of a temple so broken we cannot tell exactly where the stairs were, nor the level at which the floor lay, nor the course of even one of the walls. We unfold the squares of brocaded cloth that wrap the part of the picnic we brought for ourselves—maybe there's something here for the gods, too, maybe the smell of corn ground with lime, toasted, if not the substance. Every now and then don Mateo stirs the coals with the stick that was already here, making sure every last puff of incense gets free.

The three ethnographers are quite content not to be doing ethnography. We've joined don Mateo in asking every imaginable god to be present here on the day Eight Bird, to accept the sustenance we've offered on the hearth, we've been sniffing the smoke of that banquet ourselves, and now we're getting high on straight shots of the same liquor the stones got dizzy on, we're taking big bites from fresh tortillas and cutting through the skins of soft avocadoes. But don Mateo has something he wants to say. A story he wants to tell. The trouble is, when you're talking with people, you can't just bring in a story out of nowhere. Someone says something and a story occurs to you. Someone raises a question and the story holds the answer. But today don Mateo already has a story and we haven't raised any questions at all, much less a question that would give him a reason to tell his story. So he'll ask a question himself if he has to. A big question. He says, to no one in particular:

Why? Why?

And who knows what we'd remember of his answer if we hadn't had a tape recorder with us, just in case ethnography started to happen in the middle of a picnic.

Now here I am, not on a mountaintop in Guatemala but back at the keyboard in my study again, and I'm listening to his story again, but this time I can stop it, rewind and repeat. The words come out in cleanly broken lines. These are not the long periods of a prayer, where pauses almost get in the way, but short breaths marked off by almost equal calms, the silences of a speaker who thinks about what he's saying and wants us to think about it too. The first intelligible words on the tape, with silences before and after, are these:

Why? Why?

Not one "why" but two, a couplet of sorts but it's one unbroken roll of sound. It's fine that it scans; vigesimal beings all over the middle of the Americas say at least a few scannable things even when they're not making speeches while standing in front of stones and thin air, even when they're telling stories instead. But just this word "why" is not enough. Why what? Through our drinks that day, and his, through our throbs in the head from the day before, and his—and maybe the altitude was affecting us, too—we were having trouble seeing where he wanted to take us, or where we should have been asking him to take us, though we did have enough sense to turn the recorder on. And now, on the tape at least, something of what his big question was can be read even from the beginning of his answer. Let's play the game now, let's take up the question after all this time and ask him, "Why?" (and "Why?"), and take down his answer:

Because, truly,
Eve and Adam

were crucified in the world, Eve and Adam.
He was the first man who married.

Crucified? Eve and Adam were "crucified"? Here's a word don Mateo got from Spanish, one of "our" languages, from "our" side of the Atlantic. Does he mean to be using *crear* here, "create," instead of *crucificar,* or is he folding the New Testament back over on top of the Old? He's not far off if we consider that Christ is sometimes called "the second Adam," and certainly what happened to Adam was cruel. What happened to Eve was cruel too, though it's doubly hard to think her onto a cross. But all right. "Truly," he says, he wants us to take him at his word, he's not just making this up.

So we're about to hear the story of Adam and Eve, as told by don Mateo on the day Eight Bird on top of the mountain called Tohil's Place. Or rather the story of "Eve and Adam," he's reversed the order twice already, there's no mistake about it, he'll tell us the story of Eve and Adam, and perhaps the twist in his version will involve more than folding the New back onto the Old—though people who speak his language nearly always put "her" first when saying "him and her," or rather "her and him." But don Mateo is doing this to a pair of names that have always been spoken the other way around, all the way back to the Hebrew.

What, then, is the question before us? It would seem to have something to do with our condition as vigesimal beings. We're all descended from Eve and Adam, we are the way we are because they "were crucified in the world." And, don Mateo tells us, Adam "was the first man who married." So the question would also concern why we're still here today, after all this time. I say "we," but we don't know yet whether don Mateo intends to include himself and his own people in this "we," since he's about to tell a story that we from the Old World had thought was ours and not his—unless, of course, we want to insist that he, too, must be descended from Adam, though he didn't happen to receive enlightenment on this subject until we, or someone who got to the New World long before us, gave him the words of the Old World Book.

Here follows a lot of noise on the tape, but in the midst of the zaps and rumbles some words can be made out:

☆☆☆☆✳✳✳!! ◇◇☆☆!!!!
◇ano◇ther th✳ing that ☆de☆fea✳ted ☆us
was a de☆vi☆l
who was ✳ca✳lled the Ser◇pent.

Right here I hear myself on the tape, saying, "The Serpent?" Maybe I'm hoping it'll turn out to be a New World serpent, the Plumed Serpent even, and not just that wretched serpent in the Garden. Don Mateo simply says "Yes," it's a serpent, and the noise comes up again, we've only this hint to the turn of the plot that hasn't even got started yet, but no matter. People who live in these mountains are always folding stories back on themselves, and chances are he'll come to this place again. Whatever it was we missed, we'll be able to pick up on it later.

When the tape comes clean again we're in the midst of a different scene, a later one:

Well.
Then, yes
after that
the Lord Jesus Christ said,

now don Mateo gives the voice of the Lord Jesus Christ a magisterial tone,

"**So.**
Now—
let their sin begin."
Because they hadn't known how to sin,
Eve and Adam.
They were already adults, but they didn't know how
to sin.
So he said,
"Let their sin begin."

Here he is, the Lord Jesus Christ, already on the scene way back when. It's beginning to sound as though Adam, or even Eve and Adam, will be in the role of the second Christ. And the Lord isn't saying, "Let there be light," or "Let the earth bring forth the living

146 ➤

creature after his kind." He's saying, "Let their sin begin." Whatever the Serpent may have done under cover of those zaps and rumbles, sin doesn't come into the world until the Lord gives his say-so. And it's the practice of sin that matters, not the concept. Eve and Adam don't even know *how* to sin until Jesus says, "Let their sin begin." The Word is made flesh.

At this point don Mateo expects to hear something from us, he's beginning to wonder about us, about whether we understand what "sin" is. He turns to us, speaks to us gringos in the same tone of voice he'd use if he were getting impatient with his children:

You're still a little young.
. But not me.

Then he gets right back into his story, he asks a question about the beginning of sin and doesn't wait for us to volunteer an answer:

But why?
In order to make the world **abound.**
➤ ➤ ➤

Here he pauses longer than usual, about two seconds—that's a long time in the middle of a story—to let his answer sink in. In case we were still wondering what kind of sin it was the Lord was speaking into existence, it's the kind that makes the world **abound.** Now don Mateo repeats the same words (and repeats the same pause), but shifts his emphasis:

In order to make the **world** abound.
➤ ➤ ➤

He's not just telling his version of "our" Old World story but means to include everybody among the descendants of Eve and Adam, it's the **world** that abounds. Then he offers an interpretation, he opens the breach between text and interpretation in the midst of his own words:

So there would be more people,
there would be more
Christians.

He uses the word *cristianos* in the same way Spaniards used it when they came here from out of the Middle Ages, it's synonymous with "people." And as far as that goes, he's been baptized and so have his wife and children and many previous generations, and the same goes for the three ethnographers who happen to be with him on the mountaintop. Except that he and his forebears have never seen any contradiction between sprinkling water on babies and giving drinks of strong liquor to stones. By this time the three ethnographers don't see any contradiction either, or at least not today they don't.

Now we're ready to get back to the story, to find out what happened between Eve and Adam. Don Mateo starts out on a long high pitch, as if he were just able to bear a pain from somewhere inside him, then comes back to words again:

> Eeeeeeee Eve
> began to cry.
> ➤ ➤ ➤
> Because for Eve
> it was just a little difficult.
> ➤ ➤ ➤

So Eve's part in making the world abound is painful, just as it is in the Old World Book. And why is it difficult for her?

> Because females
> are hard
> and they are
> somewhat physical,
> I mean.

So it's not because she's being punished for something she did, but because it's in the very being of women to be more of this world than men. Women know this through their pain, the pain that makes Eve cry, but they are "hard" in the face of this pain. When don Mateo says, "somewhat physical, I mean," the tape has the sound of my voice, I'm letting go of a chuckle, perhaps a laugh of recognition at hearing a notion that sounds like one of our own. But a laugh from his audience is not what he's looking for, he turns to me to affirm

what he just said, in a gentle tone but with a dip in his pitch that
bears a hint of annoyance:

Yeeeeees—

and suddenly he narrows his eyes and sharpens his voice:

> I'm telling you the **truth.**
> It's because I'm older
> that I'm speaking to you about this question.

At this point doña Bárbara concedes him the point with "Yes." He
drops his sharp tone but he's not through defending his authority
against my chuckle:

> And also
> you've already seen my sacred book?
> You've done that already.
> All right, then.
> Mm hm.

So we're not getting the story of Eve and Adam by word of mouth
alone, he has a book. He's made this move before, and the authors
of the alphabetic version of the New World Book made a similar
move four centuries ago, saying their work was based on a prior book
in "the ancient writing." And long before that, when the only kind
of writing in this part of the world was the ancient kind, people
telling stories probably cited books, and when they were handy they
probably set them out for all to see. Don Mateo had long since
shown us his own book. He keeps it on his altar at home, hidden
behind the parapet of the tabernacle, right next to the crystal that
brings him dreams.

Somewhere, someone in these mountains probably has another
manuscript of the New World Book tucked away somewhere, or
maybe even a version in hieroglyphs. Or better yet, a hieroglyphic
book with alphabetic notes crammed into the white spaces, an
interlinear translation into Spanish, made a fistful of years ago and
lost from view until who knows when. Haven't we all been waiting
for the weighty Book that could bear the name Rosetta?

The sacred book don Mateo has at home is octavo, thin, stapled along the fold line, and battered. A lot of dust, volcanic ash, has fallen on it, and a few drops from a leaky roof. The color-lithograph illustrations are of Bible scenes and the text is a retelling, in Spanish, of some Bible story. It's the sort of thing that's handed out in Sunday school. Whatever story it is, it's not the one about Adam and Eve. But it is a book, and it stands for The Book. Don Mateo never thinks of reading it, nor does he ask his children or one of us to read it aloud for him. It's there for the fact of it, there to have its existence revealed to those who need to know of its existence. And when he's away from home it's for citing, and now that he's cited it here he takes a good bite from a tortilla and gets back to his story. The words are a little difficult to make out at first because his mouth is still full:

> Then
> Adam said to her,

and here he speaks as if to someone farther away than any of us,

> "You, Eve:
> ➤ ➤ ➤
> you have to make a shirt.
> You have to make some
> pants, you have to make everything.
> And
> with cotton."
> "And you, Adam:
> you have to work."

As Eve continues her speech don Mateo picks up the stick he's been using to stir the incense and begins to whack a stone with it. Life is going to get just as hard in his story as it got outside the gates of the Old World Eden:

> "With a p**WHACK**ickaxe,
> with**WHACK** a machete," **WHACK**
> w**WHACK**ith ev**WHACK**eryth**WHACK**ing that
> th**WHACK**at **WHACK WHACK**
> that we have here in the world. **WHACK WHACK**

So Eve and Adam tell each other what their respective lots will be, they're making a contract, it's not just coming down from on high. And come to think of it, in "our" version of the story Eve isn't even given work to do, unless it's in that line that goes, "In sorrow thou shalt bring forth children," or hidden in the line about Adam that goes, "He shall rule over thee."

Having already switched from the "you" Eve addressed to Adam to a "we" that includes you and me, don Mateo goes on about us and gets in one last whack:

> For this reason we're here
> in the world
> physically
> working. **WHACK**
> And **why?**
> Because God
> told us.

Here is physicality again, as with Eve's "Eeeeeeeee," and work is one of the things that comes along with it. And it seems that God is behind this matter of work after all, despite that conversation between Eve and Adam. But at least they did have a conversation about it, and they both have their work.

The next six lines, up there on the mountain that day, went by very fast. We can't ask the tape machine to answer questions, but this time around we can at least catch the words:

> Because Evenadam
> were a god,
> equal to Jesus Christ.
> They are the first
> humans who
> are in the world.
> ➤ ➤ ➤

So "they *are* the first humans" and "*are* in the world," but they "*were* a god." They (and we) are now working, but weren't before. And why are we working? "Because God told us." Why did he do this to us? "Because Evenadam were a god."

Let's try this one a little slower. "Eve and Adam" sounds like "Evenadam," don Mateo runs the words together as one. But then he says they "were," making them plural again, and next he says they were "a god," making them one again. It's like those pairs of gods in the Book, the New World Book, where we're never quite sure whether we're dealing with two gods or one, unless the two halves of a pair start talking to one another, as Eve talks to Adam here. And it's like Jaguar Cedar, the first of all vigesimal beings, who's a "motherfather" all by $^{her}_{him}$ self before Red Sea Turtle becomes his wife. Of course there's something androgynous about the Adam of the Old World Book too, whose name simply means "human" in Hebrew, and part of the very substance of this human became the substance of Eve—a "rib" or (as it could've been translated) a "side." Eve as the "other side" of a not-yet-divided human.

The way don Mateo tells the story, Eve and Adam were, or the god Evenadam was, "equal to Jesus Christ," but when Jesus Christ said, "Let their sin begin," and when they went to work in the world, they became mere humans, and that's why we're all here. If we ever had any potential for rivaling the gods, Jesus Christ took care of that by weighing down our very existence with physicality and by making sure there would be any number of us. We were a problem to the gods of the New World Book, too, when one of them warned the others about us by saying, "They'll become as great as gods, unless they procreate, unless they proliferate." And the Lord God of the Old World Book said, "Behold, the man is become as one of us," whatever he may have meant by "us" (and whoever he may have been talking to), just before he gave Adam and Eve the news about giving birth and tilling the ground.

Now, with the former Evenadam firmly established as the Eve and Adam of this world, with all their physicality, don Mateo is ready to move on, right past the next nine months at least:

And then
later
then, after this,
they had a son
who was c a l l e d

who was called
Pastor.
➤ ➤ ➤
And then they had another son who was called
who was called—
I have it in a book there,
I'm going to show you there,

and here doña Bárbara and don Dionisio both say "Yes," we're humoring him, here he goes with his book again,

I'll show you.

And doña Bárbara adds, "At home," yes, his book is at home. No one offers him any help with names, even though all three of us gringos know Cain and Abel. We let it go when he says Pastor instead of Cain, and never mind that the firstborn son of Adam and Eve was not a pastor. We keep Abel to ourselves as well, even when he comes right out and asks us for the name of the second son:

Then
who was c a l l e d
➤ ➤ ➤
what was this son called?

After all, we're ethnographers, not missionaries. We want to hear what don Mateo might say, what a Quiché Indian might say, without any prompting from us. What he might say if we weren't even here, never mind that plenty of other people from the Old World have reached these mountains before us. So he gives up on naming the second son of Eve and Adam and goes on:

Then—
this Pastor
➤ ➤ ➤
is more, is more—
I don't know
why
but what I'm trying to say is that
he's physical.

So Pastor is more "physical" than his younger brother, just as Eve is more "physical" than Adam. Eve's physicality is evidenced in her hardness, her endurance of the pain that comes with childbirth. How, then, do we know that Pastor is "physical"?

> Because he killed his brother.

Is don Mateo merely saying that giving birth to a child and killing a man are both grossly physical acts, or could there be something more to it than that? For the glimmer of an answer we have to look over to the west in Mexico and back to the time before Europeans arrived, where women who died in childbirth and men who died in battle were sent off to share the same celestial paradise, while people who died from other causes were sent off to earthly worlds beneath the land of the living. Don Mateo's story seems in harmony with this scheme of things, but it concerns a woman who gives birth *without* dying and a man who kills without *being* killed. Instead of going off to a celestial paradise, these two survivors have an even greater burden of physicality than other earthly beings.

When doña Bárbara heard that Pastor "killed his brother" she said "Oh," perhaps startled at the way don Mateo was giving away the main event in a story whose characters he had barely introduced. Now, having heard her "Oh," he goes back and repeats his previous words, but with emphasis added:

> He killed his **brother.**

Now don Tuncan interjects, "Wasn't it in the milpa?" which is to say in a garden of maize, squash, and beans. For the first time, one of the three ethnographers reveals that he might've heard the story before. After all, didn't Cain kill Abel in a field of grain? And wouldn't don Mateo interpret that field as a milpa? Or mightn't missionaries have told him it was a milpa? Don Mateo answers aside with a quick "Yes," seeming to accept what don Tuncan has ventured, but he doesn't let it change his course. He goes right on describing Pastor, the man who will kill his brother once his story actually gets told:

> It seems
> he had a lot of livestock.

Those of a single color
are his brother's.
And those of two colors
belong to Pastor,
he was a pastor.

So we're not dealing with Cain the gardener and Abel the herder.
Rather, both brothers own livestock. But where does don Mateo get
this division of the livestock according to colors? To find that, we'll
have to read ahead, twenty-six chapters and twenty generations
beyond the story of Cain and Abel: "And he removed that day the he
goats that were ringstraked and spotted, and all the she goats that
were speckled and spotted." It was Jacob who did that, separating his
own animals from Laban's according to a bargain they had struck,
and Jacob did indeed end up, as don Mateo has it, with "a lot of
livestock." But Laban was Jacob's maternal uncle and father-in-law,
not his brother. Jacob had a brother all right, the twin who was born
from Rebekah just ahead of him: Esau, the hunter. But it was Esau
who thought of killing Jacob, not the other way around. So it would
seem that don Mateo has put a prosperous Abel into the body of a
homicidal Cain and a prosperous Jacob into the body of a homicidal
Esau, and then called them all Pastor. No wonder he can't seem to
find a name for the other brother.

And then—
after that—
they talked.
And since young were born from those of two colors,
        only from those of two colors,
then
only the
only Pastor had
animals—
cows and bulls and however many things.
And
this what's-his-name
he didn't have anything, because

now don Tuncan interrupts, he's trying to be helpful again but his timing is bad. In saying "what's-his-name" here, don Mateo wasn't really asking for an answer, nor did he leave a big enough pause for one. But between "because" and whatever he meant to say after it, don Tuncan inserts "Abel," which may or may not be a workable name for Pastor's brother. No matter; don Mateo doesn't pick up on Abel anyway. He says "Eh?" aside and then, without waiting for don Tuncan to repeat the name (and without finishing whatever was hanging on "because"), he reasserts his claim to be telling a story. He makes the most basic of all narrative moves, saying,

> Then

and again don Tuncan interrupts. Having once decided to intervene, he wants his intervention to make a difference. Now he offers information about Abel, translated the way a missionary might translate it, saying, "He was a milpero," a gardener who planted maize, squash, and beans. He's so caught up in don Mateo's story he's forgotten that if anybody was a milpero in the Old World Book, it was Cain and not Abel. As for don Mateo, he continues straight on with the new sentence whose space he staked out with "Then":

> he said,

and here follows a conversation between Pastor's younger brother, what's-his-name, and someone else. It's a secret conversation, and don Mateo goes into it so deeply that he almost keeps it secret from the rest of us. He partly whispers, partly mutters with a tight-mouthed meanness. This could almost be an internal dialogue on the part of what's-his-name, or even an internal dialogue on the part of don Mateo. It's almost as hard to follow as that earlier part of the tape where nothing but the words "devil" and "serpent" came through, and the next thing we knew the Lord Jesus Christ was saying, "Let their sin begin." The only intelligible words are as these, in which someone is trying to turn what's-his-name against Pastor:

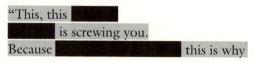

"This, this ████ ████ is screwing you. Because ████████ this is why

all ▮▮▮▮ they are all
all of two colors,
all spotted and all—"
➤ ➤ ➤

Once again we miss out on what the "because" might be, why it is
that Pastor, who has the right to all the animals of two colors, ends
up with a lot of livestock while what's-his-name doesn't have
anything. The answer given by the Old World Book is that Jacob,
who seems to have been something of a magician, cut "rods of green
poplar, and of the hazel and chesnut tree; and pilled white strakes in
them," and "the flocks conceived before the rods, and brought forth
cattle ringstraked, speckled, and spotted." Laban was left without any
solid-colored offspring for himself, and whether or not anyone
whispered in his ear (or in his head) about this, Jacob noticed that
"the countenance of Laban . . . was not toward him as before." As
for what's-his-name, we'll have to wait a bit for his reaction to the
secret voice that tells him he's getting screwed. Don Mateo leaves off
quoting that voice, but he's still concerned that what's-his-name is
getting the short end of the stick:

So none of them came out black, none of them came out
none
dark, none came out—
these—
➤ ➤ ➤

he breaks off as his children move in close and want something to
nibble on, then abandons the narrative mode long enough to tell us
that this part of his story is an origin story:

Because of this
cows remain distinct,
yes, in distinct classes.
There are
white, there are black, there a r e
roan, and there a r e all of them
because of this
this matter.

Twice he stretches the sound of the verb "are," as if to include all the colors he doesn't mention by name.

Now what's-his-name ends his secret dialogue with whoever-it-is has been telling him he's been getting screwed. He has made a decision:

> "Well,
>
> ➤ ➤ ➤
>
> by Jesus,
> I'm going,"
> he went to, to Pastor,
> he was thinking of fighting
> with his brother.

Given that it was Jesus who said, "Let their sin begin" in the previous episode, perhaps it's not altogether inappropriate that what's-his-name should swear by Jesus as he goes off to fight with Pastor. Yes, the younger brother is thinking of fighting with the elder, $\frac{\text{Jacob}}{\text{Abel}}$ is on the move against $\frac{\text{Esau}}{\text{Cain}}$. But one thing hasn't changed: the prosperous brother is the one who's in danger, in which case $\frac{\text{Esau}}{\text{Cain}}$ is on the move against $\frac{\text{Jacob}}{\text{Abel}}$. Either way, Pastor is in physical danger, like a woman in labor or a man in battle.

Before don Mateo gets around to letting what's-his-name confront Pastor, he feels the need to claim authority for his story again—only this time, instead of citing a book, the book he has at home, he asserts that his word is the *Ojer Tzij,* the Ancient Word, the Prior Word:

> This is the Ancient Word.
> Because
> the Ancient Word is, is about Pastor and the
> other son of Adam.

Back in the time when the New World Book had its first confrontation with the Old World Book, don Mateo's ancestors called the speech that came out of reading their own book the Ancient or Prior Word, and they called the speech that came out of the invaders' book *uch'ab'al Dios,* or "God talk." After more than four hundred years of preaching, the story of Pastor and the other son of Adam, if not quite the story of Cain and Abel, nor quite the story of Esau (or Laban) and Jacob, has come to qualify as part of the Ancient Word. Or else the Ancient Word has taken those stories unto itself. Either way, two brothers are about to have it out:

> Then—
> they went off.
> Since they always went to round up the
> the animals.

Now Pastor's nameless brother begins to make trouble, saying,

> "What is this?
> I'm going
> ➤ ➤ ➤
> I'm going to count the animals.
> I'm going to count the **animals.**
> And I don't have any more than before.
> Only one, two, three.
> Well, one
> is pure black. ·
> Another is pure, pure
> pure—"
> what's it called?
> Another color that's not pure black, it's not pure
> white, it's pure—
> mm.

Again the three ethnographers refuse to come to the rescue; they won't even risk putting the name of a color in don Mateo's mouth. He closes the matter with "mm" and moves back into the angry words of Pastor's brother:

> Then,
> ➤ ➤ ➤
> "You've been screwing around with me, you have
> more," he says.

This last line is hard to make out, and the problem gets worse when Pastor makes his reply. Again don Mateo goes too far inside his story for the rest of us to follow. He's thinking his characters through rather than acting them out. For Pastor's reply he uses such a tense, low, close-mouthed voice that only the fact of denial comes through:

"No.
No, ████████."

Whatever may have happened beyond an exchange of words, don Mateo is content to tell us, in a single line we've already heard anyway, what prosperous Pastor did to end the argument started by his jealous brother—and then we're off on a new episode:

He killed his brother.
Then, after that—

the next thing we know, we're hearing (or trying to hear) what will turn out to be the words of Adam, as he breaks the news of Pastor's deed to Jesus Christ:

"My Lord,
████████ these words."
Then, after that he said—
"He killed his brother."

After a marked pause, don Mateo goes back to filling in something he should have told us before he got to the words of Adam:

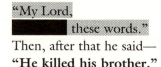

And when he killed his brother
then the blood
of the brother
wasn't
wasn't accepted by the Holy World.
The Holy World didn't accept it.
Because
he hadn't talked with the World.

The three ethnographers prick up their ears, they're always listening for twists that would move a story like this one a little farther from the Old World and closer to the New. On the tape doña Bárbara can be heard saying "Aha." Aha, it begins to sound as though Pastor *sacrificed* his brother. But when he did, the blood wasn't accepted by the Holy World, Holy Earth. Pastor didn't talk with the earth, he didn't have the words to make the sacrifice acceptable. Except for his name and his cattle, he could be a character out of the New World Book. The gods of that book, Heart of Sky, Heart of Earth, would have wanted him, as a vigesimal being, to be a "provider, nurturer," but there was something even more important for them than sacrifice. As they put it, "Our recompense is in words."

But don Mateo has not moved as far from the Old World Book as it might seem. Even there, the problem with the spilling of Abel's blood is not limited to the fact that he was killed by another human being, or that the killer was his own brother. God says to Cain, "The voice of thy brother's blood crieth out from the ground. And now art thou cursed from the earth, which hath opened her mouth to receive thy brother's blood from thy hand." So the earth is almost a character in the story, at least for this brief moment. She "opened her mouth" to receive Abel's blood, but she didn't accept it as a proper offering—or else it was God who didn't accept it, that jealous God who wanted to cut off any possibility of offerings to the earth.

Now we're ready to hear what Adam has to say about Pastor, whose blood offering wasn't accepted by the Holy World:

> Then
> he said,
> Adam did,
> "Jesus Christ,"
> he said,
> "Now then:

and here Adam speaks with sharp pain:

> **What** am I going to **do** with my **son?**
> Because for me
> it hurts me a lot, because
> because my son
> is burning ˙
> the blood

only for the Holy World.
He's burning it only for the Holy World
who doesn't accept
the cursèd World doesn't accept it."
➤ ➤ ➤

So Pastor has been *burning* the blood. Don Mateo has combined the spilling of the blood with the idea of a burnt offering. Shades of Abraham, only this Abraham has gone up on the mountain to sacrifice not his son but his brother, and he's gone through with it. But the fact that Pastor's burnt offering consists of blood makes sense right here on this mountain where the story is being told, on the day Eight Bird. The copal that still smolders on the hearth before us is made from the sap of trees, and sap is *kik'* in the Quiché language, and *kik'* means "blood." We are burning blood right here. Not only that, but the New World Book tells us that the first piece of incense ever burned on earth was a substitute for the heart and blood of a sacrifice.

But Adam thinks Pastor shouldn't be burning blood for the World, since "the cursèd World doesn't accept it." He's about to be told he's wrong:

After that he said to him,
Jesus Christ did, "No.
The World
is not cursed:
what it is, is sacred."

Jesus, of all people (or gods), comes to the defense of the World, becomes the Savior of the World in a new sense, declaring the World itself, the earth in all its materiality, to be sacred. Again the three ethnographers pay close attention; they are members of a generation of gringos who worry about the way their society seems bent on the destruction of the earth, the biosphere itself. The problem seems to go back at least as far as the Old World Book, which sets up the wrong relationship between humankind and the earth in its opening pages. God tells man to "subdue" the earth and gives him "dominion" over it, which spells disaster for the earth—and then, in no time at all, the disaster becomes mutual. Adam is told, "Cursed is the ground for thy sake," and one chapter later Cain is told, "Now art thou cursed from the earth." But don Mateo's Ancient Word has Jesus calling the earth "sacred," and the moment she hears it doña Bárbara says "Yes." Don Mateo acknowledges her response by repeating the words of Jesus:

> "The World
> is not **cursed**—
> what it is, is **sacred**,"
> ➤ ➤ ➤
> says Jesus Christ.

This time he gives "cursed" and "sacred" more punch, emphasizing the difference between them, but he makes no change in the words themselves, nor in their timing. Here is a bit of fixed text in the midst of improvisation. Indeed, in the original Spanish, these words constitute a rhymed couplet: *El Mundo no es condenado; lo que es, es sagrado.* This is the kind of statement contemporary daykeepers are apt to make in the course of their arguments with members of the Catholic Action movement, which aims to remove the stains of paganism from people like don Mateo and make them into "real" Catholics. Converts to the movement memorize their arguments in catechism classes; meanwhile, people who burn copal to the Holy World have been developing a counter-catechism. Catechists question the worship of the World, just as Adam is doing here, and counter-catechists try to straighten them out with pro-World statements liked the catchy couplet used by Jesus. *El Mundo no es condenado; lo que es, es sagrado.* But Adam resists:

> "Mm hm.
> That's all very well," he said.
> "But what I say is,
> it is cursed.
> What's to be done?" he said.
> ➤ ➤ ➤
> "You have only to clean it, and then it isn't cursed,
> this World."

So Adam and Pastor have some cleaning to do before the World will accept Pastor's offering. The kind of cleaning Jesus is talking about is partly done by prayer. When burning offerings one should always say, even before striking a match, "Make my guilt vanish." If it weren't possible for one's guilt to disappear, at least for as long as it took to present offerings down by a spring or up on a mountain, then it wouldn't be possible to set foot in a holy place without profaning it. But there is another kind of cleaning, "the washing of the plate and cup," the sweeping out of ashes from the earth and stones of the shrine itself. What vanishes then are the wrongs that may have been done during the very act of making prayers and offerings. Perhaps someone asked that illness enter the body of a neighbor, or perhaps the perfectly good words someone spoke aloud in prayer were mingled with the words of an inner voice that couldn't let go of some resentment against a neighbor. Pastor's own brother might've been thinking about the uneven division of livestock while he prayed at the very shrine where his own blood was destined to be burned. If so, that would be the root of the curse that prevents the World from accepting the blood.

In any case, having told Adam that a cleaning will set things right with the World, Jesus goes on talking about the Holy World:

> "Because
> **you must go with him,**" he said.
> ➤ ➤ ➤
> "Walk with him—
> talk with him—"

and with these words, don Mateo has made his pro-World Jesus stand the crypto-catechist Adam on his head. "Go with him," or *"Vaya con Él"*—"Him" with a capital *H*—these are the words used by Catholic catechists and Protestant evangelists only with reference to the Lord Jesus, and here Jesus himself goes right ahead and uses them with reference to the Holy World. And as if that weren't enough, he goes on to paraphrase a hymn about himself, the one whose English version goes, "He walks with me / and He talks with me." Don Mateo has accomplished a conversion, the conversion of the arch-converter himself, and he in his turn sets Adam back on the right track, here on the face of the Holy World.

The voice of Jesus' instructions to Adam is broken off, interrupted by a grander voice that speaks of the future relationship between all vigesimal beings and the World, the World as a physical entity. Don Mateo projects this voice several yards beyond the three ethnographers and his two children, as if Jesus were preaching to a small congregation right here in this clearing on the mountaintop:

> **"Your children**
> **will be**
> **earth.**
> **And they will be dust**
> **and dust**
> **and dust will be their end.**
> **➤ ➤ ➤**
> **They will come to an end."**

We've all heard something like this before: "For dust thou art and unto dust thou shalt return." But that was God speaking to Adam, driving him and Eve out of the Garden and bringing death into their lives. He passes a death sentence on the whole of humankind at a time when there has not yet been any death. But don Mateo has Jesus speaking with Adam at a time when the first human death has already occurred, the slaying of one brother by another. That makes Pastor the originator of death. Death in this part of the New World is something humans originate among themselves, not a sentence passed in advance by the gods. Don Mateo has never read the New World Book, but the same thing is true there. No one ever dies until the Quiché lords, disguising themselves as jaguars and even leaving jaguar tracks behind, start preying on members of other nations, nations whose lords they count as elder and younger brothers. And just as Pastor offers the blood of the slain to the World, so they offered blood to the world that is this very mountain, to the god, the gape who gave this mountain his name, Tohil.

Now don Mateo takes over the preaching himself, speaking all the way into the trees:

Because of this, we
we are earth
and we are dust
and dust
and dust
and dust and dust will be our end.

Then he pulls his voice back in to the two children and three ethnographers who are seated around him:

So I say to you.
➤ ➤ ➤
And so it is.
➤ ➤ ➤

➤ Trying This Erotic Thing

SILENCE, JUST A FEW SECONDS of silence mark the end of the sermon on the mountain called Tohil's Place. Don Mateo has more to say and the tape keeps moving through the recorder. Having just spoken in his biggest voice of the day, he returns, once again, to the matter of his authority:

> It seems they question this,
> Latins ask, "How do they know,
> these Indians
> these *ixtos?*"

The people in power here in the very middle of the Americas, *ladinos,* cousins of the three gringos, speak of *indios,* "Indians," and the very word seems to say, off in the distance, that it wasn't so much that Columbus came to the wrong place as that the people who were living here weren't the right Indians. But they also call them by a name they picked up from the Indians themselves, *ixtos.* It comes from Cakchiquel, the language closest to Quiché, and the original form is *xtan.* To call a serving girl in Cakchiquel, you say, *Xtan!* Like saying, *Muchacha!* in Spanish. "Girl! Come here!"

> Because there are
> some who are very mixed up, they say to me, *Ixtos.*
> *Ixtos,* they tell me.
> Yes.
> But
> the word *ixtos* is not a word.

There's no place for this word in don Mateo's Spanish, nor in his Quiché. Yes, there are Quiché words that begin with *x-* or *ix-*, making them diminutive or feminine, but those words don't end with

-os. Spanish words can end with *-os,* which makes them plural, but the *x (sh)* sound in *ixtos* is foreign to Spanish, and in fact the whole sequence *ixt-* makes this word for Indians *sound* Indian. The addition of *-os* submits these same Indians to the laws of Spanish grammar and implicitly reduces all of them, regardless of sex or age, to the status of serving girls. At the same time, *ixtos* sounds almost like the Spanish diminutive ending *-itos,* which Latins use to turn *indios* into *inditos,* "little Indians." But *ixtos,* says don Mateo, is not a legitimate word, and he goes on to stake a claim to something that is legitimate:

> Because King Black Butterfly Grandson—
> why do we have—

and then comes a noise, the flutter a machine puts on a tape when it comes to the end and stops. While the cassette is popped out, turned from Side A to Side B, and popped back in again, don Mateo goes on, probably he's naming the names of other people who were already here in these mountains, his people, when don Pedro de Alvarado arrived and then there were Latins who spoke of Indians. Latins, once upon a time, were the native people of Latium, then Romans finding themselves in the barbarian reaches of the empire were Latins, then Spaniards finding themselves among Moors were Latins—or rather Ladinos—and Sephardic Jews finding themselves among Spaniards were Ladinos, and clever Spaniards finding themselves among naive Spaniards were Ladinos, and then Spaniards who expelled the Jews from Spain and later found themselves in the Indian reaches of the new empire were Ladinos/are Ladinos, these clever Christians who know an Indian when they see one.

Now comes Side B, it begins with the flutter made by the PLAY and RECORD buttons pressed at the same time, and the rumble of a hand setting the machine down and letting go of it. Don Mateo is speaking the words of Ladinos again:

> "How
> can this man
> speak of this?
> And where did he go
> to learn these words?"

And I—it's because,
by the grace of God,
I had to study a, a book of the
interior,
the book
the sacred book.

Here the tape has my voice asking, "A book of the interior?"

Yes.
Interior book.

"What does that mean?" I ask.

The interior book?
Sacred book.
Because
I
had one some priests gave me.
Some priests
gave it to me—well, as a loan, nothing more,
they didn't give it to me once and for all.

So he was given some religious text to study, a book for *hablarse al interior,* Spanish for "speaking to oneself." That's what all reading is, in a way, but there was a time when the study of a text meant speaking it out loud, and it still means that for anyone who's learning to read and write, or studying for a part, or studying a catechism.

It's been, it's been some
some
some forty years.
➤ ➤ ➤
I had only one child when
I saw this.
And—
but still
but still I remember
the whole assignment right now.
It preached

it preached
Eve and Adam,
➢   ➢   ➢
and why
they say that Eve and Adam,
why Eve was born.

So it wasn't that book he now keeps behind the parapet of the tabernacle on his altar at home, but a book he remembers. If the priests lent him an old *Doctrina Cristiana,* a missionary tract of the sort that goes back to the sixteenth century in this part of the world, it might've preached, for example, that "Our Lord God made Eve of Adam's rib, and not of his flesh, and the reason is that flesh is neither sturdy nor hard, whereas a rib is very sturdy and very strong and hard." Hard like don Mateo's Eve. And it might've preached that the work of making Adam and Eve was done by the second of the three persons of the Trinity, the one with an earthly destiny, and not by the Father or the Holy Ghost. If it was anything like an old *Biblia Pauperum,* a Poor Man's Bible with more pictures than words, it might've even had an engraving that showed Jesus in the act of creating Adam (see opposite page).

Now don Mateo opens his invisible book of the interior and turns to one of the three gringos, it's don Dionisio, saying,

Why was Adam born, what do you say, sir?

But he knows very well he'll never get anywhere asking questions of an ethnographer, so he quickly turns the game around:

Do me the favor of saying this,
just this:
"Why was Eve born?
And why was Adam born?"
➢   ➢   ➢

No answer. He turns to doña Bárbara and don Tuncan:

You, madam, you, sir.
➢   ➢   ➢

170   ➢

No answer.

I want you to ask a question.

So this book on loan was a book of questions and answers, a catechism, and he wants the ethnographers, who ask questions all the time anyway, to ask the questions now, in the middle of a picnic, questions he's never yet heard them ask. But don Dionisio turns the game back around again, saying, "What's the question you want to ask us?" Don Mateo replies, with impatience,

How was Eve born?
How was Eve born, and how was Adam born?
➤ ➤ ➤ ➤ ➤ ➤ ➤ ➤ ➤ ➤

This time he waits long enough to make the silence embarrassing. Don Dionisio speaks at last, he starts off with, "Adam was—" and then, after a moment's consideration, chooses "sleeping."

> Ah, good.
> That's for sure.
> But how was he born?
> ➢ ➢ ➢

No answer. Don Mateo rewords his question and tries a coaxing tone:

> What did it consist of when he was born?
> Adam.

Now don Tuncan ventures an answer. "Naked," he says, and then adds, "without knowledge."

> Ah, naked, yes, he was certainly naked.
> It's worse.
> He was a *marinera*.

He was a female mariner? Even if don Mateo meant to say *marinero*, that still wouldn't make sense. The ethnographers look at one another in puzzlement, and don Mateo is surprised at their ignorance of *marineras*:

> Aren't those exported from here, from Guatemala?

"No" is all don Dionisio can say. It doesn't occur to anyone that don Mateo might have meant *marioneta*, "marionette." That's *poy* in his own language, a doll, a puppet, an effigy, anything that's been got up to look like a human being. Don Mateo's Adam is a *fabricated* person, he's just like the first people in the New World Book, who are made and modeled by the gods of Skyearth.

Now don Mateo gives up on getting answers and addresses his question *al interior:*

> **How was Adam born?**
> **Made of clay.**

In unison, and in a tone of voice that says, "So *that's* it," doña Bárbara and don Dionisio repeat the answer, "Made of clay." Triumphantly, don Mateo passes it back again:

Made of clay.

Don Tuncan is heard from here, but he only manages "Mm." Perhaps he's disappointed that don Mateo didn't say "Made of maize," which is what the New World Book says. Don Mateo hesitates a moment and then continues as if he'd left "made of clay" dangling on a high pitch when in fact it sounded conclusively low, and as if he were still telling the story that sounded as if it had nowhere to go after that sermon on the subject of dust:

➢ ➢ ➢

Adam was, when Jesus Christ said—

and he leaves this dangling too, gets a sudden gleam in his eye and looks around at all of us as he reaches inside a cloth bundle and brings out a handful of *ajache'*, a pulpy, thin-skinned fruit about the size of a plum but rounder, chartreuse on the outside and yellow on the inside, native to this part of the world and known to science as *Casimiroa edulis*. Speaking *al interior*, the name *ajache'* sounds a little ominous here, it sounds like *ajam che'*, "carved of wood," which is how the New World Book describes some marionettes the gods once made when they were trying to make humans, only these particular marionettes merely ended up as monkeys. And the Spanish name for this fruit is ominous too, *matasano*, "kills-the-healthy," which is what a no-good doctor is called, the kind we call a "quack." Sounds a little like a *manzano*, an apple, and if you ate a *manzano* as green as a perfectly ripe *matasano*, you'd get sick all right. But really, there's nothing at all wrong with this fruit.

Let's eat this, look:

and he hands the first of his ripe puppets, his bright green quacks, to don Dionisio, who says, "This?"

If you like.

Don Dionisio takes a bite and says, "Mmmmmm." It's—well, something like a plum. Don Mateo hands out quacks to the other two ethnographers, and as he does this he goes back to his suspended story, clear back to events that happened before anything he told on Side A:

> In the first place—
> "What are we going to make in the World?" she says,
> the Virgin Mary.

So Mary was there with Jesus when Eve and Adam were made. We'll never find a picture of that in a Poor Man's Bible. But we can read, in the New World Book, that it was the Grandmother of Light and of time itself who ground the maize that became the flesh of the first vigesimal beings. The Virgin Mary goes on speaking:

> "And what are we going to make
> so the World will abound?"
> ➤ ➤ ➤
> "Let's crucify Adam."

There it is again, ~~crea~~crucifix~~tion~~, the same way it was on Side A. "Let's crucify Adam" says Jesus, and Mary says,

> "Good."
> They made him.
> They made something like
> like a—a doll.
> Of clay.

So it's a doll now, *una muñeca,* don Mateo has found a word that's easy for us, not like ~~mariomarineraneta~~. Now he takes out two more quacks and hands them to his children:

> Here, take this.
> And by hand he formed
> something like a man.
> Good.
> Then,
> after Adam

has already been formed,
then a little bit later,
Adam
is very **sad.**
He's in a
in a garden
and it was called **Jordan.**
➤ ➤ ➤

He pauses a moment to let this name be known, and no one breathes
a word of Eden.

River Jordan.
In a garden that's called
River Jordan.
Then
Adam
is very s a d , sad, sad, sad.
Then,
after that,
"What are we going to do with Adam?
He's very sad, sad, very—
I don't know how it is with Adam."
Then
after that she said
she said
the Virgin Mary did,
"No.
Let's make a helper.
So that
so the World will abound."

We heard something about this on Side A, only don Mateo didn't tell
us then that Eve was Mary's idea. Now he pulls out his bottle of
bootleg liquor and takes the top off, the same bottle he used when
he anointed the lips of the stones on the altar. He holds it out within
the reach of don Dionisio:

Take it.
A little drink?

Then he turns to doña Bárbara:

A little drink?
Let's give you a little drink.

Then don Tuncan:

Don't you want a little drink?
Drink that there.
That there.

Back to don Dionisio:

Won't you take a drink?

And this time he gets "Yes."

Then, Jesus Christ said,
"Then
➢ ➢ ➢
we'll make a helper."
So it's because of this that
women
➢ ➢ ➢
are below men.
Why?
Because God
God
convinced us.

"He **convinced** us?" says don Dionisio, sounding dubious, and don
Mateo answers with just a hint of annoyance:

Y$_e{}_e$e^s.

And then she said,
because the Ancient Word was spoken by this
Virgin Mary,
"My Jesus,

look at the man,
my Jesus."
When she had told him,
this *Mariajesús,*
then he said,
"He looks
he looks all right, doesn't he?"

And Mary replies in a delicate voice,

"But no—
he's sighing."
"What are we going to do
by way of preaching
to this man?
Because this man is very sad.
Mm hm."
Then she said,
"No.
We'll make a helper.
We shall crucify the woman."
She said.
Good, the first woman
there was in the World.
Good,
then
➤ ➤ ➤
he was in a
in the midst of a
deep sleep.
➤ ➤ ➤
The man Adam.
He's in his deep sleep.
They **took** a **rib** from him,

and don Mateo touches his left side twice with his right hand as he
says,

from here

and he touches it again,

> on the left side.
> It wasn't on the right, but on the left side.

More often than not, the old books of religious instruction show Eve
coming out of Adam's right side. Perhaps don Mateo just happened

to see a picture that had her on the left. Whether he did or not, the
daykeepers of these mountains, don Mateo included, reckon the left
side of everyone's body as female and the right side as male. So Eve
comes from the female side of Adam.

> For this reason women are always
> below the shoulders of men,

and he pats his left side again as he goes on,

> here, here,
> because they were taken from here.

So she was taken.

The *Doctrina Cristiana* draws a different lesson: "Our God did not make the woman Eve from the head of Adam, lest the woman think herself greater, or surpass her husband. Nor did he make her from the foot, lest the man think, in the same way, to despise her, or keep her as a slave. He took her from the side so that, between the two of them, they should know that they are equals." But among the people of these mountains, whenever men and women sit down together, women sit on a lower level. Chairs and benches are for men, and women take their places on the ground. Even so, a rib from below Adam's shoulder is not enough to make don Mateo's Eve:

> Then
> they went to get
> clay
> and flowers,
> and everything.

So Adam's rib, which is only a part of him, is only a part of her. She has her own clay, and she even has something Adam doesn't, something taken from plants. All the men and women of the New World Book were made of plant material, but by now it's only Eve, and instead of maize it's flowers, and it's mixed with clay and bone.

> Because of this, the women
> **flower**
> a n d **every**thing.
> What is it to flower? I ask.

Here he refers to doña Bárbara without quite looking at her:

> This lady
> could say to me, "What is it
> to flower?
> What does this capacity show?"

Don Dionisio says, "To flower?" and don Mateo replies,

> To flower.

And doña Bárbara simply says, "To flower." Again the ethnographers wait to hear what an Indian might say.

What is this word?

Now he sounds annoyed:

You're not able to tell me.
No, even though you're old enough.

He looks directly at don Dionisio:

And you, sir?
Because of this, women flower.
➤ ➤ ➤

Then he turns to don Tuncan:

And you, sir?
You, too, are a minor?

And then he looks at his children:

I can't ask **you.**
To flower, it says.
➤ ➤ ➤
It's just the birth of children.

Don Dionisio says, "Oh, to flower." Doña Bárbara says, "To flower." And don Tuncan says, "Mm."

Yes, yes.
Such was the Ancient Word that
our Lord preached.
Then,
after that,
Jesus Christ said to him,
"We're going to give you a helper, Adam—"
he was the first man there was in the World.
Whether he was Latin, whether he was—

and here don Mateo cuts off the next word, which might've been "Indian." With Latin and Indian he could've covered nearly all the people of Guatemala, but even with his efforts to bring this story close to home, the possibility that Eve and Adam might've been Indians sticks in his throat. He starts his list over again:

> Latin, whether he was Spanish, whether he was a
> > gringo, whatever he was
> he was the first man
> there was in the world.
> Because from here came out all
> those who
> were to exist.
> Here.

In the New World Book, there are four first men and four first women. That's how many vigesimal beings it takes just to account for "our root, we who are the Quiché people." Other peoples—and there are any number of them—are granted their own founding ancestors. Between that book and don Mateo stand four centuries of missionaries, working to reduce multiple stories of multiple origins to one single story of one single origin, their story. Don Mateo seems to have learned his lesson when he speaks of "all those who were to exist," yet he still raises the question of Adam's ethnicity, naming only the alien possibilities. To speak as he does is to be, for the moment, an "Indian" indeed, the wrong person in the right place.

> Then
> he said
> then the Lord said,

and here don Mateo pulls out another piece of fruit, another quack, and takes a bite that makes it hard to speak at first:

> ➤ ➤ ➤
> "Very well,
> ➤ ➤ ➤ ➤ ➤
> **let the females be preached.**"
> And the **man**
> is sleeping,
> he's in his deep sleep.

They took his arm from him, they took a rib from him,
he didn't feel it.

"His arm?" asks don Dionisio, and don Mateo replies,

> Also, as well.
> They took a rib from him.
> With this the woman was preached.
> Good.
> This wasn't enough—
> they preached with earth.
> With clay.
> Good.
> Afterward,

and here he speaks in the same delicate voice he used for Mary,

> the w o m a n is sitting there

then he whispers,

> she's sitting there a a h

and then it's a loud whisper on her part, right in Adam's ear:

> "WAKE UP!"
> Then the son Adam awakened.
> ➤ ➤ ➤ ➤ ➤ ➤

Here don Mateo goes on in the third person, yet he's speaking as if
he were inside of Adam:

> He woke up, but who knows what happened?
> Like a **dream**
> the man woke up from.
> He s a w **then** that the woman was seated there,
> he was startled, he started to run away from fright.
> And then
> "N o o o, Adam, no, Adam, haven't you heard?
> Jesus Christ left me with you
> I'm your companion."
> **"Y i i i i h!**

Get yourself unglued from me,
get further away," yet she was two cords away, . . .

a cord is a measurement native to these mountains, roughly twenty
yards,

> . . . some
> two cords or some
> twenty
> yards,
> or twenty
> I don't know what.

"He was frightened," says don Dionisio, and don Mateo replies,

> He was frightened.
> "A_{dam!} A_{dam!} A_{dam!} Sit **down** man, Jesus Christ left
>   me with you, I'm your companion, I'm your
>   companion."

Now don Mateo stutters momentarily, creating a sound image of
Adam's condition:

> He st—
> he **stopped** and **stood.**
> **Because** of this **man,** there are **times** when **men** want
>   to **talk** with a **woman**
> and are fearful
> because a woman is coming.
> Because the woman—
> since this happened
> there are times when a man wants to talk,
> "I, I hm hm hm hm hm hm," now he doesn't make
>   words, since
> he becomes mute, the
> the man.
> Why does he become mute? Because
> because God made it so
> with Adam, who fled,

and here Adam starts off panting,

> "I'm going," trembling, trembling, Adam was left
>   trembling.
> Adam was left trembling.
> After this he came back.
> "And what is this?
> What?
> Little animal.
> Is it a little animal thou art?
> Art thou a little animal?"

Eve replies gently,

> "No, I'm not an animal.
> What I am is thy companion."
> Well, that's why there's this word "thou."
> Because using "thou"
> is abusive.

Eve and Adam are using familiar rather than formal address here, and they're speaking Guatemalan Spanish in particular, using *vos* rather than *tú*. Don Dionisio says, "Mm hm,"

> It's abusive.
> One should say "you."

"Yes," say Doña Bárbara and don Dionisio. They, too, have been schooled in the use of the polite *usted*, so much so that they don't know when it would be perfectly all right to use *vos*. And it doesn't help that as speakers of English, they are completely unpracticed in the use of their own "thou."

> Yes.
> "Thou."
> Before, they didn't think of this.

So familiar address came into existence with the first conversation between the first man and the first woman. Jesus and Mary, and whatever other immortals might have been around back then, didn't use it. Indeed, in this story, they never use the second person at all when speaking to one another.

> Haven't you studied?
> This "thou."

The ethnographers nod yes. Eve speaks again:

> "I am thy companion."
> "Yes."
> So they put themselves in accord.
> Then, all is well.

Here don Mateo takes up his stick and stirs the heap of burning incense on the altar. The fire crackles loudly for the next four lines.

> They are walking, walking, walking in the garden,
> in a garden that's called
> River Jordan.
> River Jordan, it is.
> But in **this,**
> in this **river**
> it's not, it's not just any water, what it is,
> is s i l v e r.

"Ah," says don Tuncan, and don Mateo replies,

> It's silver, the water is.
> *Pwaq.*

Here's a word from Quiché, don Mateo's own language, for the first time since he started this story about universal human ancestors who speak Guatemalan Spanish to one another. *Pwaq,* it's that word he didn't quite speak in the story of the fire that marked a spot on the mountain called Scribble, that money word that clanks with metal. Doña Bárbara responds with a well-worn local phrase, *"Pwaq, pura pwaq,"* Quiché *pwaq* sounding together with *pura* borrowed from Spanish. Plata, just plain plata. Silver, solo silver. Pwaq, precious pwaq.

> *Pura pwaq.*

Then,
"J a a a'!
It is great, your majesties,
there in your house."

And here's another Quiché word: *Ja'!* has the sense of "Oh, look at that!" But who are "your majesties," and what is this house of theirs—and, for that matter, who is speaking to them? It's as if the words *pwaq* and *ja'* had opened a door for don Mateo, a door that leads not only into another language but into some other story, a story with a royal palace of *pwaq, pura pwaq.* But perhaps the mind that strays there is not don Mateo's after all, but Adam's, who speaks to himself as he beholds the river of silver. Perhaps his mind is following "a pure river of the water of life" into New Jerusalem, where everything is built of precious stones and metals. If that's the river he's on, the Tree of Life should be there.

Then, after that
he spoke
this Serpent did, he's up in
a, a quack tree.

So here he is, he's twisted his way back into the story: that Serpent who disappeared with zaps and rumbles, way back at the beginning of Side A. And whether it's the Tree of Life or the Tree of Knowledge he's up in, it's a quack tree, a puppet tree.

Adam and Eve are walking
they aren't far from there

and here don Mateo bites into a quack and goes on with his mouth full,

perhaps something like twenty-five yards, I don't know when— . . .

suddenly he looks around at his audience,

. . . you understand?

We nod, but we're still not sure if this is the right garden.

But there they are,
humble,
and it bothers the woman,
it bothers the man.

Perhaps it bothers them to be humble people in the presence of the river of silver, the great house, and "your majesties." And perhaps the Serpent knows this.

Then,
after that, he said
to the first woman—
➤ ➤ ➤
it was just that far away,

he gestures toward a nearby tree.

"Look! Eve!"
They passed by only
as far away as that tree there.
"Do you eat this fruit?" "No.
No, I don't eat it, since Father would scold me.
He'd scold me."

Now the Serpent speaks insistently:

"He won't **see,** woman, **try** it, he won't **see.**"
And so it was the woman
he caused to do this, he who was in the shadows.

Don Mateo starts in on another quack, deliberately smacking his lips, and Eve says,

"A a a h."
Now she's trying this erotic thing—
"What
what flavor could this be?
There are many fruits, but those are oranges, those are
        limes, those are—"
and now she tries this, this

fruit, "What could it be?"

Now he speaks aside, as if to confide in someone, then suddenly goes
public:

> And it was a quack,
> **just plain quack, it has two**
> **it has two little pits,**

he pulls two pits from his mouth and holds them out for all to see
while he swallows the last of the flesh,

> it's really juicy.

Don Dionisio says, "Indeed," but he has no idea what don Mateo
might be leading up to.

> Why? Because this was, this was, how to put it—
> it wasn't for humans.
> The quack.
> Then,
> ➤ ➤ ➤
> she tasted
> Eve tasted that it was delicious.
> "Adam.
> Try this, it's delicious."
> "No.
> No, because he'll scold me.
> Jesus Christ will hit me." "No."

Don Mateo bites another quack.

> Then
> she said
> she said
> Eve did,
> "No.
> He
>   won't   us.
>   see
> He's
>   not   .ing.
>   com

He's not coming, so there's nothing to do but
try this fruit,
it's very delicious, and I've already tried it,
it's **delicious.**"
"Very well."
➤ ➤ ➤
He took it like this, like this:

he dangles a quack over his mouth, sighs, and brings it low enough
to munch, smacking his lips as he chews.

➤ ➤ ➤ ➤ ➤ ➤ ➤ ➤ ➤
"**Adam,** what are you **doing?**" said
Jesus Christ.

Adam cries out just for an instant and then looks bug-eyed, sounds
like he's choking:

"**Yiy!** Ghh! Ghh!"
He grabbed himself here,

he clutches at his Adam's apple, and his choke becomes a stutter:

this is, this is a
this is a, this is a, it's a, it's a
it's a, what's it called
the pit of the quack.
This is the pit of the quack.

Here he displays the pair of pits from the quack he's just eaten.

Because of this, we all have it.
Whether Latin, whether foreigner, all—

—not to mention Indians—

you understand, don't you?

he says as he looks at don Tuncan, and then he turns to doña Bárbara
and don Dionisio:

You have it here, don't
you?

By this time the three ethnographers, the two children, and don Mateo are all touching their Adam's apples.

> Of course.
> All, all, all.
> And t h e n
> he said
> our Lord did,
> "Now
> they will begin to
> to work."
> Because Eve didn't work before,
> nor Adam.
> Certainly they weren't working at anything,
> then they began to work.
> "Adam:

and in goes another quack,

> ███████," he says,
> "take up the hoe,
> take up the ax,
> and take up the machete,
> you're going to work.
> And Eve:
> take up
> take up all the machines for,
> for writ—for, for"—what're they called?—For
> weaving,

for a moment there, Eve almost got a typewriter, a *máquina de escribir* or "writing machine," but in any case she does get the archetypal machine of Quiché tradition, the one for weaving. Don Tuncan repeats "weaving" and don Mateo goes on,

> and, and, and cooking,
> and, and
> and also for

"grinding," suggests don Tuncan,

grinding.
Stones for grinding, everything.

Eve and Adam assigned work to each other on Side A, but here on Side B, Jesus Christ is giving the orders.

> For which reason
> for which **reason**
> he t h e n became sad,
> Adam did.
> "As for me," he said,

and here don Mateo makes him sound like a humble peasant,

> "it's all very well that I'm working."
> Because the situation turned out badly—
> well
> then, **Eve**
> was very sorry, because
> Adam,
> now
> they began to sin.
> She felt it was a very
> she felt it was a v e r y
> serious matter.

This would be Eve's pain again, from Side A: the pain of making the world abound.

> Then he said,

we don't know who is speaking here,

> **"Devil."**
> He said.
> **"Serpent,**
> unfortunate one," he said.
> "You are the most devilish
> of all the animals."

"Yes," says don Dionisio, sounding slightly resigned.

But why?

Don Mateo starts laughing halfway through his answer:

Because he was already cursed.

"Mm," says don Dionisio. Don Mateo stirs the incense again, and the fire crackles through the next nine lines.

> Now
> this is what the question was:
> the crucifixion of the World
> along with us
> so that we might abound.
> If it were not for this—
> and God also
> said this, that
> we were going to abound in the World.
> It's like a flower.
> It's like a **flower.**

Don Mateo's children stop listening and start playing, and one of them can be heard laughing through the next five lines.

> The flower
> is planted,
> and it goes
> and goes and goes
> and goes, then

—both children are giggling now—

> so it goes.
> If it hadn't been for—
> if he hadn't gotten involved, this
> this
> this, what's he called, this Serpent,

and here don Mateo speaks with a sort of shrug in his voice,

> then—
> the World wouldn't abound.

There would be no children.
There would be no children

—here he belches—

and there would be no
family.

➤ ➤ ➤

Such was the Ancient Word.
There, I'm going to show you some, some, some
writings there—
I should do it
today or tomorrow.
I'm going to teach you.
I have some books there
that preach everything here.

"Very well," says don Tuncan, and doña Bárbara and don Dionisio
say, "Mm." Then a rumble on the tape marks a hand taking hold of
the recorder, and a quick zap records the thumb on the STOP
button.

➤ Borrowing Lightning

BY THIS TIME THE INCENSE on the shrine was down to a mound of charcoal, sending up traces of white smoke. All that remained of the yellow tallow candles, given to the Holy World beneath our feet, was a large spot of grease, embedded with curled black lines of charcoal that had once been wicks. The white candles, the tall wax tapers for the Holy Quaternity, still had a long time to burn, but one of them was crooked now, bent by the heat while the incense was ablaze. Still laid out on one of the flat slabs of basalt in front of the hearth were the four divining bundles, the large and lumpy one belonging to don Mateo and the three neat, fist-sized ones belonging to the three ethnographers. Don Mateo looked at don Dionisio's bundle, which is to say my bundle. Then he looked at me and said,

"I want to ask a question."

"A question?"

"Yes, I want you to count days for me."

"But where? There's no table here."

"That's all right. You can do it on that rock," and he reached out to tap the largest of slabs in front of the shrine, the one I was seated right next to.

"But there's no cloth to spread on it." Diviners always spread a bright brocaded cotton cloth on their tables.

"That's all right, just do it right on the stone."

Diviners cannot refuse to answer a question, so long as the day on which they're asked has been kept. Today was a good time to ask, since the four of us with divining bundles wouldn't have come up here on the mountain called Tohil's Place in the first place unless we'd been keeping this day, unless we'd all been planning to abstain from sex and anger for the whole day. I felt awkward divining for a man who had been a diviner for who knows how many years, and speaking my lines with an accent, but I had no way out.

My bundle was on a rock beside don Mateo, but I had to go and get it myself, since no one should handle a bundle that belongs to someone else. I sat back down on the ground, scrunching up as close as I could get to the large slab and setting my bundle down at the center of it, with the mouth, which was tied shut, pointing away from me. For a moment my fingers came in contact with the stone, and I could almost see the soft cloth I wished I had with me. Don Mateo

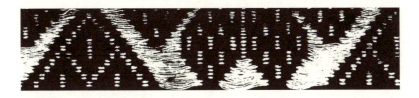

moved closer for a better view, one knee on the ground and one folded up against his breast. With a table he would've been sitting across from me, but instead he was to the left of my work surface, and when I wasn't turning to address him I was facing the shrine. It was as if the Holy World were asking the question, or don Mateo and the Holy World were asking it between them.

The motherfather who taught Barbara and myself how to divine, Pedro Sabal Paja of Altar Town, often began by crossing himself and doing an Our Father and a Hail Mary and sometimes adding The Apostles' Creed, all in Spanish, before he prayed in Quiché and made his first move toward the bundle at the center of the table. I skipped all of this, which don Mateo didn't mind in the slightest, and started in on the Quiché prayer I'd memorized—yes, memorized—from a text our teacher had dictated to us. He had composed it as he dictated, but then we studied it the only way we knew how, which was to commit it to memory word for word, like memorizing verse in school. Except that we'd made some small changes at the beginning, putting in a few words from the New World Book.

Pardon my trespass, so go the opening words, but then, instead of naming Tiox, which is to name Dios, which is to name God, what I say is *Heart of Sky,* and then *pardon my trespass, Heart of Earth* instead of Mundo, or World, and *pardon my trespass, grandmother-fathers,* all the vigesimal beings who once lived here on the face of the earth, just as I was taught, and I hold out my right hand with the cutting edge down, touching my bundle as if to divide into left and right halves, and then touch it again at right angles to make top and bottom halves, the four quarters of the World. I can feel the small, hard things inside the cloth bag as I do this.

I'm taking hold of the yellow mixture, white mixture, and here I take up the bundle in my right hand, *yellow beans, white beans, yellow seeds, white seeds,* undo the bow in the thin string that keeps the bag shut, *yellow crystals, white crystals,* unwind the turns in the string, *yellow necklace, white necklace,* gently pour the red seeds and white crystals into a pile on the black basalt, *before you, Skyearth,* and I set the empty bag and its string to my left, near don Mateo. While I mix and spread the pile, running the palm of my right hand over the seeds and crystals in circles, he finds a ten-cent piece in his pocket and places it on the bag, and the seeds and crystals click and clink as I stroke them.

I'm borrowing, just for a moment, your breath, and also what we have as our mountain, which is to say our body, and here I begin picking out the larger crystals from among the others, *I'm asking for the blessing, the favor,* place the largest crystal, not quite the length of a finger joint, on the far side of the pile, pointing away from me, this one is the mayor, the Mam, Old Man who bears the years, *for just this one clear light,* flank the mayor with a pair of aldermen, *for the sake of my work, my burden,* just one scribe, clearer than the other crystals, to the right of the right-hand alderman, and one treasurer, to the left, *my mixing, my pointing,* a pair of staff-bearers flanking the left-hand alderman and the scribe, and another pair of staff-bearers flanking them, and one more to the left.

With all ten presiding officials lined up in a tight row at the far side of my work surface, I depart from my set piece to address the longest crystal, the Mam, *Come hither, Old Man Deer, Old Man Wind,* the powerful lords of the days that bring in dangerous years, and then the next two crystals, *Old Man Tooth, Old Man Thought,* the lesser lords of the days that begin the calmer years, then *Secretary Net,* lord of the day of written records, *Treasurer Bird,* lord of the day of money, *do me a favor,* and then I pick up where I left off, *and also, yellow clouds, white clouds, the mist, the cold, the wind, walking over mountains, over plains,* I'm running my hand over the seeds and small crystals again, *and also, the large hills, little hills, large flats, little flats, large volcanoes, little volcanoes, large plains, little plains, come out and talk! They'll speak for just a moment, for just this one light, for just this one question, in the chill, in the wind,* and here I look at don Mateo, *they're speaking on this holy and precious day, in the chill, in the wind, they're speaking for a moment,* the clicking and clinking stops, *for just this one question, on the day Lord Eight Bird.*

"What is your question?" I say to don Mateo.

"It's my pig. I want to know who killed my pig."

So he wants to know just who it was he was praying about a while ago, that unknown person he wanted delivered into the hands of the apostles and the Holy Quaternity, the mountains with gaping stones on top and the lightning archangels.

"What day did it die?"

"It was three days ago."

"Very well then, today is Eight Bird, so that would be, let's see, Seven Jaguar, Six Cane, Five Tooth. It happened on Five Tooth," I conclude, and go back to running my hand over the seeds and crystals.

Come hither, Lord Five Tooth, speak for a moment, for just this one light, just this one question, for Mateo Uz Abaj, by name. Then I hesitate, wondering just how to frame this question. He's already certain someone killed his pig, rather than wondering whether the pig just died, but I start off with the question I've been taught to ask.

Does his pain have an owner? Perhaps some neighbor, some companion piled up words behind his legs, behind his arms, and again the clicking and clinking, *I'm taking hold of the yellow mixture, white mixture, yellow beans, white beans,* the seeds and crystals that can move a question into a tinted light and then, for just a moment, into bright clarity, *and also, the grandmothers, the grandfathers, they talk, they speak, for a moment, for a while, concerning this one question,* and

I stop for a moment. My eye is caught by the glint of the crystal scribe, I've almost forgotten to call the sheet lightning, the lightning that moves over distant horizons:

I'm borrowing the yellow lightning, white lightning that moves over the large lakes, the small lakes, from the place where the sun comes out, to the place where the sun goes down, four-cornered sky, four-cornered earth, may the lightning move over the horizon of my body, may I catch its reflection in my blood.

The hand stops moving. I raise it, cupped, to my mouth.

We're doing this right now, into my hand I blow a short breath, *pardon my trespass,* I grab a fistful of seeds and crystals, as many as I can tightly hold, and put them in a separate pile to the right. Then I push what's left of the original pile, the better part of it, off to the right, leaving a work space about the size of a large open book. From the right-hand pile I take the seeds and crystals, in whatever combinations come to hand, and arrange them in clusters of four, making

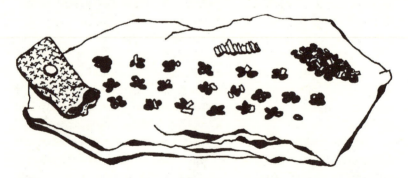

rows and files like those of a calendar, starting at upper left. If don Mateo were doing this right now he'd be praying the whole time, but I'm just about out of words. At the end of the third row I have one seed left over, which counts as a cluster but means the answer to the question will not be as certain as it would've been with an even number. Leaning back a little, I look the whole arrangement over. The mixing is done and it's time for the pointing.

Come hither, Lord Five Tooth, do me a favor, and I'm ready to count the clusters, starting at upper left and moving across the rows, pointing with my first two fingers held together, but before I can even get started I feel lightning in my blood, a twitch moving up just under the skin of my left calf, and don Mateo sees me withdraw my hand and glance down at the back of my pant leg.

"'THE WOMAN IS COMING,' it says," I say in the low but urgent voice of the blood, to no one in particular, and then in my normal voice, to don Mateo, "There's a woman involved in this." No sooner do I turn back to the counting of days than the lightning moves across the base of the big toe on my right foot, and don Mateo sees me glance at the toe of my shoe.

"'HE'S ILL,' it says," I say in the blood voice again, and then to don Mateo, "Some old man, or some important man, is ill, or will be ill, but I don't know whether he'll die," and even as I speak the lightning darts into the crease behind my right knee, and this time don Mateo sees me move that leg a little, cocking my head to glance at the gathering of the pant leg behind my knee.

"'THE TOMB,' it says," I say, giving voice to my blood once again, and then, looking over at don Mateo, "He's on his way to the grave, this old man." Again I look back to the rows of seeds, point at the upper left cluster, and this time the lightning holds back, the blood falls silent to hear the count. All the days come with auguries, but I speak only their names out loud:

Five Tooth the good road, the bad road, *Six Cane* in the house, *Seven Jaguar* before the Holy World, *Eight Bird* praying, pleading, gold, silver, *Nine Sinner* before God, *Ten Knowhow* good thoughts, bad thoughts, *Eleven Blade* lips that trample, *Twelve Rain* filling the bowl, setting the table, *Thirteen Marksman*—the lightning moves on the front of my right thigh—not in the middle, but off to one side—and don Mateo sees me glancing there.

"'THE SHRINE,' it says," the blood says, and the count stops. To don Mateo I say, "It's the shrine of your lineage, something's off center in your family. Or on your land. The table is not balanced on all four legs." Then I look back at the cluster I was pointing at when the lightning moved, repeating the name of the day, but this time I give voice to the augury that comes with it:

"This was Thirteen Marksman. 'Before the grandmotherfathers,' it says," and I add, looking at don Mateo, "It's got something to do with the ancestors, and it's been a long time." Just a trace of displeasure crosses his face. He serves as the motherfather for his lineage, and it's his responsibility to feed and pray to his ancestors for everyone else, but he says nothing. On with the count.

One Lefthanded going mad, Two Wind getting angry, Three Foredawn opening, blaming, Four Net a burden, a debt, Five Snake the enemy, Six Death bringing good, Seven Deer the motherfather, Eight Yellow ripening, Nine Thunder paying, suffering, Ten Dog jealousy, uncertainty, Eleven Monkey spinning thread, and here I reach the final seed and announce the day in a louder voice, and the augury:

"Twelve Tooth. 'The good road, the bad road,' it says. Things are on the wrong track because of what happened." There's more to this than just the incident of the pig. Don Mateo says nothing, and I continue with a second count clear through from the top, starting with the next day:

Thirteen Cane, One Jaguar, Two Bird, Three Sinner, Four Thought, Five Blade, Six Rain, Seven Marksman, Eight Lefthanded, the lightning moves under the edge of the heel of my right foot:

"'HE'S BEEN STEPPED ON,' it says," and then I tell don Mateo why he's seen me glance at my shoe: "Whoever did this deed, you've almost got him, you're just—" the lightning interrupts me, ripples the blood at the edge of the palm of my right hand:

"'HE'S BEEN GRABBED,' it says. He's almost caught. Just this much is lacking," and I show don Mateo my thumb and forefinger just a finger's breadth apart. Then I look at the cluster of seeds where I stopped counting:

"Eight Lefthanded. 'He's going mad,' it says. Whoever this is, he was crazy to kill your pig, but it's craziness that's going to grab him." And so on with the days:

Nine Wind, Ten Foredawn, the blood moves on the back of my left thigh:

"'IT ALREADY HAPPENED,' it says. The woman who's in this, I don't know, something happened between her and the man's lineage, some time ago. So says the blood." Don Mateo brightens, and I go on to take the day into account:

"Ten Foredawn. 'Blaming,' it says. Whatever happened, the man blames someone." Don Mateo gives just a trace of a nod. On with the count:

Eleven Net, Twelve Snake, Thirteen Death, One Deer, Two Yellow, Three Thunder, Four Dog, Five Monkey, Six Tooth, the lightning moves in my right testicle, I look straight down, and the only voice the blood has for this one is a chuckle.

"This woman had contact with a man," I tell don Mateo, and then I reach the single seed at the end:

"Seven Cane. 'In the house, in the home,' it says. The man who killed the pig is in your own household. Or at least you're related to him in some way." Don Mateo looks excited now:

"Raimundo Sucac! Ask if it was Raimundo Sucac Awel!" That would be the father of his eldest son's wife. Maybe that man didn't really like giving his daughter in marriage to don Mateo's son. But it's not mine to ask the questioner why he wants to test this name. I make a single pile of all the seeds and crystals again (except for the ones that serve as officials), mix again, grab a handful again, make clusters of four items each, posing the new question:

Raimundo Sucac Awel: is he the owner of this, the pain of my neighbor, my companion here? Don Mateo watches closely as I complete the last row, coming out to exactly four in the final cluster. A perfectly clear answer we'll get this time, I'm thinking, but as I reach to start the count, don Mateo puts his hand on my arm:

"It's clear! Very clear! There's no need to count. The answer is yes. It's him."

"No need to count the days?"

"No. We already know very well who it is." So I give in, though I was taught otherwise. Don Mateo himself, who is not one to be fussy about the minute details of ritual, always dispenses with counting when all he wants is a yes/no answer. An odd number of seeds is no; an even number is yes. Four seeds at the end is an even better yes than two.

This time I bring the seeds and all the crystals together (officials included), rub them a few times, pick them up by handfuls, and funnel them into the bag, down to the last clicks and clinks. Don Mateo points out a seed that slipped off the slab at some point, properly leaving it to me to pick it up, and that goes in the bag too, along with his ten-cent coin. When I've got the string wound tight and tied, I rub the whole bag between my palms a few times—it sounds like a rattle, but muffled—and then press it to my lips, putting it away in the big breast pocket of my wool shirt.

Nothing more was said about the pig that day, nor about Raimundo Sucac. But we later heard that two weeks after our visit to the mountain called Tohil's Place, the man died. That would have been on *Nine Thunder paying, suffering,* Nine Toh, Tohil's very own day.

When I heard the news, it came home to me that don Mateo had tricked me into being a sorcerer's apprentice. I should have known it at the time. Whatever is said at a shrine, so long as incense is still smoking or candles are still burning, goes on the record with that mountain and with the Holy World, goes over the telegraph line that connects the mountains together, reaches Secretary Net, is written *in the First Book, in the Second Book, on the First Shelf, on the Second Shelf.* Don Mateo had put the pig and its unnamed killer on record with his own prayers on the day *Eight Bird praying, pleading,* asking that the killer fall into the hands of the powers that be. After that, he had set me in search of the man's identity—or else put me to work confirming a suspicion he already had. In the end, the name of the late Raimundo Sucac Awel had been uttered by both of us in the presence of the smoke and candlelight.

Don Mateo, as we already knew at the time, is the kind of person who knows how to *ask for justice,* as the matter is delicately put. That's the way he would put the matter, but there are other people who would call it by other names.

Itzb'al.

Brujería.

Witchcraft.

But he uses no scraps of clothing, no nail clippings, no locks of hair, nor toads, nor poisonous brews. Candles, incense, words, and names work well enough for him. And he gets a little help from a saint he has at home, the darkly clothed figure he keeps in the same room with his brightly painted Apostle John, but on the opposite side.

➤ Let's Have a Little Drink

NOW THERE WAS NOTHING TO DO but wait. To get the full benefit from offerings, one should stay till they burn out. Or failing that, till it seems quite certain that nothing will remain unburnt. The tall wax candles went on and on, up there on Tohil's Place on the day Eight Bird, the second Sunday in Advent, and don Mateo went on taking slugs from his bottle of bootleg liquor. He was quieter now, but every now and then he gave voice to his ruminations, not turning to any of us but staring off into space.

"So, then, I am from the town of Middle. I am well-informed because I am Middle. I am Middle." Then he laughed as he added, "But who knows where my seed is. It's like I told you, then, about Adam and Eve"—yes, Adam and Eve, he had them back in the original order now—"that the first man was a guilty one. Because he killed his brother." Evenadam were a god, so that made Pastor, their eldest son, the first man. But why, so many times now, this phrase, "He killed his brother"?

Don Mateo has a brother in Middle, a man who really has a problem with drink. He's younger than don Mateo, but he looks older. When you just think of him the lightning moves on the right side of your upper lip, THE MAN DRINKS, says the blood, it means you're going to see someone drunk. He's been through three wives and lost five children along the way—the lightning moves to the tip of the little finger, A BABY DIES, it says, he's going to lose another one. A few years ago he sold some land and spent the proceeds on liquor. Don Mateo has never forgiven him for shrinking the holdings of the Uz lineage, holdings which he himself has worked hard to increase, even to the extent of going down on coastal plantations for wages, fighting his way through heat, malaria, and worms that eat you from the inside. There's no question as to which is the prosperous brother, but the younger one is so weak and humble it's hard to imagine him ever starting a fight with don Mateo, or don Mateo striking back, as Pastor did. Unless they prayed against one another. In that case, it's obvious who won.

"Because of this," don Mateo goes on, "there is an inferno for us," and then, after a little thought, "there, below, it is well," whatever he may have meant by that, perhaps just resignation. The place below, the inferior place is all that's meant by "inferno." It gets to be fiery just by the sound of it, but right next to the dark saint that stands on don Mateo's altar-on-the-other-side is an old painting, on tin, of a pink, bare-shouldered woman with long, wavy black hair, up to her armpits in flames, her face and arms upraised, her wrists in irons with dangling chains. She was probably painted as the martyred St. Agnes, her body uncorrupted by fire as she prayed, but who knows what story may be told about this picture now, or what requests may be made in its presence. Let's just say you wouldn't want anyone painting you into it.

"It's not a lie. This, too, is so," don Mateo says, perhaps still talking about the place below. Still anxious about his authority, but he's muttering, not really talking to us. He takes up his stick and stirs the coals of the incense, letting loose just a little more white smoke.

We're still under the overcast we started with, it looks as though we won't see the sun in what little is left of the afternoon. Perhaps the writers of the New World Book were thinking of this time of year when they told the story of Jaguar Cedar and Red Sea Turtle, who shivered and wandered so long in darkness on their way up here. These chilly gray days around the winter solstice, a month before the season that absolutely fulfills its name: "clear days," or "plain sun." While don Mateo wanders in and out of his inferno, I wonder about an experiment I made a couple of hours ago, when all of us were praying.

Most of what I had managed to say before the shrine was memorized, just as it was when I divined for don Mateo. But right after *Uk'ux Kaj, Uk'ux Ulew,* Heart of Sky, Heart of Earth, I had put in a few more words from the Book:

At Pisom Q'aq'al, Thou Bundle of Flames, the ark Jaguar Cedar left for his descendants, "it wasn't clear just what it was, it was never unwrapped, it was wound about with coverings," *at puch Tojil*, and thou, Tohil, whose mountain this was and might still be, *Awilix*, Lord Swallow, who might still haunt a cliff below this very ridge, and *Jakawitz*, Open Mountain, whose name might cling even now to a distant place.

When we went up on Tohil's Place, no one yet knew the name of the ancient one-legged god with the flaming forehead, the god who can be seen in the hands or cradled in the arms of the sculpted likenesses of long-dead kings and queens in abandoned cities. He was described as "the manikin scepter" by some archaeologists, and he was one of a series of unidentified gods whose images had been assigned letters of the alphabet. It was *K* that fell to his lot, and ever since then he has been God K in what scholars call "the literature." He could have done worse. *K*, whose angled appendages were fingers when it looked like this ↡, was the phonetic sign of the syllable *kaph* in Phoenician, meaning "hollow of the hand."

Tahil the ax, Tahil the torch, Tahil the flaming blade. Tahil whose leg becomes a serpent whose mouth is wide enough to swallow a person. I can say that now, and I can see it, but there on the day Eight Bird I could see nothing. Heart of Sky, Heart of Earth already made sense, even then. In the Book of the Jaguar's Spokesman, from far to the north, I had read that the heart of heaven is a bead of jade, or turquoise, and don Pedro of Altar Town had told us the heart of a great mountain is gold and silver. These were easy to envision, even when caught between a solid overcast and the solid ground. But as for Tohil, all I could see on top of his mountain was a hunk of basalt about the size and shape of a face mask, its only features a series of parallel ridges running across it, one of them declared to be a mouth by don Mateo. Not a carving, but a natural stone anointed with liquor. Not even when I shut my eyes did anything present itself. Just the sounds. *Tojil, Awilix, Jakawitz.*

Don Mateo went on tippling all this while, but no longer was he in the fire, no.

"And I love my friends and I love my brothers and everyone," he said, and looked around. Here we all were again.

"And, thank God that all of us are children of God." Or I think that's what he meant to say, but in place of *Gracias a Dios* he said

Ojalá, resulting in something more like, "Would that all of us were children of God." Perhaps Raimundo Sucac Awel was still at the back of his mind. Or that woman in the painted flames. But behind his Spanish *Ojalá* we can hear a medieval Moor saying, "Would to Allah!" A Moor who might one day be burned by Christians.

"You, madam, sirs, love me," he said, looking around at us, "and I love you. Mm." The third ethnographer, don Tuncan, was looking at the bent candle, the one that had been closest to the fire, bending even more by now, almost forming the Greek letter Γ. He answered don Mateo this way:

"The earth loves the candle so much." Don Mateo, struck by these words, turned to doña Bárbara and said,

"But it doesn't go out. It's yours. It's your precious candle." No one spoke for a moment, and then I began whistling. However the tune may have come into my head, it was a Bach recessional.

It wasn't long before don Mateo said,

"Yes. Let's have a little drink, madam, sirs." He offered the bottle, and don Tuncan was the first to accept.

"Tzam," he said, which means "liquor" here but sounds like the word for nose. He took his swallow and passed it on to doña Bárbara, who said,

"Tzam." Don Mateo replied,

"Yes, *tzam.*" She swallowed and passed the bottle to don Dionisio, who said,

"Tzam." He took his turn and passed the bottle back to don Mateo, who took another swig and then said,

"Takest thou the last one, now." We all laughed as the last round began.

"After this little stay here," said don Mateo, "after this we'll go. This is my word to you, yes."

"Jo'," said don Dionisio, which means, "Let's go." Don Mateo answered,

"After this, *Jo'.*" Doña Bárbara said,

"Jo'." Don Tuncan said,

"Jo'." And finally don Mateo said,

"All right, then."

On our way down to the jeep, parked by the side of the road that leads from Holy Cross Many Trees to St. Andrew Plaster House, I finally had my vision of *Tojil, Awilix, Jakawitz.* Once it came I couldn't get the picture out of my mind.

Broken statues.

Scattered rubble.

Some of the pieces missing.

No splinter of wood, no shred of cloth.

No fragment of inlay, no trace of paint.

Not a single small bead of precious stone on the anthills around this place, brought up from below.

"Dead gods," I thought.

➤ Ripples on the Still Black Sea

WHEN THREE MOONS HAD PASSED and the count of days was reaching Six Net, I found myself standing before a movie set, looking into it from the same spot where a camera once stood. It was an interior scene from an ancient civilization. In the center, before an open window, was a heavy tripod vessel, closed with a heavy lid. It looked a little like a Chinese bronze, but more like a ceramic incense burner in the style of Teotihuacan, the Place of the Gods. They had made it just for this set.

"It holds the Waters of Eternity," they told me, and then I saw it suspended above the still black sea. The vessel tilted forward, opened, and emptied out, and where the water fell it spread shining, sparkling, radiating ripples over the surface of the darkness. A slim young man ran from somewhere out in the sea, skimming right over the ripples of light, and came ashore just ahead of the first one. His shoes were waiting for him, or his sandals, just where he'd left them on the beach. He inserted a wooden platform into one of them and then slipped his foot into place on top of it, putting all his weight on that one leg.

"That's Aladdin," they told me, but the moment I woke up I knew they were wrong. He did have a way to make fire, they were right about that, but I could've told them who he really was.

"He's the sound of thunder. Smoke of obsidian. Sets fire to his sandal by turning his foot."

Night brought the dream and inside the dream it was night. Why I had ever hoped to see a fallen god make a move in daylight, even if only on his own mountain and only in my mind's eye, I don't know. The daimons of the mountains turned to stone when they were caught in the open by the light of the first sunrise, and they turned to stone all over again in glare of the fire that came with Peter

Pallid. As far as that goes, it's never been the way of gods, here or anywhere else, to walk around on the face of the earth in broad daylight, with all the substance of someone casting a shadow on the ground.

The day Five Foredawn brought the dream: day of concealment, day of opening. It's in the way of Foredawn to promise light but only give a hint of it. During the night, Five Foredawn handed the dream over to the next day, Six Net, a good one for paying a debt. Net is *k'at* and daykeepers sometimes find it right to think from *k'at* to *k'atik,* "to burn." He who had refused to show himself by day came forth on ripples of light and found a place where he could stand, ready to burn his foot all over again. Perhaps he was making payment for the sound of his name and the smell of incense up there in the ruins of his temple, three moons ago.

The moon of Six Net was a little short of full, I mean the moon in the night outside the dream, and perhaps it was a bright but unseen moon that gave light to the ripples on the sea within the dream. Down in the ruins of a city in the lowlands, from the time when Tohil was Tahil, there is an inscription that tells us how it was with the moon when Tahil made the first of all his appearances. The city was not the one whose emblem was the bat, in the east, but rather a place whose emblem was the egret, the kind we call the snowy egret, in the west. Palenque is the name it goes by today, and Tahil has a temple there, dedicated in the year the Old World calls 690. In the sanctuary, on a stone tablet, a scribe recorded a hypothetical date for the coming of Tahil, complete with a note on the moon. It happened, so he wrote, 3,050 years before the completion of the temple, and the moon was almost full.

I can still see the shine on that black sea. Obsidian black. Obsidian worked by tapping and chipping, glints off ridges and valleys where flakes flew off.

Ten days later I met a man who was selling white plates and clear glasses, all secondhand but spotless, displayed on a table in front of his house. He was a little on the heavy side, dark with a moustache, in his late fifties perhaps, and wore a brimmed black hat. Behind him was a storeroom with the door standing ajar, and I went to take a look inside. Just as I stepped over the doorsill someone shrieked in my left ear and I woke up.

This dream was handed over by Two Cane, a day of the house, to Three Jaguar, a day that belongs to the Holy World, the earth, the mountains. According to don Pedro of Altar Town, there are indeed times when the spirit familiar of a mountain takes the form of just such a man as the one I saw. The dishes and glassware that belong to mountains are the hearths where offerings are served. When a new motherfather is installed, says don Pedro, the first thing that must be done is "washing the cup, washing the plate, washing the gourd jar," which is to say that all the ashes must be swept out of the shrines the novice will use, to give him a fresh start. This had already been done in the dream, as if to show me a path beyond that of a mere day-keeper, but then I went right past the dishes, wanting to know what was back there in that storeroom. If indeed I saw anything inside, the shriek made me forget it, all the worse for coming from the left. But this doesn't necessarily mean I shouldn't have gone in there at all. Don Pedro would say that the next time I find myself on that threshold, I should look to the left to see who or what is there, instead of waking up too soon.

I had seen that dark man with the moustache once before, all the way back before the dream of the daimon who stood on one leg. I was in a hilly town, alone in a room and looking through a window. It was a festival day, and there were people all over the open slope across the way, some sitting, some standing, all of them dressed in the same light blue cloth, cut in different shapes and styles. None of them saw me looking, but then I saw *him*, wearing a dark suit and a black hat, and in that moment I felt lost in time, somewhere out of the present—or else not knowing when the present was. From the window I caught his eye and asked him,

"What day is it?" and he said,

"It's January 18, 1937."

"The eighteenth?"

"Yes, January 18, 1937." I searched all over the room for a pencil and paper, found them on a cluttered table, and wrote down the date and read it. Then I awoke, amazed, and wrote it down again.

This dream came on the night when Thirteen Snake, day of the big enemy, became One Death, day of unexpected favors. Counting back to 1937, the day inside the dream was Two Thunder, Two Toh, a day of Tohil, but I'm sure that man wasn't him. As for the year, I hadn't been born or even conceived back then. No wonder I hadn't known where I was, or when. The year points to a story told by don Pedro, the one that took place "in '36 or '37, when all kinds of papers were asked for," and a man on his way to market failed to take heed when a squirrel ran left across his path. The squirrel entered a hollow tree and looked out at him, trying to warn him that he'd left his papers at home and would end up looking out the window of a jail. So there I was, not knowing what day it was, looking out my own window in a town where everyone else was outdoors. I had trouble finding my papers, but once I got the date written down I escaped the dream. Daykeepers should always know where they are in time, whether it's today or whichever day they get to by counting forward or back.

The dark man did me a favor, as befits the day One Death, and he was also trying to do me a favor when he displayed the dishes and glassware. But One Death, by its number, brings the smallest favor of any day named Death, and it comes the day after Thirteen Snake, which harbors the biggest enemy. It was a narrow scrape, with the easy out of waking up, just as it had been when the house of Two Cane turned out to contain the scream of Three Jaguar. Whenever that man appears there is danger near, whether he shows himself beforehand or waits till the dreamer is already in trouble. It happens that way with don Pedro, too. Many months before my dreams, he had told us what happened to him on the night when Three Blade became Four Rain.

Don Pedro was walking along with the two of us when he suddenly felt drunk, and the next thing he knew he started to vomit. But what came out of his mouth was animals—they looked like pumas and jaguars, only they were small, the size of house cats, yellow and gray. But there were lots of them, and they wanted to bite him, or grab him, it seems, and they surrounded him. Then the dark man with the moustache was there, and he grabbed don Pedro by the arm and took us all inside a square wooden booth. The animals ran round and round the booth, but there was no way they could get inside.

When don Pedro awoke he was trembling, and even when he told us about it a day later he was in a sweat. He remembered that the three of us had once talked about going on a trip to a town with a famous image of St. Simon, a trip we never got around to.

"Blade is the day of gossip, or the day when one says what one wants and then has a loss of will. One fails to comply with one's own desire. We haven't offered anything to St. Simon, but he has a way of finding out when someone thinks of coming to him, and perhaps he sent this dream."

"What about that dark man?" we asked.

"It was the Holy World who was helping us. And he seemed to be fifty-five or sixty, so he was a great mountain, like the Great Place of Proclamation. He's the one who helped us, he hid us in that little house. That's the way it is: the World always helps."

But I kept thinking of that dark saint don Mateo keeps in the town of Middle, the one who has an altar all to himself, on the wrong side of the room. Black hat, black moustache, heavy build. And who is he? St. Simon, says don Mateo. Mountains are different: they have dark skin. St. Simon, like any other person who once lived here on earth but has flesh and blood no longer, has a pale face.

➢ Grandfather Judas

BROTHER SIMON, AS HIS VISITORS sometimes call him, sits bolt
upright in a wooden armchair on a dais covered with sky blue ceramic
tile. Today, as always, he wears a tailored suit of the finest woolen
cloth. Some years ago he preferred black, or dark blue, but today he
wears blue gray, and tomorrow it might be tan with a powder blue
pinstripe. His dress shirt is solid white, but he has other white shirts
with discreet, widely spaced brown stripes running through them. His
necktie is bright red, but he has others that range into maroon. The
President of the Republic once remarked, after seeing his wardrobe,
    "From the looks of it, he has more ties than I do!"
    Spread from Brother Simon's lap down to his ankles is a bath
towel, solid purple today but with floral patterns printed on white
some other time, placed there to protect his pants. His visitors are
given to sprinkling his legs and feet with liquor, and the towel catches
most of that. For the same reason he wears black rubber boots in
place of shiny leather dress shoes. Although he is seated, he has a
silver-tipped mahogany walking stick in his right hand, holding it like
a baton—or like a scepter. With his left hand he receives bills of
various denominations, each of them folded in half. They spill over
into his lap, almost covering the fat bundle of cigars someone
brought him earlier today. Draped around his shoulders he has a
small red rayon scarf with white polka dots and black outlines of
roses, a machine-made item, but he also possesses scarves made by
the people of these mountains, woven on the backstrap loom with
handspun cotton thread, wide red and purple bands divided by
delicate stripes of varied widths and colors, scarves large enough to
fold in half and still cover most of the front of his suit jacket, the
shiny silk fringes dangling into his lap.

Brother Simon is never without a hat pulled down a little below his hairline, always with a high creased crown and a broad brim curled up at the sides, Stetson-style. Today it's white and made of fine straw, but on other days it would be black or dark blue and of finely shaped felt. As for his face, it's always the same. A light complexion but with something of a gray cast, a somewhat pointed chin thrust forward just a little, thin lips slightly open, long black moustache combed to the sides and down past the corners of his mouth, ears on the small side, black sideburns cut off straight just above the level of the earlobes. His eyes are large, glassy, and wide open, staring straight ahead and slightly upward. He never looks down at his visitors, who have to climb a short flight of stairs at his right just to bring their heads up to the level of his knees, then climb down the matching stairs to his left. The tapestry hanging behind him today depicts the Last Supper.

St. Simon, as all the visitors name him (whether they call him brother or not), sits within a spacious wooden tabernacle with fluted columns at the corners, painted solid glossy black, and glass sides. He is crowded from both sides by massive bouquets of gladiolas, roses, and carnations, all of them pink or red. On the walls to either side of the tabernacle hang testimonials in longhand or block letters, graceful calligraphy or manual typescript, on every color and cut of paper, in wooden frames behind glass or mounted on cardboard and wrapped in plastic, and others embroidered on cotton cloth, cut into wood, or even engraved in marble and set into the wall.

"Gratitude to St. Simon for having helped with the marriage of my daughter." Gertrude Bigtoad.

"As a remembrance of Brother Simon for having helped me with the return of my wife with the children." John Mary Pascual.

"Thanks to Brother Simon for having cared for my little animals while I went to work on the coast." Cyril Chili Ant.

The authors of the notes come from as far away as Los Angeles and El Salvador. A large placard in English proclaims,

"The rainbow is a bridge between peoples." Anonymous.

Michelle Suárez, from the town of Under Ten Deer, was cured of a bad stomach that had troubled her for twenty years before she

drank the Waters of St. Simon on the recommendation of her Indian maid. The waters come from the washing of his clothes.

In front of St. Simon's dais, in place of pews and kneeling benches, are rows of long tables where the devoted stand, burning whole bunches of candles and setting fire to whole packs of cigarettes. They are no longer allowed to burn anything directly at his feet, so they rap him on the shins with their unlit candles and then take them to the tables. Several years ago, it seems, their ardor reached the point of setting him on fire, burning not only his clothes but his wooden image. A local artisan made a new and more life-like replacement, with smooth painted gesso on the hands and face and glass eyes of the kind a one-eyed person might wear. The walls of the temple are still blackened beyond what one would expect from candles alone, and by now many a visitor has left a negative handprint, nearly always the right hand, and written a name and date with a wet finger. On the walls near the entrance are posters of the Socialist Party.

Years before the fire, St. Simon had his picture taken (see above). He sat on his chair outdoors, in front of the temple, holding up his baton in the usual manner. He was a little heavier then, kept his moustache curled up at the corners, and wore a flower in his lapel. This black-and-white photograph has been reproduced by means of halftone plates made from a positive print, and photo-offsets shot from reproductions printed from those plates, and Xeroxes of offset reproductions, and Xeroxes of Xeroxes. By now there are people who say, or at least there are people who claim to have heard other people say, that this is a photograph of St. Simon himself, taken while he still walked this earth in the flesh. About a century ago, they are said to say. A wealthy local Latin who gave food and money to poor Indians, someone read somewhere.

St. Simon is not permitted to show his face in any church, at least not while a priest is around, but he finds a home in chapels maintained by religious fraternities and on household altars all over these mountains. The temple where he caught fire is his grandest establishment. It is located south of Tohil's Place, across three or four mountain ranges but still to the north of the great volcanoes of the Pacific rim, in the town of St. Andrew Obsidian, on a street corner well away from the parish church. After the great earthquake of 1976, it was rebuilt with a reinforced concrete framework, walled in with red brick. The low-pitched roof is made of precast sheets whose principal ingredients are cement and asbestos, but the gable end at the facade is outlined with two rows of red tiles. At the peak there is no cross, which makes the whole place look like a fundamentalist mission. Just below the peak is a spotlight, aimed to illuminate the walled courtyard in front, and hanging from the front corners of the eaves is a pair of ornamental cast-iron lanterns with dark yellow glass. The round-arched windows are set within the front gable end and high up on the side walls, steel casements with rippled panes of solid blue, yellow, or green. The facade is pierced by a pair of arched doorways, framed in steel and with steel tympanums and double steel doors, all painted blue. White Gothic lettering on the lintels identifies the left doorway as Entrance and the right as Exit, but only the entrance is open today.

The steps of the temple of St. Simon are of concrete, and the courtyard is paved with concrete. Those who have not only candles but incense to burn rap their packets of copal on St. Simon's legs and then, when they have finished their work inside the temple, they burn it at the foot of the steps, in line with the entrance. In the courtyard and on the street outside are the stalls of vendors of candles, cigars,

PRAYER TO ST. SIMON

O! powerful St. Simon; I, a humble creature disdained by all, come to prostrate myself before thee that thy spirit might aid me in all my acts and in all danger whenever needed.

If it be love, thou shalt stop the man I want stopped, if it be business, never shalt thou fail because thy spirit permitteth not witches greater power than thine own: if it be an enemy, tis thou who must prevail, if they be secret enemies, they will be gone in the moment I name thee. O! powerful Simon, I offer thee thy cigar, thy tortilla, thy shot of liquor, and thy little candles, if thou wouldst save me from any danger in which I might find myself and when they sue me for debts that I cannot pay at the moment, I ask thee that the judge be overcome and on my side, in thy name that all remain forgotten and I ask thee in the name of the one whom thou didst sell for thirty pieces of silver and they were given to the most needy.

»»»»»»»»»»»»»»»»»»   «««««««««««««««««««

painted plaster-of-Paris images of St. Simon in two sizes, and pocket-sized leaflets and booklets containing prayers and instructions in Spanish, all without names of authors, places, publishers, or printers.

Supplicants pray at St. Simon's feet and pray again at the candle tables, but they don't look at pieces of paper while they do it—except for that young Quiché man from Altar Town, who consults a list of the names of the people who hired him and other names they wanted him to mention. Everyone speaks rapidly and almost without

Thus I wish that thou wouldst work for me thy miracles I ask of thee. O! Judas Simon, I call thee brother on every occasion, because thou art indeed on the earth, in the mountains, plains, woods, cities, countryside, hamlets and houses.

EXPLANATION

Every person who makes use of this prayer, must comply with true devotion, above all, in faith.

Place a water glass of liquor, a cigar, three tortillas, bread and a scarf. All together, but on the floor, if this is not done, there is no effect.

In order to call upon St. Simon tap the water glass three times. Plot everything before beginning and if you wish to avenge yourself, this prayer is sufficient, for whatever you desire be it evil or else good.

»»»»»»»»»»»»»»»»»»   «««««««««««««««««««

pauses—except for that thin Latin lady at the table over there, who takes one deep drag after another from her cigar and blows all the smoke toward St. Simon. Everybody is talking but her, yet the whole place is quiet, all those words reduced to murmurs. In churches or at mountain shrines, you can catch some of the words, but here at the temple of St. Simon it seems as though people don't want anyone else to know what they're saying. It is only from their candles that their stories can be read.

Other saints get white candles, or sometimes yellow, but St. Simon gets them in every color. The SIGNIFICANCE OF CANDLES is explained in the leaflets, and some vendors have framed, large-print versions hanging behind their counters:

> RED: Love, Faith and Will.
> GREEN: Business and Prosperity.
> BLUE: Work and Luck.
> PINK: Sickness or Health.
> BLACK: Enemies or Vengeance.
> SKY BLUE: Money, Happiness, Travel and Study.
> VIOLET: Vices and Evil Thoughts.
> YELLOW: Protection for Adults.
> WHITE PARAFFIN: Protection for Children.
> WHITE TALLOW: Protection against Witchcraft.

But just who is this St. Simon, that priests keep him out of church? In the New part of the Old World Book, there are nine Simons. First among the Twelve Apostles is Simon Barjona, whose name was changed to Peter by Jesus. But in these mountains St. Peter, with his key, is the patron of diviners, distinct from St. Simon.

Whoever St. Simon of the colored candles may be, he is not the other Apostle Simon, also known as Simon the Zealot or Simon the Canaanite. As the saint of choice in money matters, he has more affinity with Simon of Samaria, the sorcerer who was baptized by Philip. When this Simon saw Peter and John laying hands on converts he offered them money, saying,

"Give me also this power, that on whomsoever I lay hands, he may receive the Holy Ghost." Peter answered,

"Thy money perish with thee."

And then there is the Simon of "James, and Joses, and Simon, and Judas," the four brothers of Jesus. One of the pamphlets on sale outside the temple in the town of Obsidian gives Brother Simon the double name Judas Simon, and indeed there are many people who say he is Judas.

But which Judas? There are six Judases in the New Old World Book. There is, for example, Judas Barsabas, a Jewish Christian who went to Antioch with the Apostle Paul. And the Apostle Judas Thaddaeus, brother of the Apostle James. The pamphlet that comes with the plaster-of-Paris images of Brother Simon of Obsidian offers a prayer with these lines:

"I believe firmly in thy great power, which hath manifested always through thy holy miracles ever since that glorious 28th of October, day of St. Judas Thaddaeus, on which thou didst make an apparition of thyself in the lands of Guatemala." Ordinarily Brother Simon appears only in dreams, but on that day—who knows what year it was—he appeared in broad daylight in a valley full of hot springs and geysers, near the town of Bathers, far to the west of St. Andrew Obsidian and a short distance south of Under Ten Deer. There he met a Quiché man who happened to be a namesake of the Apostle Philip, baptizer of Simon the sorcerer, talking with him and granting him favors.

In the temple at Obsidian, an old and heavily varnished wooden image of St. Judas Thaddaeus occupies a small, poorly lit tabernacle at the foot of the stairway that descends from Brother Simon's left. Instead of looking straight ahead, as most saints do, St. Judas Thaddaeus is always shown with his head turned toward his own right, which in this case makes it seem that the people descending the stairs have caught his attention. It happens that he shares his day, October 28, with a fellow apostle, St. Simon the Zealot, which brings us back to Brother Simon as Judas Simon.

And then there is Judas Iscariot, thirteenth at table but twelfth among the apostles, whose father's name was Simon. Two brothers of Jesus, a pair of apostles, a son and his father: all of them Judas and Simon. Whoever Judas Simon of the pamphlets may be, they say his thirty pieces of silver "were given to the most needy." As for Judas Iscariot of the Old World Book, when he realized that Jesus would be crucified, he returned his thirty pieces to the priests in the temple at Jerusalem, saying,

"I have sinned in that I have betrayed innocent blood." They replied,

"What is that to us? see thou to that." And he cast down the silver and went away to hang himself.

For their part, the priests used the silver to buy "the potter's field, to bury strangers in." Of course. Who could be more needy than those with no one to bury them? Without names, even.

Some years ago, on Holy Saturday in one of the streets of Guatemala City, a crowd gathered for the customary burning of an effigy of Judas Iscariot, with a papier-mâché head and a body of stuffed clothing. Most of the people, Latins, were there to enjoy themselves, but they were dismayed when two Indian children began to cry, begging that nothing be done to hurt Brother Simon. The Latin children of the neighborhood shoved the Indians aside and dragged Judas over the pavement to the foot of an electric power pole, where they hanged him by the neck.

The next day, Easter Sunday, Judas was nowhere to be found. Some people claimed to have seen the two Indian children in the street during the night. They had lowered Judas from the pole with great care and made away with him.

In the towns around the Lake of the Puppet Trees (or Quack Trees), which lies between Obsidian and Under Ten Deer, the effigies made for Holy Week are called Maximón, a single word with two words in its past, Mam Simón. Mam, Old Man or Grandfather, is the name of the lord (or four lords) of the days that take a solar year out when it is eighteen score days old and bring a new one in five days later. The rhythm is always the same, without any leap years, so the change slowly drifts backward through the seasons. At present it takes place in late February, but when The Very Noble and Very Loyal City of St. James of the Knights of Guatemala was in its last days, it happened during the spring. That was when Mam and Judas Simon became one.

On April 15, 1773, Mam Thought took the old year away on Three Thought, which happened to fall during Holy Week, on Thursday. Five days later Mam Wind, the most violent of the four lords, brought the new year in on Eight Wind. Five score days after that, on Four Wind, twin earthquakes came ten minutes apart and wrecked the city. Two score days after that, on Five Wind, a further earthquake wrecked whatever repairs had been done by then. The government of Guatemala moved eastward to a village called the Hermitage, soon to become Guatemala City.

On April 15, 1774, Mam Wind took the old year away on the day Four Wind, and five days later Mam Deer brought in the new year on Nine Deer. On Thirteen Wind, which came eighteen score days after the twin earthquakes of the previous year and fell on the eve of the feast of St. James, the name of The Very Noble and Very Loyal City of St. James of the Knights of Guatemala was officially changed to Antique (Antigua) Guatemala.

In the time before the coming of the Old World Book, the five-day transition from one year to the next saw the adoration of an image of the incoming Mam, adorned for the occasion and brought to the house of the principal lord of a town. In our time, in the town of St. James at the Water, the clothes of Mam Simon are washed in the Lake of the Puppet Trees on the night of Holy Monday and his image is assembled on the night of Holy Tuesday, after which he is brought to a small white chapel in front of the parish church and hanged on Holy Wednesday. He stays there all day on Thursday, the day that brought the adoration of the Mam in 1773, and on Good Friday he is taken down and dismantled. During the other eighteen score days of the year, his ancient counterpart stood at one of the four entrances to a town, rotating among them year by year. Mam Simon, for his part, spends this time hidden away in the house of the Fraternity of the Holy Cross.

The fraternity keeps Mam Simon's wooden head and body wrapped in a bundle, his wooden mask in a glass box, and his clothes in a chest. The wood is that of the flute tree, bearer of the red seeds of divination. It is said that a small idol is concealed inside the body, made of precious stone or metal. The mask is unpainted, with carved parallel lines indicating a wrinkled forehead, eyebrows, eyelashes, and a moustache and goatee. His mouth is open just wide enough to hold a fat cigar.

When Mam Simon is fully assembled, he wears a shirt, pants, and sash that are all made locally and in the current style, which these days means that his pants have rows of flowers, leaves, and birds embroidered around their white-and-purple striped legs in every available color. His shirt cannot be seen because he wears a suit jacket over it, blue serge in the past and red mohair today, and over that, hanging from his shoulders and neck, a score or more of scarves of silk and cotton. His hat is a Stetson with a red silk scarf tied round the band and hanging down in back, and his boots are fancy, tan with the toe tops closed in by alternating cream and tan thongs in a twill pattern, or else black-and-white wingtips with squared toes.

There is some talk that Mam Simon has a wife. Her name is Mary Magdalene.

Before Mam Simon was made, they say, there were twelve brothers in St. James at the Water who caught fish in the Lake of the Puppet Trees and sold them in The Very Noble and Very Loyal City. It took them three days to get there on foot. Six were married and six were bachelors.

In those times, people from St. James were capable of seeing into the distance, and it happened that one of the married brothers, while he was on the road one day, realized that his wife was with another man. Sure enough, when he got back into town, someone told him his wife was having an affair.

One time the fisherman came home earlier than he was expected. His wife and her lover were frightened when they heard him coming. She told him to hide under the bed, in the hope that he could slip away as soon as her husband went to sleep. Or perhaps when her husband had to go outside to piss.

Her husband could see nothing when he entered, but he knew perfectly well that his wife's lover was under the bed. He had bought bread, chocolate, and liquor especially for this occasion, and he called to the man to come out and enjoy a feast with himself and his wife. But the man was too afraid to move, so he told him,

"It doesn't matter. You've merely been helping my woman to be fruitful. And since God has said that sins should be forgiven, I forgive your sin, and hers as well."

Finally the man came out from under the bed. It was one of the husband's bachelor brothers. He shared the meal and then thanked his host. As he left, the husband told him,

"If you came back tomorrow, that wouldn't matter either."

The next time the six married brothers came back from a trip to the capital, someone told them that each of their six bachelor brothers had been with one of their six wives. They said,

"Yes. We already knew that, and this time we intend to do something about it." Among themselves they said,

"Now we must put a caretaker on this earth, a guardian for our women."

"Why don't we make an image?"

"Yes. It should be someone who speaks, since the saints spoke in ancient times. And they worked miracles."

"But what kind of wood should we use?"

"Pine?"

"No."

"Cedar?"

"No, because cedar is sacred. All the saints are made of cedar."

They went into the woods on a mountain near St. James to look for a tree, and when they came to a flute tree, it spoke to them. With a machete, they cut a figure from it, dressed it, and put a mask on it. Then they told it,

"You will live here on the earth, taking care of our women."

The figure agreed by moving its head up and down. When they walked back down the mountain, he walked along with them.

After that the figure was seen walking here and there all over the place, and some of the people of St. James began to object. Sometimes it appeared to be a man, sometimes it appeared to be a woman. Either way, whoever saw it was in for trouble. Whenever a man slept with it, he would die three days later. A young woman turned up pregnant but denied that she had ever slept with a man. When the baby came into light it had short legs, a long trunk, and a lined face. Just like the figure.

Often the figure went walking in the streets in the form of a beautiful blonde woman, and boys would come up and flirt. People realized who this was when they noticed her hands, which had only four fingers.

Now there were those who said the figure should be disabled. They suggested that if the head were turned backward with the mask still in front, it wouldn't be able to speak any more. But the men who had sculpted it in the first place decided that it could serve as a representation of Judas, and ever since then the day of its feast has been Holy Wednesday.

In 1914, a bishop came to St. James at the Water with the purpose of burning Mam Simon, but he was stopped and thrown out of town. In 1950, the leader of the Catholic Action movement, himself a priest, arrived in town. He banned Mam Simon from the rites of Holy Week, but people ignored him. A couple of months later, on June 6, which fell on the day One Sinner, this priest and two others secretly slipped into the quarters of the Fraternity of the Holy Cross. They destroyed Mam Simon's head and made away with his mask.

Afterward, it was rumored in St. James that the Pope, impressed with the power of Mam Simon, had called him to Rome. But then came another story that the priests had abducted him, and that they had been armed when they did it. A newspaper columnist in the capital remarked that the partisans of the Epistles had become packers of pistols.

When the members of the fraternity demanded that Mam Simon be allowed to make a return appearance during the next Holy Week, the priests told them the mask had been burned. So then the members did the only thing they could do, which was to make a new head and mask for Mam Simon. As Holy Week of 1951 approached, they sent a telegram to the President of the Republic, asking permission to dress Mam Simon for his usual appearance. When this was granted, they took him to a chapel in the cloister adjoining the parish church. The next year the resident priest complained that the chapel was noisy and too near his bedroom, so they took Mam Simon to the market instead. The year after that they found a place for him on the porch in front of the church.

Nowadays the fraternity carries Mam Simon to a small chapel, completely covered with whitewash, on the bare earthen plaza in front of the church. The building is square, with a pyramidal pinnacle at each corner, and domed. Once upon a time it served as a baptistry. There is a pediment over the door, but whether or not it ever had a cross at the peak of it, it has none now.

As for the old mask of Mam Simon, the one supposedly burned by the priests, it has long since turned up in the Musée de l'Homme in Paris.

Some years ago, a strange thing happened to Mateo Uz Abaj at the Lake of the Puppet Trees, but on the opposite side of it from St. James. It happened near the village of St. George at the Lake, which is perched on a shelf a thousand feet above the water, across a small bay from the tourist hotels and weekend condominiums of the town called Puppet Trees.

The slope below St. George steepens until it drops straight into the bay, but there is a trail that goes part way down. Don Mateo and some other people, about fifteen in all, were guided down this trail by a man from St. George. They brought along bunches of candles, packets of incense, a bottle of beer, and a little liquor. Don Mateo was wondering,

"What are we, what are we, what are we going to see?"

The upper part of the slope is mostly wooded, but at the end of the path is a rock outcropping with a cave in it. The guide arranged the offerings of the pilgrims on the ground at the mouth of the cave and began to speak on their behalf, standing with his back to the lake.

Suddenly, before the prayer was finished, a man came out of the cave, a big man, tall, foreign-looking, and he ran past everyone, they heard a noise behind them, twigs snapping and rocks falling. When they went to look, and it was clear that the man had gone right over the edge of the cliff.

Not everyone saw the man come out, but everyone heard him. And who is he?

"The one who came out is, well, St. Simon. It's a spirit, is what I'd say," says don Mateo.

He has an image of St. Simon in his house in the town of Middle, the kind they sell in St. Andrew Obsidian, glossy paint on cast plaster of Paris. It's on the same small altar with the woman in flames, across the room from the larger altar dedicated to St. John.

"This is a bad road one takes," says don Mateo. "There are words, and it's the words that do the work."

And if someone else has done an evil with St. Simon?

"Then one must fix it with St. Simon, one must ask St. Simon's pardon. Four times for the question of fighting in the house. And one has to spend a lot."

It doesn't take thirteen days?

"No, only two days, twice each day. One spends four ounces of incense, and eight wax candles at one cent apiece. With some flower petals, a white rose. And with a pint of drink, and one bottle of water. And one prays the Our Father, the Hail Mary, and the Creed, and one prays to St. Peter and St. Paul, even though this is St. Judas."

St. Simon sits in his chair to the burning woman's left, his face pink, his hat and suit a blue so dark it's almost black, a pink dot on the lapel for a carnation, white shirt, red necktie, the whole figure on a green base, and the whole casting inside a tabernacle with a glass door, the wood frame painted red. Spread on the altar itself is a handwoven cotton tablecloth, pink with red and white pinstripes, protected with a thick sheet of clear plastic. To the woman's right is a dark green bottle of bootleg liquor, corked. Between her and St. Simon, leaning up against his tabernacle, are candles still inside the newspaper some vendor wrapped them in, and on top of the tabernacle are a few packets of copal incense, the small kind, each piece about the size of a nickel. Slightly to the left of St. Simon's feet lies an artificial flower, a pink rose on a leafy stem.

Enameled figure, glass bottle, plastic rose leaves, sheet of plastic over the tablecloth: all give back a glitter to the flashbulb. Directly in front of St. Simon, in a homemade holder of unfired clay, a candle burns with its own light. It was placed there by this man who sometimes asks for justice, this man who wanted the name of the killer of his pig to be named while the smoke still rose, that cloudy day up there on Tohil's Place.

Well then, what color is this candle, caught in a color photograph?

It's red.

And what does that mean?

Here it is in the pamphlet: "RED: Love, Faith and Will."

➤ Proper Respect for a Stone

IN THE TOWN OF MIDDLE, not far down the road from don Mateo's place, there once lived a married couple—I don't remember their names, but he was a Latino from Guatemala City and she was a gringa from the Florida panhandle. He was employed on a local road construction project, funded by an international relief agency, and she collected the handwoven blouses Indian women wear. They quarreled constantly, loudly enough for people to hear his shouts and roughly enough for people to see her bruises. Their house was down in a gulch, and the woman who rented it to them had a reputation as a grave robber.

Late one evening the man sat at a table with don Mateo and they talked about roads. Don Mateo said there were two roads, a white one and a black one. He drew a straight line on the table, leading in the same direction he himself was facing, and said it was the white road. It was difficult and sometimes hard to make out, but straight, and it led to the Place of Light. Then he drew a second line, forking off to the right from the straight one, and said it was the black road. It was easy and lined with flowers, but it led to the darkness of the Place of Fear, the place where Blood Gatherer, the father of Blood Moon, still lived. Down that road went Catholics who were fond of reciting arguments they'd learned from catechisms, Protestant evangelists and all their converts, people who murdered their own parents, and Gypsies who put on minstrel shows.

One afternoon don Mateo and his wife, doña Leona, heated up their sweat bath. He cut sprigs of fresh-smelling rue for bathers to brush themselves with, and she prepared food they could eat when they came out. The man from down the road accepted an invitation to enter the bath, and when he came crawling back out through the low door, don Mateo offered him a freshly boiled thorn to eat—or at least "thorn" is what it's called in Quiché. It's a fruit that grows on a vine, and it's green on the outside, covered with thorns, greenish white and somewhat grainy on the inside, and tastes like a potato. The man knew the thorns would be soft and easy to peel off after boiling, but he refused to eat. In fact, no one had ever seen him accept food from the hand of an Indian.

Much to don Mateo's annoyance, the man and woman continued to quarrel. They'd been asking lots of questions about local customs, so don Mateo offered to brush both of them all over with a single pine bough and then bury it. That, he said, might cure their quarreling. Or else they could each take a turn at wearing the same shirt and then he'd bury that. They weren't interested.

Finally don Mateo offered to give them a stone with a gape to keep in their house, the largest stone in his personal collection. This, they accepted. He told them it wouldn't be dangerous unless they forgot to feed it, or unless they quarreled in front of it. On the days Four, Eight, and Nine Wind, and on days named Tooth or Jaguar with those same numbers, they were to light tallow candles in front of it and pray in Quiché, saying, *Come hither Lord Wind, come hither all daughtersons of St. Peter, you who stay there in the Place of Light,* and they were also to mention the owners of the place the stone came from, saying, *come hither, World of Rose and Mosquito.* Then they were to splash it with liquor, taking care that some of this ran into the mouth and saying, *This is my water, the tip of my nose, given for you.*

Why St. Peter? St. Peter was the owner of all the gapes. Why the tip of the nose? Just a local expression for a strong drink. And then be careful not to quarrel.

The face of the stone was at least six or maybe five times larger than a human face. Don Mateo poured liquor on it and said a few words over it before he let it go. He showed them where the mouth was, running the tips of the first two fingers of his right hand all around the lips of a long crevice and then through the length of the crevice itself, making sure no spot was left dry. The stone was so heavy it took three men to lift it. The man and woman took it home in their microbus and gave it a prominent place in their bedroom. That wasn't such a good place for it, since stones don't like to be near a man on top of a woman any more than they like to be near a fight, but don Mateo let it go.

Not long afterward the couple threw a party. Most of their guests were people who worked for the international agency, but they also invited don Mateo, who arrived early. The stone looked neglected to him, and he warned the couple that it might commit a sudden act of violence unless he fed it right away. When the other guests began to fill up the house, the candles were burning and the mouth was wet. A hired hand of the agency, a local Quiché who'd been going to catechism classes for some time, was wandering around the house. Suddenly he found himself face-to-face with the stone, and he was outraged. To everyone, and to no one in particular, he declared, in Spanish,

"There is only one God in heaven and here on the earth!" By the tone of his voice he dared anyone to tell him anything different, but the host and hostess ignored him and don Mateo was nowhere to be seen. The catechist then set to drinking, and when he left, long after everyone else had gone home, he got no farther than the shoulder of the road before he lost what was left of his balance and went down. There he remained, shouting over and over again at the top of his voice, on and on for hours in the darkness until he passed out,

"There is only one God in heaven and here on the earth!" The whole time he was flat on his back in the dirt. When he came to, it was already late in the morning. Someone walking by on the way into town had taken his shoes, so he went home barefoot.

Still the couple quarreled, and then came the morning of a day named Blade—I don't remember what the day's number was, but the Lord Blade rules over fights, especially fights with words. He gave the woman a dream in which she saw five identical white cups and knew the middle one was hers. Someone wanted to fill that cup with dirt, but she tried to prevent it. Suddenly all the cups became cars, and she woke up.

A few days later, while her husband was driving a pickup truck belonging to the international agency, he hit a patch of loose gravel on a turn and rolled it. The roof of the cab was smashed in and he was battered and bruised. He ended up with a bad limp.

When I last went by their house they'd moved out, but don Mateo gave me some further news. They'd gone to Guatemala City, he said, and one night the man thought he heard someone breaking into his microbus, parked on the street in front of their house. He ran outside with a pistol, and sure enough there were thieves, three of them. One of them shot him in the face and he died right there. His wife went back to Florida. And the stone?

Don Mateo has it.

➢ Notes

WORDS FROM MAYAN LANGUAGES, when they appear in italics, are written in the new alphabet of the Academia de las Lenguas Mayas de Guatemala (1988), except that vowels have been reduced to the five found in early documents. With the following exceptions, consonants may be pronounced approximately as in English: *j* is like Spanish *j*, with the tongue farther back than for English *h*; *l* is like Welsh *ll*, with the tongue farther forward than for English; and *q* is like Hebrew qoph, with the tongue farther back than it would be for English *k*. Two other Mayan sounds are found in English, but are spelled differently: *tz* is like *ts* in English "bats," and *x* is like English *sh*. The glottal stop, which is equivalent to *tt* in the Scottish pronunciation of "bottle," is indicated by *'*; when it follows a consonant, it is pronounced simultaneously with that consonant. Vowels are approximately like those of Spanish or Italian. Stress is nearly always on the final syllable of a word.

The day names of the Quiché version of the Mayan divinatory calendar have been translated into English throughout. In the following key, the Quiché names are followed by their Yucatec counterparts:

Deer	*Kej*	*Manik'*
Yellow	*Q'anil*	*Lamat*
Thunder	*Toj*	*Muluk*
Dog	*Tz'i'*	*Ok*
Monkey	*B'atz'*	*Chuen*
Tooth	*E*	*Eb*
Cane	*Aj*	*Ben*
Jaguar	*Ix*	*Ix*
Bird	*Tz'ikin*	*Men*
Sinner	*Ajmak*	*Kib*
Thought	*No'j*	*Kaban*
Blade	*Tijax*	*Etz'nab*
Rain	*Kawuq*	*Kawak*
Marksman	*Junajpu*	*Ajaw*
Lefthanded	*Imox*	*Imix*
Wind	*Iq'*	*Ik'*
Foredawn	*Aq'ab'al*	*Ak'bal*

Net	*K'at*	*K'an*
Snake	*Kan*	*Chikchan*
Death	*Kame*	*Kimi*

Preface

The scores for translations from tape recordings, wherever they occur in this book, follow a method I have been using since 1970. For further examples, together with discussions of the importance of timing, amplitude, and tones of voice in oral performances, see D. Tedlock (1983, 1990c).

Breath on the Mirror

Popol Vuh is the name of the sacred book of the Quiché Maya, often referred to as "the Book" or "the New World Book" in the present work. The literal meaning of the name, properly spelled *Popol Wuj* in the present-day official alphabet for Quiché, is "Book of the Mat," referring to the mat a council of lords sat on. For a complete translation, see D. Tedlock (1985); the events referred to in the present chapter are narrated on pp. 163-70. The illustrations in this chapter, which give the Quiché text for the translated passages that follow them, are from the surviving manuscript of the Popol Vuh (folios 34r, 35r-35v), which is reproduced in full in Ximénez (1973).

Jaguar Cedar, the name of the eldest of the first four humans ever made, is composed of *b'alam,* "Jaguar," and *k'itze,* which may be derived from *k'ische',* given as a term for cedar in the colonial dictionaries of Coto (1983) and Guzmán (1984).

Red Sea Turtle, the name of the eldest of the first four women ever made, is composed of *kaqa,* "red," and *paluma,* which is close to *palama,* given by Coto (1983) and Guzmán (1984) as a term for sea turtle. In the manuscript of the Popol Vuh, *caka* (the old spelling of *kaqa*) is miscopied as *caha* (folio 34r), which makes no sense, but the Title of the Lords of Totonicapán (reproduced in Carmack and Mondloch 1983) has the correct form (folio 8r).

Vigesimal beings, or humans, are called by terms meaning "twenty" in all Mayan languages *(winaq* in Quiché), referring to the sum of the fingers and toes. The English word "vigesimal" means "pertaining to the number twenty" or "counted by or based on twenty." The Mayan number system is vigesimal (based on twenty) rather than decimal (based on ten).

Holy Cross Many Trees, the name of a Guatemalan town, is translated from Santa Cruz Quiché, in which the last word is more properly *k'iche',* meaning "many trees."

Thirteen numbers and twenty names form the basis of a 260-day divinatory calendar that came into use in Mesoamerica at least 2,500 years ago and continues in use today in about sixty Mayan towns in Guatemala; its workings are explained more fully in a later chapter, "Two Rhythms at Once." The multiple meanings given to the day Eight Bird in the present chapter—Call, Cry, Metal, etc.—are divinatory interpretations. The best source on the ongoing life of the calendar and its use in divination is B. Tedlock (1982).

Split Place, Bitter Water Place is *Pan Paxil, Pan K'ayala'* in Quiché; the Mam Maya, who live nearby, call it *Paxal* (Miles 1981).

She Who Does a Favor and He Who Puts in Order, the names of the patron deities of diviners, are translated, respectively, from *Xmukane* and *Xpiyakoq*, as given in the Popol Vuh (D. Tedlock 1985:369-70).

Jaguar Night *(B'alam Aq'ab')*, Not Right Now *(Majukutaj)*, and Dark Jaguar *(Ik'i B'alam)* were created immediately after Jaguar Cedar (see above), the four of them together being the first humans on the face of the earth. The last of these names is derived from a lowland Mayan language of the Cholan family; in Chol itself, *ik' bolay*, "dark predator," is a term for the jaguar (Josserand and Hopkins 1988).

Motherfather, or *chuchkajaw*, is the Quiché term for the priest-shamans, always men, who head patrilineages (see B. Tedlock 1982:74-82). In the Popol Vuh this term is used for the first four humans (D. Tedlock 1985: 165-67), who are implicitly androgynous until the first four women are created.

Skyearth is *kajulew* in Quiché, composed of *kaj,* "sky," and *ulew,* "earth," which together make a term for world.

Heart of Sky *(Uk'ux Kaj)* and Heart of Earth *(Uk'ux Ulew)* are the names or epithets of the creator gods in the Popol Vuh. Mountainplain is *juyub'taq'aj* in Quiché, combining *juyub'*, "mountain," and *taq'aj*, "plain," which together make a term for the surface of the earth.

Prawn House *(Chomija)*, Water Hummingbird *(Tz'ununija')*, and Macaw House *(Kaqixaja)*, in that order, were created immediately after Red Sea Turtle (see above), the four of them together being the first women on the face of the earth. Water Hummingbird's name is spelled *tzununiha* in the Popol Vuh manuscript (folio 34r), which leaves the question open as to whether -*ha* might be *ja,* "house" (as in the names of the other two women) or *ja'*, "water." The matter is settled by the Annals of the Cakchiquels (Brinton 1885:112-13), where the name appears as *Tz'ununa' (4,ununaa* in the orthography of the manuscript). Like *ja', a'* means "water," and *tz'unun,* by itself, means "hummingbird." The mystery as to what a "water hummingbird" might be is solved by the Tirado (1787) dictionary, which defines *tz'ununja'* as a bird with "a long beak, white breast, colored green but with white wing tips, frequenting rivers." The only Mesoamerican bird of that description is *Chloroceryle americana,* the green kingfisher.

Daykeeper, or *ajq'ij,* is the Quiché term for diviners who address their questions to time itself, in the form of the lords of the days of the 260-day calendar.

Those who look into the middle, or *nik' wachinel,* is an old Quiché term for diviners; that one of the things they did was to look into water is mentioned by Coto (1983, in the entry for *adivinar).*

Sunbringer, or *iqok'ij,* literally "carrier of the sun or day," is a Quiché term for Venus in its role as the morning star.

Seven Macaw *(Wuqub' Kaqix)* and Shield *(Chimalmat),* during the era preceding the one during which human beings were made, had falsely played the roles of sun and moon (D. Tedlock 1985:89-94, 330, 360).

Fistful of Boys is *Omuch' K'ajolab'* in Quiché, which could also be translated "Four Hundred Boys"; they became the stars we call the Pleiades during the same era in which Seven Macaw and Shield became the stars of the Big and Little Dipper (D. Tedlock 1985:96-97, 342).

The Great Eastern City

Tulan or Tolan was the name (or part of the name) of at least a dozen places in Mesoamerica, the ruins now known as Tula, near Mexico City, being just one of these. Pilgrims went to such places to seek the status of nobility and the trappings that went with it, which is what the leaders of highland Guatemalan nations were doing when they went to the eastern city of the Popol Vuh. In Quiché and in Cakchiquel (the language most closely related to Quiché), the word *tolan* was also used for abandoned places, or places so desolate that only insects could be heard (Basseta 1921, Coto 1983, Varea 1929, Ximénez 1985). I suspect that the authors of the Popol Vuh were not so much giving us a place name as they were removing the eastern city to a distant era. For their account of the city, see D. Tedlock (1985:171-76).

Zuyua, as a place name, is even more of a problem than Tulan or Tolan; so far, no one has pinned it on a map or even settled the question of which language it comes from. In the Book of Chilam Balam of Chumayel, from Yucatán, Zuyua is given as the place of origin for riddles that must be answered by a person seeking lordship (Roys 1967:88-98, 125-31).

Seven Caves, Seven Canyons *(Wuqub' Pek, Wuqub' Siwan),* as an epithet for the eastern city, points in two different directions. On the one hand, Seven Caves suggests the place of origin claimed by speakers of Nahuatl (the language of the Aztecs), which is called Chicomoztoc or "Seven Caves" in their language. On the other hand, they make no mention of Seven Canyons, which may refer to a city with seven districts. In Quiché, a city as a whole is referred to by the double term *siwan tinamit,* which combines the word for canyon (or canyons), referring to the lower districts, with the word for citadel, referring to the high place where the lords of a city would dwell (D. Tedlock 1985:314).

Copán comes closer than any other Mayan site to fitting the role of the ancient eastern city, beginning with the fact that it lies due east of the Quiché heartland and is connected to it by valleys and ridges that run east-west. It is the Annals of the Cakchiquels (Fire Trees) that tells us the city visited by the highland nations was the eastern member of a group of four cities and that its insignia was a bat (see D. Tedlock 1989:10, 21n). The cities that may have formed a group of four with Copán were Palenque, at the west end of the Mayan world, and Calakmul and Tikal, north and south of one another in the middle of that world (Marcus 1986:11-22). On the phonetic reading of the Copán emblem glyph see Looper (1991); he mentions the possibility that the site is named after the solitaire *(xwukpik* in Chol) but then chooses a different bird, the motmot, with a similar name *(xwukip).* The transcription of the solitaire's cry is adapted from Davis (1972:174), and the account of the cry's meaning comes (with my translation) from the Annals of the Cakchiquels (Brinton 1885:76-77). The Quiché and Cakchiquel term for this bird is *chajal siwan,* "guardian of the canyon."

The first and last dates in the inscriptions of Copán, expressed in Mayan terms, are 8.6.0.0.0 and 9.19.11.14.5 (Schele and Freidel 1990:309, 343). Here and elsewhere in the present book, equivalents of Mayan dates on the Christian calendar (Julian version) are given according to the correlation number (584,283) that best fits the historical evidence (see Thompson 1960:303-10, Bricker and Bricker 1986:54, and D. Tedlock 1992).

Tree-stone is *che' ab'aj* in the text of the Popol Vuh (appearing twice on folio 35r); on the decipherment of Cholan Mayan words with the "tree-stone" meaning in the inscriptions of Copán, see Schele and Stuart (1986).

New Sky on the Horizon and Sire of the Dagger appear as *Yax Pak* and *U Sit Tok'* in the Copán inscriptions, translated by others as "First Dawn" and "Patron of Flint" (Schele and Freidel 1990:483, 494). *Pak* is from a highland language, occurring in Cakchiquel words that refer to the eastern sky at dawn (Coto 1983).

K'ab'awil, the term for the gods (or icons) received at the eastern city, carries a sense of naming that remains quite clear today in the word *k'ab'a* or *k'aba,* which is found in Kekchi (Haeserijn 1979), a language of the Quichean branch of the Mayan family, and in Chol (Josserand and Hopkins 1988), Mopán (Ulrich and Ulrich 1976), and Yucatec (Barrera 1980). For a discussion of the "open mouth" meaning of *k'ab'a* in Quiché, see D. Tedlock (1985:247-48).

Tohil *(Tojil)*, the patron deity of Jaguar Cedar, and his Classic Maya counterpart—called GII, God K, the Manikin Scepter, K'awil, and Tahil in the Mayanist literature—have attributes that are summarized by D. Tedlock (1985:365) and Schele and Freidel (1990:414). In both Quiché (Ximénez 1985) and Chol (Josserand and Hopkins 1988), there are two different verb stems that take the form *toj*, one of them for paying and the other for making thundering noises. The play on words that brings together a pine torch and a piece of obsidian is discussed by Schele and Miller (1986:49).

Lord Swallow, the patron deity of Jaguar Night, is *Awilix* in the Popol Vuh (folio 35v), *Awilis* in the Title of the Lords of Totonicapán (folio 10v), and *Wilix* in Ximénez (1985). *Kwilix* in Kekchi (Haeserijn 1979) and *wilis chan* in Chol (Josserand and Hopkins 1988) are both terms for swallow (the bird). The *a-* on the front of the name might have originated in *aj-*, which means "person of" or "he of" in a wide range of Mayan languages, or it might have resulted from a combination of *ajaw*, which is "lord" in most Mayan languages, with *wilis* or *wilix*.

Open Mountain *(Jakawitz),* the patron deity of Not Right Now, is like Tohil and Lord Swallow in having a name that makes sense in a Cholan language like that of the eastern city. In Chol itself, *jak* is "to strip off" and *witz* is "mountain" (Josserand and Hopkins 1988). The writers of the Popol Vuh seem to have understood the name in this way when they contrasted *Awilix*, who was given a home in a forest, with *Jakawitz*, who was placed on a *saqi juyub'* (folio 39r), a "clear (or treeless) mountain" (for this sense of *saqi* see under *saq* in Varea 1929).

Middle of the Plain, the patron of Dark Jaguar, is *Nik'aj Taq'aj* in Quiché.

White Dagger is *Saqi Toq'* in Quiché; this name is used only with reference to a sacrificial knife.

Birds and breechclouts *(tz'ikin* and *ch'uq)* might seem far-fetched as a word play on ears and elbows *(xikin* and *ch'uk)*, but it must first be said that Mayans in general are given to punning (see D. Tedlock 1985:265-66 for Quiché examples). The possibilities for a play on *xikin*, the term for ear, begin with the fact that it was also used for such appendages as a long handle on a cooking utensil (Varea 1929). *Tz'ikin*, the generic term for bird, is the commonest Quiché metaphor for penis, an alternative metaphor being *pich'*, the term for a red-headed woodpecker (Guzmán 1984, Tirado 1787, Varea 1929, Ximénez 1985). Classic Maya lords did penance by bleeding their penises rather than their ears (Schele and Miller 1986: chap. 4), and bloodletting is precisely what Tohil tells the future Quiché lords to do with their so-called *xikin*. As for what he tells them to take stitches in, that is written as *chuc* in the imprecise orthography of the manuscript (folio 38r) and may be read as either of two words: *ch'uk*, which is indeed "elbow," and *ch'uq*, which refers to covering by means of cloth (Tirado 1787) and specifically to the covering of a man's genitals (Basseta 1921). In the present context "elbow" makes a better fit with "ear" if we insist on a pair of terms for body parts, but if we consider the stitching, then a cloth covering works better. The covering serves in turn as a metonym for what it covers, or else as a metaphor for the foreskin, which was the site where blood was drawn. The method was to pass a cord through it (as if sewing). According to a later Popol Vuh passage (folio 42v), the penitents who took these stitches prayed to Tohil for their *achijilal*, which literally means "manhood" but is also, according to Tirado (1787), a figure of speech meaning "virile member."

Great Hollow with Fish in the Ashes is *Nim Xob' Karchaj* when first mentioned in the Popol Vuh (folio 13v) and later *Nim Xol* (folio 38r). *Xob'* and *xol*, respectively, are the Kekchi (Haeserijn 1979) and Quiché (Ximénez 1985) terms for a hollow. The location in question is that of a present-day Guatemalan town eight kilometers east of Cobán, named San Pedro Carchá in printed sources but often called *Nim* ("Great") *Karcha* in Kekchi, the Mayan language spoken there. Among the contemporary Kekchi, *Karcha* is said to be composed of *kar*, "fish," and *cha*, "ashes."

Painted Town River is called Río Cahabón in Spanish, from Kekchi *kaj*, "town," and *b'on*, "painted" (Haeserijn 1979). Rumbling Intestine Canyon is *K'ulk'u Siwan* (badly written as *cul, cuziuan* on folio 14r of the Popol Vuh), combining Kekchi *k'ulk'uch* (listed under *culcutc* in Haeserijn 1979) with the Quiché term for canyon *(siwan)*. Mouth of the Change of Canyons is *Chuchi' Jalja Siwanub'* (folio 14r), an entirely Quiché name; it may refer to the entrance of the cave (actually a system of caves) where the Río Cahabón goes underground forty kilometers east of San Pedro Carchá. The cave is called Semuc today, translated here as Ravenous Cave on the basis of Kekchi *semok*, referring to irresistible desires including hunger (see under *sem* in Haeserijn 1979). After the Mouth, according to the Popol Vuh, come Spiked Rapids *(Jalja Ja' Simaj)*, Blood River *(K'ik'iya')*, and Pus River *(Pujya')* (D. Tedlock 1985:110-11, 134).

Place of Fear is *Xib'alb'a* in Quiché and many other Mayan languages. In the Popol Vuh it is ruled by One Death and Seven Death *(Jun Kame* and *Wuqub' Kame)*, who are named for two dates on the divinatory calendar.

Watching for the Great Star

One Marksman *(Jun Junajpu)* and Seven Marksman *(Wuqub' Junajpu),* named for two days on the divinatory calendar, are the sons of He Who Puts in Order and She Who Does a Favor, the patrons of diviners.

Blood Moon is *Xkik'* in Quiché, a name in which *x-* means "little" or "she of" and *kik',* which means "blood," contains a pun on *ik',* "moon." Blood Gatherer, her father, is *Kuchuma Kik'.* Her full story is told in the Popol Vuh (D. Tedlock 1985:114-19).

Marksman or *Junajpu* is named for a day (but without any number). His twin brother is Little Jaguar (or Hidden) Sun or *Xb'alanq'e,* a name composed of *x-,* "little"; *b'alam,* "jaguar" in Quiché or "hidden" in Kekchi; and *q'e,* "sun" or "day" in Kekchi. In Kekchi, the sun is called *b'alamq'e* when it is hidden at night (Haeserijn 1979). The adventures of the twins are told in the Popol Vuh (D. Tedlock 1985: part 3).

Farewell *(Chi Pixab'),* the mountain where the highland nations divided, is still known by this name today; it is located seven kilometers west of San Andrés Sajcabajá, Guatemala. The three nations that split off from the Quiché, according to the Popol Vuh (D. Tedlock 1985:177), were the Cakchiquel (Fire Trees), Rabinal, and Tzutuhil (Bird House).

Swallow's Place is *Pawilix,* shown as "Awilix" on a map in Fox (1978:44).

Middle is called Chinique in Spanish, a name that may be derived from *chi nik'aj,* "at the middle."

Tohil's Place *(Patojil)* is marked "Tojil" on a map in Fox (1978:44).

The Death of Death

Thirteen Wind and the other dates assigned to events in this chapter have been reconstructed on the basis of the Popol Vuh, whose narrative offers various calendrical signposts (D. Tedlock 1985:42-46), and the Mayan hieroglyphic book known as the Dresden Codex, which contains an astronomical table dealing with Venus (Thompson 1972:62-71). My efforts at reconstruction were inspired by the Mayan authors of the inscriptions in the seventh-century temples of Palenque. Not content with dating mythic events by the divinatory calendar, they attempted to fix them in absolute historical time as well (Schele 1987, D. Tedlock 1992).

The story of how the Dresden Codex found its way to Europe is told by Coe (1992:77-79). In any given pass across the five pages of the Venus table in this book, the periodicity of Venus is described five times (one period to a page), with the five periods together lasting eight solar years. The first of the five different occasions on which Venus reappears as the morning star always falls on a day named Marksman, and the first of the five occasions on which it reappears as the evening star always falls on a day named Death. In the Popol Vuh, which tells the story of the divine actions that lie behind these events, the gods whose victories are marked by the appearance of the morning star are One and Seven Marksman and (later) Marksman and Little Jaguar Sun, while those whose victories are marked by the evening star are One and Seven Death.

The Dresden table shows three different ways of keying the events of Venus periods to their positions within solar years. What the Popol Vuh story requires is two different Venus events that happen to fall on days whose gods rule the current solar year, with one such event coming during the fifth Venus period (D. Tedlock 1985:145, 149, 288-90). Only one of the keys to the table (given on line 14 of each page) fits this description. It is the key that went into effect on the Mayan date 11.0.3.1.0 (June 13, 1227). If Marksman and Little Jaguar Deer were conceived as paying homage to Seven Marksman (their deceased uncle) on the day that bears his name, and if that day was marked by the rebirth of Venus as the morning star, then it would have come on 11.1.15.9.0 (June 5, 1259), when the key of 11.0.3.1.0 was still in effect. The moon was full on that day, as stated at the end of the present chapter.

Earthquake is *Kab'raqan* in Quiché, from *kab'a*, "pile of earth" (Varea 1929) and *raqan*, "his legs."

"Sweet poison" translates Quiché *ki'*, which means both "sweet" and "poison" and also designates the drink known as pulque in Mexico.

"They saw three suns in one day" is a Quiché statement recorded in the seventeenth century by a Spanish colonist in Guatemala (Carmack 1981:129).

White Sparkstriker

Copal incense, called *pom* in a wide array of Mayan languages, is made from the resin in the bark of the incense tree, *Bursera bipinnata*.

White Sparkstriker *(Saq K'oxol)*, who appears only briefly in the Popol Vuh (D. Tedlock 1985:182), is discussed in detail by B. Tedlock (1986).

Black Butterfly Grandson of Many Hands is *Tekum Umam K'iq'ab'* in Quiché, composed of *tekum*, a "large black butterfly that flies with great speed" (Tirado 1787); *umam*, "grandson of"; *k'i*, "many"; and *q'ab'*, "hands." In Spanish he is called by the truncated name Tecun Umam, which leaves "grandson of" dangling. His grandfather was the namesake of an earlier Many Hands, the most powerful king in Quiché history (see D. Tedlock 1985:213-19, 224, where the name appears as Quicab).

"Never has there been such bitterness," and other lines from the play whose main characters are Black Butterfly and White Sparkstriker, are my translations from the version of the Spanish text published by Asociación Tikal (1981). For a general study of the play, including the transmission of its script by means of manuscripts, see Bode (1961).

The mirror at the center of the sky is placed there in a story told by the Kekchi Maya (Thompson 1930:132).

Three Maidens at the Bath

Tohohil (or *Tojojil* in modern orthography), as a name for the Quiché people, appears in the Annals of the Cakchiquels (Brinton 1885:82-83).

Tohil's Bath is *Ratinib'al Tojil* in Quiché.

Lust Woman *(Xtaj)* and Bath Woman *(Xpuch')* are the only maidens who figure in the Popol Vuh version of the attempt to seduce Tohil, Lord Swallow, and Open Mountain (D. Tedlock 1985:189-92). The *x-* that prefixes their names means "little" or "she of"; *taj* is "desire" and *puch'*, from Kekchi, is "wash" (Haeserijn 1979). The third maiden, with the ironic name Often Married, appears in another version of the story, told in the Title of the Lords of Totonicapán (folio 13v). Her full name is *K'ib'atz'un Ja*, in which *ja* is "house" (referring to her lineage); *k'i* is "many" and *b'atz'un* seems to be a nominalized form of a verb stem for "marry" that appears as *b'atz'o-* in Varea (1929).

The Wailing Woman, best known by her Spanish name, *La Llorona*, is the subject of tales told throughout Guatemala, as well as in Belize (Craig 1991:35-36), the Valley of Mexico (Davis 1946:109-16), and northern New Mexico (Kraul and Beatty 1988).

Altar Town is known to speakers of Spanish by the Nahuatl name that was given to it by Alvarado's Mexican allies, Momostenango, referring to the numerous outdoor altars found there. The Quiché name was and is *Chuwa Tz'aq,* "In Front of the Monument." The shrines mentioned in the present chapter are all within a half-hour's walk to the west of the town center: One's Place *(Junab'al)* or Water's Place *(Paja'),* Eight's Place *(Wajxaqib'al)* or Small Place of Proclamation *(Ch'uti Sab'al),* and Nine's Place *(B'elejib'al)* or Great Place of Proclamation *(Nima Sab'al).* The places named in the story told by don Pedro, Thistles *(Pala')* and Big Mountain *(Nima Juyub'),* lie a little farther west.

St. Christopher Hot Springs is known to speakers of Spanish as San Cristóbal Totonicapán; the last word, meaning "hot springs" in Nahuatl, is a direct translation of the town's Quiché name, *Miq'ina'.* It lies directly south of Momostenango, on the Pan American Highway.

Jealous Seeds and Crystals

The flute tree is *Erythrina rubrinervia;* it has no English name and its Quiché name *(tz'ite)* doesn't refer to anything except the tree itself, so I have translated its Spanish name, *palo pito.*

The Language of the Animals

For more on Quiché dream interpretation, see B. Tedlock (1981, 1987).

The names of the four sacred mountains on the boundaries of Altar Town (Momostenango) are given in an old orthography that makes things easier for speakers of English. In the new orthography of the Academia de las Lenguas Mayas (see the first of all the notes), Quilaha is *Kilaja,* Socob is *Sokob',* Tamancu is *Tamanku,* and Pipil stays the same.

St. Francis the High is known as San Francisco el Alto in Spanish; it is located between Momostenango and San Cristóbal Totonicapán.

The Gathered Range, which Guatemalans think of as an extension of the Andes of South America, is called Sierra de los Cuchumatanes by speakers of Spanish. In Quiché, both *kuchuma* and *tan* mean "to gather." I have never been able to determine the location of the specific mountain don Pedro names as Mines *(Minas).* It is supposed to be near the town of Drinking Water, or *T'alb'in* in Mam Maya (the language of the area), which is known in Spanish as Chiantla, a name of Nahuatl derivation but of uncertain meaning. The nearby town of Deep Pool, or *Chinab'ajul* in Mam, is also given a Nahuatl name by speakers of Spanish: Huehuetenango, meaning "Walled Town."

Two Rhythms at Once

The motherfather who goes to the four directional mountains on days numbered eleven is called *chuchkajaw rech tinimit,* "motherfather of the town"; for more on his duties, see B. Tedlock (1982:35, 81-82).

On the Road to Ruin

Puppet Trees is *Panajachel,* a name composed of *pan-,* "at"; *ajache',* referring to a tree *(Casimiroa edulis)* called *matasano* in Spanish; and *-l,* indicating a place where such trees grow. The wood of this tree is used for carving and carpentry, and the name itself suggests *ajamche',* literally "woodcarving," a term used for puppets in the Popol Vuh (folio 4r). For speakers of Mayan languages, the town of Puppet Trees and the lake on whose shore it sits have

➤ 243

the same name, but speakers of Spanish know the lake as Atitlán, which simply means "At the Water" in Nahuatl. Landslide Place, the site of the lake of the north, is *Chi'ul* in Quiché, and Sweatbath House, the town whose boundary it marks, is *Tujal Ja,* called Sacapulas in Spanish. Dripping Place, the site of the eastern lake, is *Tz'ujil,* and Among the Rocks, the town whose boundary it may mark, is *Xol Ab'aj,* known to Spanish speakers as Joyabaj. Mirror Water or *Lemoa',* the middle lake, is between Santa Cruz Quiché and Chichicastenango.

Black River, or Río Negro, is also known as the Chixoy, a name of Mayan derivation but of unclear meaning. It is the principal source of the Río Usumacinta, whose name is Nahuatl and may mean "Revered Monkeys" (Arriola 1973).

For the full story of recent violence in and around Holy Cross Many Trees (Santa Cruz Quiché), see Carmack (1988). Events like those described in the present chapter took place in many other towns in the early 1980s, bringing to a climax a period of strife that began when the U.S., acting on behalf of large corporate interests, intervened to overthrow the elected government of Guatemala in 1954 and laid the foundations for the system of military rule that continues (with or without a civilian front) to this day (for documentation see Immerman 1982). During the direct military attacks on civilians in the 1980s, the principal suppliers of arms and equipment were the U.S. and Israel (Institute for Policy Studies 1983).

Guard Post is a translation of Atalaya, the Spanish name for the eastern part of the ruins of the ancient Quiché capital. Rotten Cane, or *Q'umaraq Aj* in Quiché, is known to speakers of Spanish by a Nahuatl name with a similar meaning, Utatlán. Bearded Place is *Chi Ismachi* and Ilok Place is *Piloqab'.*

Two pairs of Quiché kings, Lord Plumed Serpent *(Ajaw Q'ukumatz)* and Lord Holy Sweatbath *(Ajaw K'otuja),* and (coming two generations later) Many Hands *(K'iq'ab')* and Cauizimah, are singled out for special attention by the authors of the Popol Vuh (D. Tedlock 1985:208-18). The story of the successors (another seven generations later) who adopted the surnames Rojas and Cortés is told by Carmack (1981:321).

Peter Pallid (Pedro de Alvarado) gives an account of his thoughts and deeds at the Quiché capital in letters addressed to Hernán Cortés (Mackie 1924).

Great Monument of Tohil is *Nima Tz'aq Tojil,* listed along with other temples in the Popol Vuh (D. Tedlock 1985:218-19). I have relied on Carmack (1981: chap. 9) for the identification of various ruined buildings at Rotten Cane. The first North American visitor to write about the ruins was the famous traveler John Lloyd Stevens (see Stevens 1841: chap. 10). The Spanish priest who had written about them a century and a half earlier was Francisco Ximénez (see Ximénez 1977:80), who also made the only surviving copy of the Popol Vuh.

The emblems of Quiché kingship named in the present chapter were acquired after the founding of Open Mountain, on a pilgrimage to the lowlands (perhaps to Chichen Itzá) that probably took place in post-Classic times. The list is somewhat altered from the one given in my translation (D. Tedlock 1985:204) of the Popol Vuh (folio 48v), due to a reconsideration of dictionary sources. Sparkling powder *(tatil)* and yellow ocher *(q'an ab'aj)* are listed as *titil* and *q'ana ab'aj* (literally "yellow stone") by Coto (1983), who describes them as cosmetics formerly used by persons who were being installed in lordships; Basseta (1921) lists *titil* as a "bright powder." The tobacco gourd is *k'us b'us,* from Yucatec *k'us,* "tobacco" (a variant of *k'uts),* and *bux,* "small wild gourd for keeping ground tobacco" (Barrera 1980). The food bowl is *kaxkon,* from Nahuatl *caxcomulli,* "bowl (for eating)" (Molina 1970).

For reports on excavations at Rotten Cane, see Wauchope (1965:65-69) and Wallace and Carmack (1977). The buildings of Iximché, the Cakchiquel capital, were also covered with polychrome paintings (see Guillemin 1965:16-17).

Under the Twine, Under the Cord is *Xeb'alax, Xek'amaq* in Quiché, located somewhere along the boundary that now divides Santa Cruz Quiché from Chichicastenango (the next town south). The Popol Vuh puts this place "at" *(chiri)* Chulimal (folio 53v), which is the northernmost district of Chichicastenango.

The kings named Three Deer *(Oxib' Kej)* and Nine Dog *(B'elejib' Tz'i')* receive only a brief mention in the Popol Vuh (D. Tedlock 1985:224).

Under Ten Deer *(Xe Lajuj Kej),* so named because it is below a mountain with the calendrical name Ten Deer, is now the second-largest city in Guatemala. Its present-day official name, of Nahuatl derivation, is Quezaltenango (with the *t* missing from the quetzal), but most Guatemalans, whether Mayan or not, refer to it orally as *Xelaju.*

The Hanging of the Kings

The source for most of the details of Black Butterfly's actions is a Quiché document known as the Título C'oyoi (Carmack 1973:282-84, 301-4). The main source for Peter Pallid's (Pedro de Alvarado's) side of the story, as in the previous chapter, is his own letters (Mackie 1924). I have reconstructed the timing of the events that bring the two men together by working backward from the date given in the Annals of the Cakchiquels (Brinton 1885:176-77) for the burning of the Quiché kings, which is Four Net *(Kajib' K'at).* The division of the year called Third Stick of Firewood is *Rox*

Tzij in Quiché, in which the first word means "third" and the second is translated on the basis of entries for *tzij* in Ximénez (1985) and Coto (1983), where it figures in verbs for setting fire to something and in nouns for candles and firewood.

Blood River, called *K'ikel* in the Título C'oyoi (Carmack 1973:283), appears on maps as Río Xequiquel; it runs into the Río Salamá halfway between the Pan American Highway and Quezaltenango, directly in front of the Motel del Campo.

The occasions on which Alvarado found himself trapped in Cholula and Mexico City (Tenochtitlán) are detailed by Díaz del Castillo (1963:189-201, 282-306). For the Popol Vuh version of the demise of the Quiché kings (folio 55v), see D. Tedlock (1985:224); for the Annals of Cakchiquels (Fire Trees), see Recinos and Goetz (1953:120). The translation of Alvarado's questions about gold is my own, from the Cakchiquel text of the Annals (Brinton 1885:180). On the use of torture by the Inquisition in Yucatán, see Clendinnen (1987). For a more general discussion of the European use of torture in obtaining testimony from Mayans, and of the use and misuse of such testimony by European and Euro-American scholars, see D. Tedlock (1993).

Eyes and Ears to the Book

"Superstitions and falsehoods of the devil" are the words of Fray Diego de Landa, who oversaw the burning of Mayan books in Yucatán (see Tozzer 1941:77-78, 169).

For more on the anonymous authors of the alphabetic version of the Popol Vuh and their possible identity, see D. Tedlock (1985:59-61). My description of its hieroglyphic predecessor is based on the few surviving books (or fragments of books) written in the Mayan script, especially the one called the Dresden Codex (Thompson 1972). What I call "the thirteen houses of the road of light" is the Mayan zodiac, which is set forth in the Paris Codex (Bricker and Bricker 1992).

"The lighting of all the skyearth" is *tzuk' ronojel kajulew* in the Popol Vuh (folio 1r). I have translated *tzuk'* (spelled *tzuk* in the manuscript) as "lighting" on the basis of *tzuk'u-*, which appears in various colonial and modern dictionaries as a verb stem for placing a light (such as a candle or torch) in a high place (Varea 1929, Ximénez 1985, Maynard and Xec 1954, García et al. 1980). After this statement comes a long story that accounts, among other things, for the origin of the sun, moon, and stars. Near the very end of the book comes a description (quoted in the present chapter) of the divinatory use of its hieroglyphic predecessor (D. Tedlock 1985:219).

"Mirror words" and other Mayan notions about the relationship between language, writing, and the world are discussed in D. Tedlock (1988). Both the *ajpop* title of the present chapter and its reverse, the *pop ajaw* of Copán (see p. 13), are well attested in hieroglyphic texts (Lounsbury 1989:229-31). My interpretation of the *aj* and *po* glyphs starts from the arguments given by Lounsbury (1989) and Coe (1992:199-200) but runs more deeply into myth and ritual than they do. Both of them offer general introductions to Mayan writing, but the most comprehensive single account to date is that of Mathews (1991). On the "planting" of ears of corn *(äj)* on the day named *Aj,* see D. Tedlock (1985:42, 133-34, 283-84). The vowel in *Aj* is pronounced something like the first *a* in "Mayan," while the one in *äj* sounds more like the second *a*.

On the calabash tree *(Crescentia cujete)* and the use of its hollowed fruit as a vessel for beverages made of cacao, see McBryde (1947:57). For the full context of the toast the authors of the Popol Vuh propose to their readers, together with the story of the origin of the calabash, see D. Tedlock (1985:105-15).

The independent Mayan kingdom that held out until 1697 was Tah Itza (also known as Tayasal), centered on an island in the largest lake of the Petén region in Guatemala; for a full history, see Jones (1989).

On Francisco Ximénez and his works, see Carmack (1973:189-92). The town where he was parish priest when he copied the Popol Vuh, which I have called St. Thomas above the Nettles, is known to speakers of Spanish as Santo Tomás Chichicastenango, the final word being Nahuatl for Nettles Citadel. Mayans know the town as *Chuwila',* "Above the Nettles." Ximénez used his copy of the Popol Vuh as an appendix to a larger work he entitled *Arte de las tres lenguas 3a3chiquel, quiche y 4,utuhil,* which is to say, "Grammar of the Three Languages Cakchiquel, Quiché, and Tzutuhil," the manuscript of which is now in the Newberry Library in Chicago. For the full text of his letter to the Virgin Mary, see Ximénez (1985:21-41). On the Bundle of Glory (or Fire) to which he compares her, see D. Tedlock (1985:198, 329).

The Trap Door

Stone Voice is located a short distance southeast of San Cristóbal Totonicapán, with the Pan American Highway running along the base of it on the south and west sides. It is called *Kanchawox* locally, which sounds like a rapid Quiché pronunciation of the Spanish words *canchal,* "rocky place," and *voz,* "voice." The rocks with the crevice are called *Kampanab'aj,* combining Spanish *campana,* "bell," with Quiché *ab'aj,* "rock."

Too Steep a Slope

Dawning Point *(Saqirib'al)* is not so much a specific place name as an epithet in the Popol Vuh, where it is applied to Tohil's Place *(Patojil)*, Swallows' Place *(Pawilix)*, and Open Mountain *(Jakawitz)* (folio 39v). St. Andrew Plaster House, located northeast of Santa Cruz Quiché, is known to speakers of Spanish as San Andrés Sajcabajá, the final word coming from Quiché *saqkab'a*, "plaster" (Basseta 1921), and *ja*, "house." Duncan Earle has pointed out to me that the mountain peak directly to the south of the town center, labeled on maps as Cerro Chuiscarbal, is probably the Dawning Point don Mateo had in mind.

Don't Tell Anyone

Mundo, Santo Mundo, and Diosmundo, or "World," "Holy World," and "Godworld," are favorite present-day Quiché ways of invoking the ultimate terrestrial deity in prayers. At the local level Mundo divides up into mundos, "worlds," which are individual sacred hills and mountains as distinct from the entire globe.

Thanks Be to the World

Tohil's Place, as an archaeological site, is described by Fox (1978:50-51).

The Story of Evenadam

The cleaning of shrines, which is carried out at the shrines of a lineage when a new motherfather succeeds to office (B. Tedlock 1982:76), is called *ch'ajb'al tasa, ch'ajb'al china, ch'ajb'al mulul*, "washing the cup, washing the plate, washing the gourd jar."

Trying This Erotic Thing

For an example of a missionary *Doctrina Cristiana*, printed in Mexico City in 1548, see Orden de Santo Domingo (1944); the passages translated in the present chapter are from folios 139v-140v. The illustrations in this chapter are typical of the woodcuts in fifteenth-century works of religious instruction from western Europe. The one of Jesus creating Adam from earth is from Schedel (1493), and the one of Jesus pulling Eve from the side of Adam is from Henry (1987). Whether or not don Mateo himself ever heard arguments or saw illustrations taken from or inspired by such early sources, there is no doubt that Quichés and other Mayans of the colonial period did so, formulating their versions of Bible stories accordingly.

Grandmother of Light *(Ratit Saq)* is one of the epithets of She Who Does a Favor *(Xmukane)*, who was introduced in the first chapter.

Borrowing Lightning

Mam, the title given to days that can bring in solar years, means "old man" or "grandfather."

Let's Have a Little Drink

Book of the Jaguar's Spokesman, or Book of Chilam Balam, is the name given to various works from Yucatán that were written, like the Popol Vuh of Guatemala, as alphabetic substitutes for hieroglyphic books. Available in English translation are the books from the towns of Chumayel (Roys 1967), Maní (Craine and Reindorp 1979), and Tizimín (Edmonson 1982). For the passage about the bead of precious stone, see Roys (1967:91).

Ripples on the Still Black Sea

The dreams in this chapter are from longer series I have woven into a long poem whose parts are organized by the divinatory calendar (D. Tedlock 1990a). On the timing of Tahil's first appearance, see D. Tedlock (1992); the inscription in question is in the Temple of the Foliated Cross at Palenque (Schele 1987:104-16). The interpretation of the Palenque emblem glyph is discussed in D. Tedlock (1990b) and Schele and Freidel (1990:468); it was Floyd Lounsbury, in discussions with other scholars, who first brought a white wading bird into the picture.

Grandfather Judas

St. Andrew Obsidian is San Andrés Itzapa, a Cakchiquel town located a short distance northwest of Antigua Guatemala. The name Itzapa is from Nahuatl Iztapan, meaning "place of obsidian"; in Cakchiquel the local river is called *Ruya'l Chay*, "River of Obsidian" (Arriola 1973). The town is the site of the principal image of Brother Simon *(Hermano Simón)* or St. Simon *(San Simón)*. My written sources on him and his devotees include various anonymous leaflets and pamphlets sold in public markets (one of which is translated on pp. 217-18) and the written testimonials that line the walls of his chapel; I have also benefitted from discussions with Anna Blume. The site of his apparition on the day of St. Judas Thaddaeus, the town of Bathers, is Zunil (near Quezaltenango), famous for its hot-spring baths. The name may be based on the Quiché verb *su'*, "to clean with a cloth" (Basseta 1921).

Maximón *(Mam Simón)* is the Brother Simon or St. Simon of towns along the shore of Lake Atitlán. On the Maximón of St. James at the Water, which is to say Santiago Atitlán, my principal sources are Mendelson (1965) and Molina (1983). The story of the origin of Maximón, as retold here, is based on the version given in Spanish by Mendelson (1965:131-33). The divinatory dating of the theft of the mask is my own, as is the dating of the merger of the Mam rites with those of Holy Week. The transformation of "partisans of the Epistles" into "packers of pistols" is my translation of a Guatemalan journalist's quip that turned *epistoleros* into *pistoleros,* recounted to me by Enrique Sam Colop.

The Very Noble and Very Loyal City of St. James of the Knights of Guatemala, or Muy Noble y Muy Leal Ciudad de Santiago de los Caballeros de Guatemala, is known today as Antigua Guatemala, or just plain Antigua, which means "ancient" or "antique." I chose the latter translation because the modern town's efforts to create a colonial atmosphere tend toward preciousness. For a short history of Antigua see Long and Bell (1988); the calculation of divinatory dates for the events recounted here is my own.

St. George at the Lake is San Jorge de la Laguna, on a hill above Panajachel.

Proper Respect for a Stone

The plant that bears the fruit called "thorn" *(k'ix)* is *Sechium edule*. Speakers of Spanish know it as *güisquil* in Guatemala and *chayote* in Mexico, the former name of uncertain derivation and the latter from Nahuatl.

➤ Bibliography

Academia de las Lenguas Mayas. 1988. *Lenguas mayas de Guatemala: documento de referencia para la pronunciación de los nuevos alfabetos oficiales*. Guatemala: Instituto Indigenista Nacional.

Arriola, Jorge Luis. 1973. *El libro de las geonimías de Guatemala: diccionario etimológico*. Seminario de Integración Social Guatemalteca pub. 31. Guatemala: José de Pineda Ibarra.

Asociación Tikal. 1981. *El baile de la conquista: texto del Municipio de Cantel, Quezaltenango*. Guatemala: Piedra Santa.

Barrera Vásquez, Alfredo. 1980. *Diccionario maya cordemex, maya-español, español-maya*. Mérida: Ediciones Cordemex.

Basseta, Domingo de. 1921. "Vocabulario en lengua quiché." Paleography by William Gates of a manuscript (?1698) in the Bibliothèque Nationale, Paris. In the J. P. Harrington collection, National Anthropological Archives, Smithsonian Institution, Washington, D.C.

Bode, Barbara. 1961. "The Dance of the Conquest of Guatemala." In *The Native Theatre in Middle America*, edited by Margaret A. L. Harrison and Robert Wauchope, pp. 204-97. Middle American Research Institute Publications 27. New Orleans: Tulane University.

Bricker, Harvey M., and Victoria R. Bricker. 1992. "Zodiacal References in the Maya Codices." In *The Sky in Mayan Literature*, edited by Anthony F. Aveni, pp. 148-83. New York: Oxford University Press.

Bricker, Victoria R., and Harvey M. Bricker. 1986. *The Mars Table in the Dresden Codex*. Middle American Research Institute Publications 57:51-80. New Orleans: Tulane University.

Brinton, Daniel G. 1885. *Annals of the Cakchiquels*. Philadelphia: Library of Aboriginal American Literature.

Carmack, Robert M. 1973. *Quichean Civilization: The Ethnohistoric, Ethnographic, and Archaeological Sources*. Berkeley: University of California Press.

————1981. *The Quiché Mayas of Utatlán*. Norman: University of Oklahoma Press.

————1988. "The Story of Santa Cruz Quiché." In *Harvest of Violence: The Maya Indians and the Guatemalan Crisis,* edited by Robert M. Carmack, pp. 39-69. Norman: University of Oklahoma Press.

Carmack, Robert M., and James L. Mondloch. 1983. *El título de Totonicapán: texto, traducción y comentario.* Centro de Estudios Mayas, Fuentes para el Estudio de la Cultura Maya 3. México: Universidad Nacional Autónoma de México.

Clendinnen, Inga. 1987. *Ambivalent Conquests: Maya and Spaniard in Yucatan, 1517-1570.* Cambridge: Cambridge University Press.

Coe, Michael D. 1992. *Breaking the Maya Code.* New York: Thames and Hudson.

Coto, Thomás de. 1983. *Vocabulario de la lengua cakchiquel.* Edited by René Acuña. México: Universidad Nacional Autónoma de México.

Craig, Meg. 1991. *Characters and Caricatures in Belizean Folklore.* Belize: Belize UNESCO Commission.

Craine, Eugene R., and Reginald C. Reindorp. 1979. *The Codex Pérez and the Book of Chilam Balam of Maní.* Norman: University of Oklahoma Press.

Davis, E. Adams. 1946. *Of the Night Wind's Telling: Legends from the Valley of Mexico.* Norman: University of Oklahoma Press.

Davis, L. Irby. 1972. *A Field Guide to the Birds of Mexico and Central America.* Austin: University of Texas Press.

Díaz del Castillo, Bernal. 1963. *The Conquest of New Spain.* Translated by J. M. Cohen. Baltimore: Penguin.

Edmonson, Munro S. 1982. *The Ancient Future of the Itza: The Book of Chilam Balam of Tizimin.* Austin: University of Texas Press.

Fox, John W. 1978. *Quiche Conquest: Centralism and Regionalism in Highland Guatemalan State Development.* Albuquerque: University of New Mexico Press.

García Hernández, Abraham, Santiago Yac Sam, and David Henne Pontious. 1980. *Diccionario quiché-español.* Guatemala: Instituto Lingüístico de Verano.

Guillemin, Jorge F. 1965. *Iximché: capital del antiguo reino cakchiquel.* Guatemala: Instituto de Antropología e Historia de Guatemala.

Guzmán, Pantaleón de. 1984. *Compendio de nombres en lengva cakchiqvel.* Edited by René Acuña. México: Universidad Nacional Autónoma de México.

Haeserijn V., Esteban. 1979. *Diccionario k'ekchi' español.* Guatemala: Piedra Santa.

Henry, Avril. 1987. *Biblia Pauperam: A Facsimile and Edition.* Ithaca: Cornell University Press.

Immerman, Richard H. 1982. *The CIA in Guatemala: The Foreign Policy of Intervention*. Austin: University of Texas Press.

Institute for Policy Studies. 1983. "Behind Guatemala's Military Power." In *Guatemala in Rebellion: Unfinished History*, edited by Jonathan L. Fried, Marvin E. Gettleman, Deborah T. Levenson, and Nancy Peckenham, pp. 128-34. New York: Grove.

Jones, Grant D. 1989. *Maya Resistance to Spanish Rule: Time and History on a Colonial Frontier*. Albuquerque: University of New Mexico Press.

Josserand, J. Kathryn, and Nicholas A. Hopkins. 1988. "Chol (Mayan) Dictionary Database." Final Performance Report to the National Endowment for the Humanities. Photocopy.

Kraul, Edward Garcia, and Judith Beatty. 1988. *The Weeping Woman: Encounters with La Llorona*. Santa Fe: The Word Process.

Long, Trevor, and Elizabeth Bell. 1988. *Antigua Guatemala*. Guatemala: Impresos Industriales.

Looper, Matthew G. 1991. "The Name of Copan and of a Dance at Yaxchilan." *Copán Notes* 95.

Lounsbury, Floyd. 1989. "The Ancient Writing of Middle America." In *The Origins of Writing*, edited by Wayne M. Senner, pp. 203-37. Lincoln: University of Nebraska Press.

McBryde, Felix Webster. 1947. *Cultural and Historical Geography of Southwest Guatemala*. Institute of Social Anthropology pub. 4. Washington, D.C.: Smithsonian Institution.

Mackie, Sedley J. 1924. *An Account of the Conquest of Guatemala in 1524 by Pedro de Alvarado*. New York: The Cortes Society.

Marcus, Joyce. 1986. *Emblem and State in the Classic Maya Lowlands*. Washington, D.C.: Dumbarton Oaks.

Mathews, Peter. 1991. *Maya Hieroglyphic Weekend*. Cleveland: Cleveland State University.

Maynard, Gail, and Patricio Xec. 1954. "Diccionario preliminar del idioma quiché." Mimeograph.

Mendelson, E. Michael. 1965. *Los escándolos de Maximón: un estudio sobre la religión y la visión del mundo en Santiago Atitlán*. Seminario de Integración Social Guatemalteca pub. 19. Guatemala: Tipografía Nacional.

Miles, Suzanne W. 1981. "Mam Residence and the Maize Myth." In *Culture in History: Essays in Honor of Paul Radin*, edited by Stanley Diamond, pp. 430-36. New York: Octagon Books.

Molina, Alonso de. 1970. *Vocabulario en lengua castellana y mexicana y mexicana y castellana*. México: Porrua.

Molina F., Diego. 1983. *Las confesiones de Maximón.* Guatemala: Artemis y Edinter.

Orden de Santo Domingo, los Religiosos de. 1944. *Doctrina cristiana en lengua española y mexicana.* Facsimile of 1548 edition, printed in Mexico City by Juan Pablos. Colección de Incunables Americanos 1. Madrid.

Recinos, Adrián, and Delia Goetz. 1953. *The Annals of the Cakchiquels.* Norman: University of Oklahoma Press.

Roys, Ralph L. 1967. *The Book of Chilam Balam of Chumayel.* Norman: University of Oklahoma Press.

Schedel, H. 1493. *Das Buch der Chroniken.* Nuremberg. In the John Carter Brown Library, Brown University, Providence.

Schele, Linda. 1987. *Notebook for the Maya Hieroglyphic Writing Workshop at Texas.* Austin.

Schele, Linda, and David Freidel. 1990. *A Forest of Kings: The Untold Story of the Ancient Maya.* New York: William Morrow.

Schele, Linda, and Mary Ellen Miller. 1986. *The Blood of Kings: Dynasty and Ritual in Maya Art.* Fort Worth: Kimbell Art Museum.

Schele, Linda, and David Stuart. 1986. "Te-Tun as the Glyph for 'Stela.' " *Copán Notes* 1.

Stevens, John Lloyd. 1841. *Incidents of Travel in Central America, Chiapas, and Yucatan,* vol. 2. New York: Harper & Bros.

Tedlock, Barbara. 1981. "Quiché Maya Dream Interpretation." *Ethos* 9: 313-30.

———1982. *Time and the Highland Maya.* Albuquerque: University of New Mexico Press. (Revised version 1992.)

———1986. "On a Mountain Road in the Dark: Encounters with the Quiché Maya Culture Hero." In *Symbol and Meaning beyond the Closed Community: Essays in Mesoamerican Ideas,* edited by Gary H. Gossen, pp. 125-38. Studies on Culture and Society 1. Albany: Institute for Mesoamerican Studies.

———1987. "Zuni and Quiché Dream Sharing and Interpreting." In *Dreaming: Anthropological and Psychological Interpretations,* edited by Barbara Tedlock, pp. 105-31. Cambridge: Cambridge University Press.

Tedlock, Dennis. 1983. *The Spoken Word and the Work of Interpretation.* Philadelphia: University of Pennsylvania Press.

———1985. *Popol Vuh: The Mayan Book of the Dawn of Life.* New York: Simon & Schuster.

———1988. "Mayan Linguistic Ideology." In *On the Ethnography of Communication: The Legacy of Sapir,* edited by Paul V. Kroskrity, pp. 55-108. Other Realities 8. Los Angeles: University of California at Los Angeles, Department of Anthropology.

————1989. "Writing and Reflection among the Maya," *1992 Lecture Series Working Papers* 4. College Park: University of Maryland Department of Spanish and Portuguese.

————1990a. *Days from a Dream Almanac.* Urbana: University of Illinois Press.

————1990b. "Drums, Egrets, and the Mother of the Gods: Remarks on the Tablet of the Cross at Palenque." *U Mut Maya* 3:13-14.

————1990c. "From Voice and Ear to Hand and Eye," *Journal of American Folklore* 103:133-56.

————1992. "Myth, Math, and the Problem of Correlation in Mayan Books." In *The Sky in Mayan Literature*, edited by Anthony F. Aveni, pp. 247-73. New York: Oxford University Press.

————1993. "Torture in the Archives: Mayans Meet Europeans." *American Anthropologist* 95:138-51.

Thompson, J. Eric S. 1930. *Ethnology of the Mayas of Southern and Central British Honduras.* Field Museum of Natural History, Anthropological Series 17, no. 2. Chicago: Field Museum Press.

————1960. *Maya Hieroglyphic Writing.* Norman: University of Oklahoma Press.

————1972. *A Commentary on the Dresden Codex.* Philadelphia: American Philosophical Society.

Tirado, Fermín Joseph. 1787. "Vocabulario de lengua Kiche." Manuscript in the Tozzer Library, Harvard University, Cambridge.

Tozzer, Alfred M. 1941. *Landa's relación de las cosas de Yucatan.* Papers of the Peabody Museum of American Archaeology and Ethnology 18. Cambridge, Mass.

Ulrich, E. Matthew, and Rosemary Dixon de Ulrich. 1976. *Diccionario bilingüe maya mopán-español, español-maya mopán.* Guatemala: Instituto Lingüístico de Verano.

Varea, Francisco de. 1929. "Calepino en lengua cakchiquel." Paleography by William Gates of a manuscript (1699) in the American Philosophical Society library, Philadelphia, Pennsylvania. In the Gates collection, Brigham Young University library, Provo, Utah.

Wallace, Dwight T., and Robert M. Carmack. 1977. *Archaeology and Ethnohistory of the Central Quiche.* Institute for Mesoamerican Studies pub. 1. Albany: State University of New York at Albany.

Wauchope, Robert. 1965. *They Found the Buried Cities: Exploration and Excavation in the American Tropics.* Chicago: University of Chicago Press.

Ximénez, Francisco. 1973. *Popol Vuh*. Facsimile with paleography and notes by Agustín Estrada Monroy. Guatemala: José de Pineda Ibarra.

————1977. *Historia de la provincia de San Vicente Chiapa y Guatemala, Libros I y II*. Sociedad de la Geografía e Historia de Guatemala, Biblioteca Goathemala 28. Guatemala: Tipografía Nacional.

————1985. *Primera parte del tesoro de las lenguas cakchiquel, quiché y zutuhil, en que las dichas lenguas se traducen a la nuestra, española*. Edited by Carmelo Sáenz de Santa María. Academia de Geografía e Historia de Guatemala, special pub. 30. Guatemala: Tipografía Nacional.